Shelter on the Journey

Priscilla Solano

Foreword by Douglas S. Massey

Shelter on the Journey

Humanitarianism, Human Rights, and Migration

TEMPLE UNIVERSITY PRESS
Philadelphia • Rome • Tokyo

TEMPLE UNIVERSITY PRESS
Philadelphia, Pennsylvania 19122
tupress.temple.edu

Copyright © 2024 by Temple University—Of The Commonwealth System
of Higher Education
All rights reserved
Published 2024

Library of Congress Cataloging-in-Publication Data

Names: Solano, Priscilla, 1978– author. | Massey, Douglas S., writer of
foreword.
Title: Shelter on the journey : humanitarianism, human rights, and
migration / Priscilla Solano ; foreword by Douglas S. Massey.
Description: Philadelphia : Temple University Press, 2024. | Includes
bibliographical references and index. | Summary: "This book surveys the
social life and contested meanings in migrant shelters in Mexico,
probing the interactions between refugees, humanitarian staff, and
outside interests. The author finds that these interactions construct a
human rights discourse in favor of freedom of movement"— Provided by
publisher.
Identifiers: LCCN 2023042560 (print) | LCCN 2023042561 (ebook) | ISBN
9781439921524 (cloth) | ISBN 9781439921531 (paperback) | ISBN
9781439921548 (pdf)
Subjects: LCSH: Refuge (Humanitarian assistance)—Mexico. | Humanitarian
assistance—Mexico. | Immigrants—Services for—Mexico. |
Refugees—Mexico—Social conditions. | Mexico—Emigration and
immigration. | Central America—Emigration and immigration. | United
States—Emigration and immigration. | BISAC: SOCIAL SCIENCE / Emigration
& Immigration | SOCIAL SCIENCE / Anthropology / General
Classification: LCC HV640.4.M6 S64 2024 (print) | LCC HV640.4.M6 (ebook)
| DDC 305.9/069140972—dc23/eng/20240130
LC record available at https://lccn.loc.gov/2023042560
LC ebook record available at https://lccn.loc.gov/2023042561

♾ The paper used in this publication meets the requirements of the
American National Standard for Information Sciences—Permanence
of Paper for Printed Library Materials, ANSI Z39.48-1992

Printed in the United States of America

9 8 7 6 5 4 3 2 1

For my son, William

Contents

Foreword: Humanitarianism in an Age of Global Apartheid by Douglas S. Massey	ix
Acknowledgments	xv
List of Abbreviations	xvii
Introduction: We All Have the Human Right to Emigrate but Not to Immigrate	1
1. "They Walk as Fugitives": Situating Shelters and Transit Migration	27
2. "I Was a Migrant and You Gave Me Shelter": The Open Ethos and Social World of the Shelter	52
3. "Of Course There Is a Difference between Charity and Solidarity": The Power of Giving	77
4. "The Shelter Is a Garden in a Mine of Oil": The Humanitarian Project under Threat	106

viii / Contents

5. "That They Do Not Keep Expressing That Mexican Territory
Is a Cemetery for Central Americans": Advocating Free
Dignified Transit   129

Conclusion: Dreaming on the Journey   153

Notes   161
References   163
Index   183

Foreword

Humanitarianism in an Age of Global Apartheid

Douglas S. Massey

In her insightful book *Shelter on the Journey*, Priscilla Solano undertakes a deep and nuanced analysis of the political, practical, and moral complexities posed by the rising tide of humanity currently passing through Mexico toward the United States. For most of the twentieth century, the situation along the Mexico-U.S. border was not very complicated: Mexico was the leading source of both legal and undocumented migrants to the United States, accounting for 99 percent of all border apprehensions. After 1980, however, Mexico also became a country of passage for transit migrants from Central America. U.S. political and military intervention in the region during the 1980s unleashed waves of violence and economic destruction that displaced many thousands of people. The result was a steady outflow of migrants seeking refuge from poverty, civil conflict, and violence, conditions that have been exacerbated in recent years by global climate change.

While Nicaraguans were welcomed as political refugees from the leftist Sandinista government, Salvadorans, Guatemalans, and Hondurans from the region's Northern Triangle were not. Most of those displaced from these countries headed north without documentation, joining the much larger migration of unauthorized Mexicans heading toward the U.S. border. Initially, the Central American outflows were modest in size and little noticed alongside the multitude of Mexicans. Beginning in 2000, however, undocumented Mexican migration began to slow, and after 2008, the net inflow turned negative, rendering Central American migrants suddenly visible to the United States at a time when their numbers were also rising.

From 2008 to 2018, the annual number of Mexicans apprehended at the U.S. border dropped from 653,000 to 152,000, while the number of non-Mexicans apprehended rose from 52,000 to 244,000. Since 2018, traffic through Mexico and the number of border apprehensions have surged to record levels. In 2019, the total of migrants apprehended rocketed to 852,000 with 71.4 percent coming from the Northern Triangle and just 19.5 percent from Mexico. Although total apprehensions fell during the pandemic year of 2020, thereafter they surged to new heights, reaching 1.7 million in 2021 and 2.2 million in 2022.

Over the last two years, Northern Triangle migrants arriving at the border have been joined by a new wave of Mexicans fleeing the disruptions of climate change and COVID-19. Moreover, for the first time, the number of Mexicans and Central Americans has been augmented by an unprecedented upsurge in migrants from other regions. In 2022, 33.4 percent of those apprehended at the border were from Mexico, 23.5 percent were from the Northern Triangle, and 42.8 percent were from other countries, notably Venezuela, Cuba, and Haiti. That year, the share of migrants from outside Mesoamerica suddenly exceeded the share from either Mexico or the Northern Triangle, creating a complex humanitarian emergency characterized by multiple causes, multiple actors, and multiple sources.

This humanitarian crisis, as elaborated in this book, stems not just from an increase in the number of migrants seeking refuge in the United States but more importantly from the migration policies prevailing in Mexico and the United States. Both nations are signatories to the Universal Declaration of Human Rights, which contains two important clauses: everyone has the right to leave any country including their own, and everyone has the right to seek asylum from persecution in other countries.

Under accepted international human rights law, both countries are therefore bound by the principle of *non-refoulement*, which holds that no one may be returned to a country where they would face cruel and inhumane treatment or suffer other irreparable harm. Despite the United States and Mexico formally honoring this rule in principle, its fulfillment in practice has been undermined by a steady process of securitization in which immigrants and immigration have been framed as grave threats to national and international security. Throughout the world, securitization has entailed ever more repressive state actions to prevent migrants from exercising their rights under international law.

In the United States, the budget of the department known as Customs and Border Enforcement rose 3.5 times to $20.9 billion from 2003 to 2020, and the budget for Immigration and Customs Enforcement rose 2.9 times to $9.3 billion. These inflated budgets generated 8.4 million apprehensions at the border and 4.1 million deportations from the U.S. interior. In Mexico, meanwhile, the federal government has created a system of some sixty detention centers that from 2001 to 2021 incarcerated some 3.0 million migrants and undertook 2.6 million deportations.

In 2019, the president of Mexico also created a sixty thousand-person national guard to combat unauthorized migration, and in 2020 the U.S. president announced that all migrants seeking asylum along the Mexico-U.S. border would immediately be returned to Mexico, intensifying an already fraught humanitarian crisis. *Shelter on the Journey* focuses on the dire circumstances of transit migrants and humanitarian workers over the past decade in Mexico, a nation whose "corridor of death" is one powerful example of the grave, endemic humanitarian harms that have been built into the structure of the global market economy.

A fundamental contradiction of contemporary globalization stems from its attempt to selectively integrate factor markets. Whereas the free cross-border movement of goods, capital, commodities, services, and information is guaranteed by powerful institutions resting on binding multilateral agreements, such as the International Monetary Fund, the World Bank, the World Trade Organization, and the SWIFT financial system, the movement of people within the global economy is overseen by weak institutions such as the International Organization for Migration and the International Labor Organization, which are authorized to monitor migratory flows and recommend best practices but have no power to impose immigration policies or labor practices on nation states.

Thus, although the Universal Declaration of Human Rights guarantees the right of *emigration*, it recognizes no right of *immigration*. As a result, global markets for labor and human capital are not free to equilibrate, creating highly segmented market structures. Although people have a right to leave their country of origin and petition for asylum elsewhere, to file such a petition, they first must get to a potential country of asylum; to preclude this eventuality, nations in the Global North have increasingly outsourced immigration enforcement to nations in the Global South. As this book details, this outsourcing has important ethical and human consequences manifested in mobility and the migrant shelter site. Moreover, even if migrants make it to the border of a country potentially offering asylum, political leaders always seem to find ways of turning them away, violating both international treaty obligations and domestic legislation but paying no political price.

A second fallibility lying at the core of contemporary globalism is its reliance on the burning of fossil fuels, propelling global climate change forward to increase the number and intensity of severe weather events while degrading the environment to create widespread population displacements. Climate change increases pressures on institutionally weak, underresourced governments in the Global South, raising the odds of state failure generating even more migrants. Thus, although the number of global immigrants rose by 60 percent between 2001 and 2021, the number of forced migrants of concern to the United Nations High Commissioner for Refugees rose by a factor of five. We increasingly live in a time of forced migration.

A final debility of the current global market economy is the uneven distribution of its costs and benefits across the socioeconomic distribution. The evidence clearly shows that over the past several decades, income gains from globalization have accrued disproportionately to persons in the top 1 percent of earners. Those located in the tenth to fiftieth percentile also made significant gains, enough to pull many in the developing world out of poverty. The fewest gains went to persons below the tenth percentile and those lying between the fiftieth and ninetieth percentiles, with the latter being composed mainly of middle- and working-class individuals in the developed world. To put it bluntly, the poor in the emerging economies of China and India were lifted out of poverty at the expense of the middle and working classes in Europe and North America.

In the United States and other wealthy nations, this global redistribution of income has driven forward a xenophobic populist nationalism that hugely complicates efforts to manage the rising tide of migrants rationally and humanely. The result is a system of global apartheid in which nations in the North seek to hold migrants at bay in the South while accepting limited numbers of well-educated professionals as residents and importing as many temporary workers as necessary without accepting responsibility for their wants and needs as human beings. Even as the United States deported 6.4 million migrants from 2001 to 2021, it simultaneously recorded 53.8 entries by legal temporary workers, underscoring the rank hypocrisy of current policies.

A core feature of global apartheid today is the strict spatial separation of the world's rich from the world's poor across rigid national boundaries. The concept of global apartheid was introduced in 1978, but until now no attempt has been made to measure the degree of separation between the world's rich and poor. Although there are no official statistics enumerating the world's rich by country of residence, the World Bank does tabulate the location of the world's poor and nonpoor (see https://data.worldbank.org/topic/11).

Drawing on data covering 159 countries containing 97 percent of world inhabitants, I computed two commonly used indices to measure the degree of segregation between the world's poor and nonpoor across national boundaries from 2000 to 2020—the degree to which the poor are isolated with other poor people in poor nations. Here, poverty is defined as an average income threshold of $6.85 per day in 2017 U.S. dollars adjusted for purchasing power parity (about $2,500 per year). As this threshold obviously

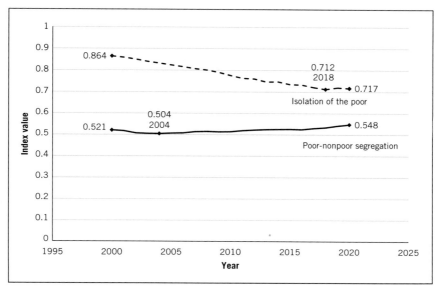

Figure F.1 National-level segregation between the world's poor and nonpoor and the national isolation of the world's poor, 2000–2020.

indicates a high degree of poverty, the nonpoor population it implicitly defines can hardly be considered rich. Thus, the indices provide a very conservative indication of the degree to which the poor are segregated and isolated in the world today.

Segregation is measured by the index of dissimilarity, which gives the proportion of the world's poor persons who would have to exchange places with nonpoor persons in other countries to achieve an even distribution across nations. Isolation is measured by the P* isolation index, which states the proportion poor in the country inhabited by the world's average poor person. By convention, index values of 0.60 and above are considered high and those from 0.30 to 0.60 are considered moderate. As shown in Figure F.1, the degree of segregation between the world's poor and nonpoor people has slowly but steadily risen since reaching a minimum index value of 0.504 in 2004, with a noticeable acceleration after 2015 to peak at 0.548 in 2020. Although the isolation index fell steadily from 0.864 in 2000 to 0.712 in 2018, thereafter the decline stalled, and the index finished at 0.717 in 2020.

As of 2020, in other words, the average poor person lived in a country where 72 percent of the residents were also poor; desegregating the world's poor and nonpoor would require 55 percent of the poor to exchange nations with nonpoor. As high as these figures are, they vastly understate the separation and isolation of the world's poor from the world's rich, illustrating the huge gulf between the social worlds of the Global North and Global South on the planet today. No wonder, then, that refugees see migration as a greater and greater imperative despite increased policing of transit. And no wonder that the places where refugees gather, such as the shelters discussed in this book, evidence a growing transnational politics of mobility rights. In reading this book, it is important to bear in mind that the humanitarian disaster unfolding in the North American migration corridor today is not some idiosyncratic peculiarity of a single world region. It is emblematic of the entire system of migration in a world of global apartheid. Widespread and systematic violations of human rights are never fluke outcomes of regional circumstances but inevitable byproducts of conditions built into the structure of the global market economy. Priscilla Solano's careful analysis of Mexico's ongoing humanitarian crisis has important lessons for concerned citizens throughout the world.

Acknowledgments

This book, like many others, was born as a PhD project idea that later became a dissertation and, after extensive revision, became this book. But that is not the only story of this book; it blossoms from seeds my father planted on questions about social justice, charity, and doing good and was born in my personal history of becoming a migrant.

I have spent almost two decades thinking about help and migration. While all errors are, of course, mine, this project would never have been possible without the practitioners, academics, migrants, family, and friends that supported the materialization of this book. This project was fed by multiple conferences, lectures, seminars, and workshops with very generous intellectuals along the way. I will unfortunately miss most, but from the academic community I wanted to especially thank Bridget Anderson, Åsa Lundqvist, Fatima Raja, Leisy Abrego, Noelle Brigden, Douglas Massey, Göran Djurdfeldt, Malin Åkerström, Mikael Sundström, Abdhulhadi Khalaf, Axel Fredholm, Ninna Nyberg Sørensen, and Julia O'Connell Davidson. You either have read extensively, commented on a draft, or supported the making of this project. I also benefited greatly from visitorships during my PhD and post-doc and thank all of those I shared my work with across the years. I especially thank Micheal Keith and Bridget Anderson for hosting me at COMPAS, Oxford; Ramon Grosfoguel in the Department of Ethnic Studies, Berkeley University; Adalberto Santana at the Centro de Investigaciones sobre América Latina y el Caribe, UNAM; and Douglas Massey in the Office for Population Research, Princeton University, who was a greatly appreciated intellectual mentor and powerful inspiration. I must also extend my immense gratitude to Ryan Mulligan, from Temple University Press who has guided and supported this process from the outset.

This project could not have become a reality without the protagonist of this book, to whom I refer as Priest Alberto. You opened the doors to the field with full transparency. I have deep respect for you and your commitments, and I express my greatest gratitude to having had the possibility to follow your work. The missionaries, priests, human rights defenders, and migrants play the most important role in this knowledge production, and their voices are of unsurmountable value to the humanitarian debate. In the field, I was received with open arms. I am grateful to such a long list of persons that I know I will not do them justice, and due to anonymity, I cannot mention most. I need to thank all the organizations that so generously participated in this project: IOM, CNDH, AI, Voces Mesoamericanas, and MSF. To all the persons I met during my time in Mexico, from migrants to human rights defenders, you marked my life forever. I am incredibly grateful for your generosity in sharing your experiences. I must thank the person who gave me an entry point into the field, Jorge Durand from the University of Guadalajara. I am especially grateful for the friendship and guidance in the field of Karla, Nacho, Celeste, Lupita, Carlos, Alberto, Lala, Luz, El Charro, Fatima, and Chapín and to Horacio Horta, Jimena Horta, Andres Reyes, Angel Zermeño, Alberto Reyes, and Carlos Stone for their outstanding hospitality.

Then there is *la familia*. Although death and distance have separated us, I could never have done this without our story. My father, you left us, but you are with me every day of my life. I thank you for being an example of integrity, kindness, and generosity. I especially thank you for teaching me to stand for what I believe in and for not being afraid of doing the right thing. My mother, you have taught me strength, as a woman and mother, to move forward in life even in the most difficult circumstances, and to do so with love. You have always extended your support in every possible way you could. *Te admiro mucho.* My brothers, you work with great passion and conviction to cause change in your work, and that is inspiring. Finally, my dearest William, you are *the reason* I could climb this mountain. You bring so much love, wisdom, and joy into my life every single day. *Estoy eternamente agradecida de tenerte en mi vida. Junto a ti el mundo es posibilidad. . .*

Abbreviations

AI	Amnesty International
CIDH	International Commission for Human Rights
CNDH	National Commission for Human Rights
DIF	Institute of Integral Development of the Family
DPMH	Dimensión Pastoral de la Movilidad Humana (Pastoral Dimension of Human Mobility)
ICRC	International Committee of the Red Cross
INGO	International nongovernmental organization
INM	Instituto Nacional de Migración (National Institute for Migration)
IOM	International Organization for Migration
MHC	Estaciones migratorias (migration holding centers)
MSF	Médecins Sans Frontières
NACC	North American Competitiveness Council
NAFTA	North American Free Trade Agreement
NGO	Nongovernmental organization
OHCHR	United Nations Office of the High Commissioner for Human Rights
PRI	Partido Revolucionario Institucional (Institutional Revolutionary Party)
PROVICTIMA	Public Ministry of Social Attention to Victims of Crime

REDODEM	Red de Documentación de las Organizaciones Defensoras de Migrantes (Network for the Documentation of Migrant Defense Organizations)
SEGOB	Secretaria de Gobernación (Governance Secretariat)
SJM	Servicio Jesuita de Migrantes (Jesuit Service of Migrants)
SPP	Security and Prosperity Partnership
STD	Sexually transmitted disease
U.S.	United States
UNHCR	United Nations High Commissioner for Refugees

Shelter on the Journey

Introduction

We All Have the Human Right to Emigrate but Not to Immigrate

> We have to be clear that the Earth belongs to all of us, and that God did not create any borders. Borders are only manipulations to protect interests. Through borders can pass—and this the most cynical knows—they can pass arms, drugs, human smuggling; everything can pass except legal workers.
>
> —FATHER ALBERTO

It is morning, one day in 2011, in a shelter for migrants on the main route from Central America to the United States, traversing Mexico. A couple of members of a film crew have arrived, looking for a shelter to be the location for a movie. The film, *La Jaula de Oro* (*The Golden Dream*; Quemada Díez 2014), is about three teenagers from slums in Guatemala transiting Mexico on their way to the United States for a better life. The members of the film crew meet the staff in the dining hall and explain what they are planning, describing how they want to portray the shelter. As we sit down, we learn that the freight train known as La Bestia, the Beast, has just arrived, with hundreds, maybe a thousand, migrants on top of its carriages (see Fig. I.1). The train derailed previously, so migrants have already waited for a couple of days in the previous community. Father Alberto, the founder of the shelter, prepares to welcome the migrants, and the film producers jump into their car and rush toward the tracks, not knowing what to expect. The priest simply runs out of the front gate, which opens onto the tracks. I follow. Hundreds of migrants start pouring off the train. The priest waves at them and shouts: "Welcome! In the shelter we have food for everyone. There is food for everyone in the shelter!" He repeats this several times. There is happiness in the faces of many migrants to see a priest and a group of people welcoming them. For some, it is like a victory, as if they have made it to safety. Amid all the cheers and welcoming, a local man approaches the priest. The priest's assistant, who always follows him, starts filming to document what is happening. This man shouts "*Pollero!*" (a term used interchangeably with *coyote*,

Figure I.1 The Beast (freight train), 2011.

referring to persons who smuggle people across borders, typically from Latin America to the United States) at the priest, swearing and threatening him, dampening the atmosphere for some minutes. Migrants are directed to the shelter. In the shelter, migrants will receive a hot meal, a place to rest, and, most importantly, traveling companions, volunteers, and religious actors to support them in a welcoming space.

At this moment of crisis in the journey, given the train derailment, solidarity seems to be at its peak. The priest, volunteers, and humanitarian actors are all there to welcome the migrants. A sense of opportunity lingers. Everything seems better in a journey filled with risk, abuse, threats, and xenophobia. There is food, camaraderie, help, and many supportive words from the volunteers and the priest. As dawn breaks, others arrive, doctors and lawyers, coming to the shelter to offer their services, including "repatriation" services by the Grupo Beta, a rescue and protection group of the National Institute for Migration (INM), an agency under Mexico's Secretariat of the Interior. If done by the INM itself, these actions are known straightforwardly as "deportations."

Moments of welcome are transient experiences during an arduous journey; they are very much needed for survival, to alleviate suffering, and, most importantly, to move on. They go to the very heart of humanitarian work in

Mexico—upholding and supporting dignity in transit. Yet in this cusp of solidarity also exists threat and the criminalization of those being helped and those who help. In order to continue to provide dignity, solidarity, and survival, organizations like this shelter are conscientious about how they tell their story to observers, whether the objecting local man, the film crew, or government authorities.

During my time volunteering in shelters, attending human rights events, and traveling across Mexico with human rights defenders and on my own, I observed a tense, perplexing contrast between security and humanitarianism, making the migrant both victim and criminal, the humanitarian worker both savior and *pollero*, and the humanitarian act both criminal and morally compelling. I was reminded that migration controls and border enforcement are one reason why migrants reach the gates of the shelter, but not the only reason.

We all have the human right to emigrate according to the Universal Declaration of Human Rights, Article 13,[1] but we do not have the human right to immigrate. This makes the process of migration fraught with danger for many who fall between the cracks. At their most critical, these dangers can be life threatening. In February 2020, the Migration Data Portal reported that since 1996, seventy-five thousand migrants have died or disappeared crossing borders across the globe; the actual figure is certainly much higher, as most migrant deaths go unrecorded. The situation in transit is no better. Between 2006 and 2012, more than seventy thousand migrants in transit simply disappeared in Mexico (Mesoamerican Migrant Movement 2016).

Migration has been a survival and life-saving strategy at times of emergency, threat, and insecurity across human history. Yet today, "irregular" transit migration is described—or denounced—as a humanitarian crisis in many parts of the world: in Mexico, Turkey, Greece, Spain, and Morocco, to name a few. While there is general consensus that nobody deserves to die for transiting a country or crossing a border undocumented, humanitarian actors do not agree on what help or rights undocumented migrants deserve to uphold their dignity in movement or whether this movement should be free or controlled. Even aside from the risks and precarious conditions migrants experience during transit, migration without documents is punishable and subject to persecution by the authorities and society at large. This book provides evidence of the need to scrutinize the indirect violence, up to death, exerted by border enforcement and migration controls in Mexico and the United States as the latter extends its physical border to traverse Mexico as a vertical border, one not acknowledged by nation-states.

This is a book about *shelter on the journey* along a unique humanitarian trail that runs through more than ninety-six shelters that have emerged on the routes across Mexico that migrants, mainly Central American, take to reach the border of the United States. Shelters are largely run by faith-based civil associations and staffed by religious actors and volunteers who style themselves as human rights defenders—mostly Mexicans who want to do something about the horrible circumstances experienced by migrants transiting the country. A few shelters also attract "apolitical" international humanitarian actors and inherently political government actors.

In these shelters, transit migrants can eat, sleep, rest, and take a shower. Most importantly, they find an oasis: a safe space on an otherwise violence-filled journey. Migrants receive advice on dangers they may encounter on their journey and how to avoid them. They meet other people like themselves, from other countries, undergoing the same travails. They share their experiences, support to each other, and receive support from shelter staff and other humanitarian actors. These encounters, even if short lived, provide much-needed hope to endure the arduous journey north.

The work of human rights defenders for migrants extends beyond shelter walls. Human rights defenders not only distribute information to migrants but also actively denounce the transit migrant situation, identifying who has died on the journey and why; support victims of rape and abuse; provide legal advice; attempt to counter xenophobia in transit communities; and gather in a social movement that lobbies for free transit visas and dignified transit framed along the lines of human rights. They give spiritual support to migrants and pray with and for them. Human rights defenders also document, quantify, and systematize the abuses suffered by migrants and convey this information to the Mexican government and international actors. The reality they share in political dialogues, caravans, the media, and published reports surpasses official figures and, often, our imagination.

Beyond the analysis of humanitarian actors, which are dominated by Western perspectives, these activities constitute a politics of dignifying transit migration in shelters. By adducing this politics of dignity, this book seeks to address the central place of human worth and threat in relation to freedom of movement within the global divides between South and North. The dignity experienced and framed in encounters within the shelter site reaches beyond the freedoms expressed in the Universal Declaration of Human Rights to include solidarity, recognition, and free transit.

In this book what is thought of as "shelter on the journey" is faith-based humanitarianism and human rights activism shaped by discourses and practices that emerge from the bottom up, as struggles and spatial disputes to support free transit, and as acts of assistance to relieve suffering in movement. Shelter sites and the practices and discourses they house may at times support the control and regulation of movement.

The main aim of this book is to outline the constraints and opportunities faced by shelters in "humanizing" freedom of movement as universal through assistance, advocacy, and accompaniment and the potential of these local sites for social transformation. The other aim is to explore the actual practices and consequences in alleviating suffering in transit and rebelling against state practices. As part of the shaping of this new politics of dignity in transit, some sets of practices as humanitarian are accompanied by peace and security goals that even if indirectly support policing, surveillance, and border controls yet this book argues that state violence and impunity does not go uncontested by this humanitarian trail even with its limitations, hence its importance.

Finally, this book considers the constraints faced by shelters run far deeper than state structures and lie at the heart of power struggles between liberal principles of freedom, security, and peace and capitalist-based inequalities nascent in receiving states in the Global North. Liberal humanitarianism is infused with assumptions about these liberal principles, and these assumptions and definitions hold the humanitarian project hostage. The deep contradictions within liberal humanitarianism, confronted with criminalized, poor bodies, do not begin and end at the border; they cast a shadow everywhere, demarcating Northern privilege and Southern "human waste" and (re)produce precarious migration for, primarily, the poor. Shelters serve and struggle with migrants in this shadow raising important questions about the meaning of universal freedom of movement.

The "Wall of Violence"

Central to the argument of this book is that freedom, security, and peace are not arbitrary collections of principles upheld by modern states. These principles have interpretations and implications from North to South in the humanitarian crisis currently denounced by civil society in Mexico. Migration-driven crises are no novelty, nor is the distribution of help to migrants in transit. What is new is how and why migration security is being framed and managed as both a criminal and humanitarian issue—and how the humanitarian project itself is facing important threats for this very reason.

In Mexico, the situation of transit migration has been denounced as a humanitarian crisis by civil society of "invisible victims" (Amnesty International 2010), a "wall of violence" (a term coined by Bricker 2008) resulting in a *corredor de la muerte* (death corridor). The wall of violence is composed of impunity, borders, and controls, yet it remains unacknowledged by the Mexican state and the international community. This two-sided wall, functioning both to enact violence on migrants and to uphold peace and freedom for the privileged, comprises the state's claim to legitimacy.

6 / Introduction

In Mexico, transit migration took place in the shadows until it hit the headlines with the 2010 Tamualipas tragedy (FM4 Paso Libre 2013). In August of that year, the state of Tamaulipas was the site of one of the worst massacres on Mexican territory. Seventy-two undocumented migrants, fifty-eight men and fourteen women, mostly from Central America, were kidnapped, tortured, and murdered, their bodies piled in a ditch on a ranch. The migrants were kidnapped and executed by the Zetas, the powerful criminal syndicate controlling the territory. This horrific incident attracted considerable attention from a plethora of actors: academics, the governments of Mexico and other Latin American countries (Coyuntura 2010), NGOs (nongovernmental organizations), and international human rights actors including Amnesty International (AI) (Amnesty International 2011a). The massacre made transit migrants visible, and the issues they faced—such as violence, insecurity, and vulnerability—were situated within the broader debate on human rights between civil society and the state (FM4 Paso Libre 2013). In 2015, the Network for the Documentation of Migrant Defense Organizations (REDODEM) titled its report *Migration in Transit: The Face of an International Humanitarian Crisis* (*Migración en tránsito por México: Rostro de una crisis humanitaria internacional* [REDODEM 2015]).

There are many forms of violence, abuse, victimization, and economic precarity suffered by transit migrants in Mexico extending to Mexico's southern border. In understanding violence as it affects the wall of violence circling transit-precarious migration, Galtung's (1969) most notable distinction is useful: considering "whether or not there is a subject (person) who acts" (ibid. 170). Violence, he notes, can be distinguished between "personal" and "direct," where there is an actor committing the violence, and "structural" or "indirect," where there is no actor. Even though indirect violence is not committed by anyone, this type of truncated violence is highly meaningful (ibid.). Mexicans refer to it as *inseguridad* (insecurity) (Boehm 2011): an environment characterized by the impunity of the authorities (Chillier and Varela 2009:71) combined with the commercialization of migration, manifest in the collaboration between corrupt local officials and criminal networks, notably the Zetas, la *Mara Salvatrucha*, and hired assassins from the drug cartel of the Gulf and *el Señor de los trenes* (the Lord of the trains) (Díaz 2013). Looking at structural violence, we also see that immigration policies position the "bad" migrant as having exclusive responsibility for the immigration process (Sassen 1999:8) and becoming the target of its control. Not focusing on structural issues has led to erasure of geopolitical and translational economic dynamics, which feature an uneven distribution in the global market economy in which international migrations are embedded, controlled, criminalized, and securitized, as elaborated in the foreword of this book by Douglas Massey.

Mexico has also been facing the spreading power of the Narco since the Partido Revolucionario Institucional (Institutional Revolutionary Party, PRI) left power in 2006. Crime rates have risen as cartels have gained power, and corruption continues (Davis 2006; Grillo 2011, 2012; Magaloni and Zepeda 2004; Ochoa 2015). To this set of dangers to refugees and migrants, we can add the U.S. context of controlling borders and migration and high levels of regional violence. Honduras and El Salvador have ranked at the top of homicide rates in the world for many consecutive years (UNODC 2021).

Another obstacle faced by migrants and sustained by the state bears greater mention: poverty, which drives migration and remains absent from most official humanitarian agendas. There is no legitimation of suffering from poverty in the refugee protection regime, yet shelters in Mexico often assist the mobile poor. Scholars have engaged with the issue of illegality as a racial and ethnic issue (see, e.g., De Genova 2004; Menjívar 2021) and the humanitarian crisis as one of increased security. But these are also issues of capital and class.

On the ground, politicians and humanitarian actors certainly realize that one of the key humanitarian issues in transit linked to illegality is poverty and destitution. Yet when push comes to shove, this issue invariably pales in comparison to other hierarchies of suffering prioritized by states to legitimate movement, such as torture, political persecution, and violence. While the situation of the transit migrant cannot be encapsulated by poverty, the displacement of poverty as an exclusively *developmental* issue obscures its relationship to violence, an exclusion produced by migration and border regimes and the ambiguous relationship poverty has to humanitarian intervention. This book focuses on this gap and how shelters engage movement in relation to liberal humanitarianism and human rights activism coming from the locality.

The Violation of Dignity in Transit: Criminalization

In order to have a satisfactory conception of dignifying movement, we must explain the reality of its violation. Such understanding goes beyond bouncing humanitarianism and security off one another. We learn most about dignity when we learn what it means to be wronged, humiliated, degraded, dehumanized, excluded (Margalit 1996), demonized. Within the context of transit migration, I also account for classifications based on socioeconomic and geopolitical power asymmetries in the region that demarcate who is deemed "worthy" to be mobile, and whose movement is threatened.

The violation of dignity described by human rights defenders working in shelters relies on cultural, contextual, and temporal frames that hold up migrants as criminals in the public domain. In theory, the wall of violence should not legally exist. Mexico has decriminalized migration since 2007 and has led a strong human rights discourse with its Central American neighbors. Yet there is an important disjuncture between what is set on paper and what happens on the ground. Indeed, the criminalization of migration concerns those populating the humanitarian crisis denounced by shelters.

Despite no general consensus: "Transit migration is commonly understood as movements of people from a supposed country of origin through various countries *en route* until they arrive in a supposedly final destination" (Düvell 2012:412). Transit migration as with any other category is a category that has been problematized by scholars (Collyer et al. 2012; Collyer and de Haas 2012), especially in relation to dichotomous characterizations as time/ space and location/direction. Of relevance to this book is that transit migration in general has been linked to the absence of legal status— often "identified as irregular migration, human smuggling, human trafficking and organized crime" (Düvell 2012:417; see also Collyer and de Haas 2012:469). From the 1970s, irregular migration began to be reported to international bodies; this is the point when irregular migration began to be treated as a criminal issue internationally. In the Americas during the 1980s, the tripartite response of the United States, Canada, and Mexico was very much a security-driven cooperation arrangement. It became a model promoted by the International Organization for Migration (IOM) (Düvell 2011:79–82) and had a domino effect in the region. Criminalizing "illegal aliens" has been traced in the case of the United States to the 1996 Illegal Immigration Reform and Immigration Responsibility Act (IIRIRA) and the 1996 Antiterrorism and Effective Death Penalty Act (AEDPA) (Abrego et al. 2017). The relationships between transit mobility and crime have therefore been unavoidable and denounced as part of the problem, not the solution.

More recently, the precarious conditions of migration have been framed as "border wars" in Aviva Chomsky's words (2014:2–3); she depicts Nogales, Sonora, on the U.S.-Mexican border as feeling like a warzone. Gledhill (2015) depicts the situation as a "new war on the poor," and Massey (2020) refers to a war based on an exclusionist climate stemming from U.S. policy decisions made in 1965 that continue to this day and have resulted in one of the most oppressive environments for immigration in the history of the country. Stumpf (2013)[2] terms the situation a "crimmigration crisis," noting that contemporary immigration law has so much overlap with criminal law that they are difficult to separate. Consequently, the sovereign state now "has the power to punish and the power to express moral condemnations" (ibid. 59), and the apparatus of the state is being used to expel from society those deemed criminal migrants. This has created a growing excluded population and fragmented society in ways that go beyond the effects of the migration control regime (ibid. 59–60). Menjívar et al. (2018) show how this process is racialized and gendered in the case of the United States.

In the case of Mexico and the United States, the effects of criminalizing migration have become more visible in the last twenty years, with more restrictive and repressive approaches to national security in both countries. Moreover, operations and programs designed to control the crossing of irregular migrants are increasingly framed as strategies to combat organized crime. These include Operativo Guardián (Operation Guardian, 1994), the Border Partnership Agreement (between the United States and Mexico in 2002), ASPAN (2005), Iniciativa Mérida (Mérida Initiative, 2007), *Iniciativa mas allá de Mérida* (DPMH 2012:32; U.S. Department of State 2011a). These agreements have multiplied the police and military presence along the borders and, as human rights defenders shared during my fieldwork, shifted civilian perceptions of the migrant. Scholars confirm that border enforcement has had a ricochet effect, with more crime spreading across border areas (Castles 2003; Cornelius et al. 2004; Durand and Massey 2004).

Farther north, more reprehensible strategies have been used, as with the dehumanization of Latin American migrants by the Trump administration in the United States. The former president referred to migrants from Central America as animals in a roundtable with California officials regarding sanctuary cities. In his words, "People are trying to come into the country, but we are stopping them. We are taking people outside the country. You would not believe how bad these people are. These aren't people, these are animals." (BBC 2018). In June 2015, in his candidacy announcement speech, Trump spoke of migrants as rapists and criminals.

> When Mexico sends its people, they're not sending their best. They're not sending you. They're not sending you. They're sending people that have lots of problems, and they're bringing those problems with us. They're bringing drugs. They're bringing crime. They're rapists. And some, I assume, are good people.

Beyond ethnicity and race, illegal mobility itself—not considering the role of the nation-state in its production—has been framed as a problem to be eradicated. Equating a specific social group to animals or criminals, designating them under a specific legal category, in this case "illegal," indoctrinates the majority group into believing that it would be better off without said group, that it is a problem necessary to stamp out. In this way, violence against civilians becomes normalized or made invisible. Donald Trump believed his remarks apply to "two maybe even three million people." As Abrego et al. (2017) note, the danger in producing such a fiction lies in the goal of producing at least that number of persons who can be incarcerated and deported as criminals. In short, the humanitarian crisis is not only defined by the irregular transit migrant situation but also framed by those with the power to address the crisis as an unidentifiable humanitarian subject.

Mexico has been engaged in a contradictory discourse regarding the criminalization of migration (Calavita 1995), given its strong opposition to the application of this migratory framework to its own citizens. The Mexican state claims not to criminalize migration by law, yet it provides a clear example in its operations and programs. The process of decriminalization in Mexico has been taking place since mid-2007. In August 2008, then-president Felipe Calderón met with Honduran president Manuel Zelaya and went as far as to call immigration a human right (EFE 2008). Ten-year prison sentences were abolished, and the Mexican state began to refer to those entering the country as "administrative irregularities." The Mexican state has taken important precautions in how it frames controls on irregular migration, always promoting a human rights discourse. Article 2 of the Migration Law of May 25, 2011 (Congreso General de los Estados Unidos Mexicanos 2016), stipulates that

> The principles on which migration policy of the Mexican state should be based are the following: Unrestricted respect for the human rights of migrants, nationals, and foreigners, irrespective of their origin, nationality, gender, ethnicity, age, and migratory situation, with special attention to vulnerable groups such as minors, women, indigenous people, teenagers, and people of the "third age" [by which is normally meant above sixty-five] and also victims of crime. In no respect will an irregular migratory situation in and of itself constitute the perpetration of a crime, nor will the migrant party be judged as engaging in illicit activities for finding him/herself in an undocumented situation.[3]

In practice, the deportation and/or detention of migrants implies the criminalization of migration even if not described as such by the law. This fact remains unchanged by the use of euphemisms such as "repatriation" for deportation or *estaciones migratorias* (migration holding centers, MHC) for detention centers. The International Commission for Human Rights (CIDH) denounces such practices as criminalizing the migrant (Milenio Digital 2014). This book sustains and adheres to the understanding of the criminalization of migration as detaining or holding and punishing migrants and henceforth refer to migration as criminalized in Mexico.

The Violation of Dignity in Transit:
Insecurity and Borders

Liberal principles of security, freedom, and peace are not transferable but up for interpretation. These principles present a complex interaction of global divides between North and South at a level of staging and enforcing border controls as a security concern. The "securitization of borders" as a term describes the management of borders as an (in)security issue. In Mexico, *inseguridad* (insecurity) is everywhere and spreads in different ways—as if airborne. Insecurity has intersected freedom of movement not only across borders but within them in the country.

When it comes to migration, the United States context is highly relevant to what happens in Mexico and to Mexico's management of borders and migration under a national security framework. As stated in a civil society report, the wall of violence is not only physical but also a border in the national security politics that persecute the migrant from the north to the south of Mexico as much as the migrant from the south to the north (DPMH 2012:32). In the Mexican context, human rights defenders interpret the demarcation of the border as vertically crossing Mexican territory (DPMH 2012).

It is not Trump's physical wall but a de facto wall of persecution made by security politics. Scholars, the media, and civil society have tried to shed light on the ways border enforcement and the implementation of migration controls seep beyond the physical demarcation of the border between Mexico and the United States. Academics such as Vogt have defined the Mexican-U.S. context as an "arterial" border (Vogt 2018), looking at economies of risk and violence. Monsiváis (2003) speaks of the *frontera portátil* (portable border), extending our understanding of the physically demarcated border. He shows how the portable border is everywhere in the reproduction of city life and is also demarcating where a person has more worth, where they can demand rights.

Other scholars have examined the sense of "deportability" carried by the migrant across their journey and at their destination (Peutz and De Genova 2010); and another body of literature looks at state power through the creation of documents (i.e., identification cards, passports, and the like) as an important marker of the boundaries the state attempts to delineate and to implement what we come to understand as "documentary regime" (see Torpey 2000). This linkage to documents is especially complex in this context, given that not only noncitizens but also citizens, the deported (including

12 / Introduction

deported criminals), and indigenous minorities transit the country. Mexico continues to be one of the most important migratory corridors in the world.

In the 2012 fiscal year alone, the United States spent $17.9 billion on its main immigration enforcement agencies and the U.S. Visitor and Immigration Status Indicator Technology. Border patrol personnel doubled over seven years to 21,370 agents in 2012. The southwestern U.S. border with Mexico was the most heavily funded. Visas and travel screening forming a virtual border were set as the first line of defense (Meissnner et al. 2013:2–4). In 2010, resources from the Mérida Initiative were used by the United States to make donations of eighteen biometric sets through the Security and Prosperity Partnership (SPP) between Mexico and the United States. Among the SPP's many programs and agreements is the Mérida Initiative, or Plan Mérida (Fogal et al. 2010; Villareal and Lake 2009). During June 2011, the biometric information of 28,610 foreigners from Guatemala and Belize had been collected (INM 2011:20). This practice continued and in 2018, $75 million were destined for more scanning equipment to transmit biometric data from Mexican jails directly to the Department of Homeland Security (Partlow and Miroff 2018).

The Migrant Protection Protocols issued in 2019 shuffled in another set of issues. This protocol allowed the U.S. government to return individuals entering without appropriate documentation to Mexico while the individuals await their immigration proceedings. The MPPs were terminated in 2021, yet were ordered to be reimplemented by court order (Department of Homeland Security 2022).

Through the power asymmetries between states, origin and transit must adapt and legitimize underlying assumptions behind the interests of destination states, be it perceptions of the capacity of states to attract skilled workers (Betts 2010, 2011:20–21) or common interests to combat crime. Moreover, there is a North-South divide marked by the domination of receiving states (Castles and Wise 2008; Düvell 2011; de Haas 2005). In this context, Mexico's border enforcement has been doing the work of the United States, extending the border well beyond the borderlands (Brigden 2018; Vogt 2018; Wolf 2022).

This extension is exemplified in the form of border outsourcing through direct funding from the United States to Mexico's border enforcement (as described previously) and policy steering through political pressure and agreements in the North American Free Trade Agreement (NAFTA). The outsourced enforcement of borders in the Global South are not unique to Mexico and have also been noted in other parts of the world; for example, on the Euro-African borderlands (Andersson 2014; see also Gammeltoft-Hansen 2006).

Beyond its cooperation and agreements with the United States, Mexico has had a two-faced policy concerning migration security, freedom, and peace. As noted earlier, the Mexico state has decriminalized migration and promoted a human rights discourse concerning irregular migrants yet engages in detaining and deporting migrants. At a border enforcement level, *Programa Frontera Sur,* established in the Peña Nieto administration in 2014, ostensibly had two aims: to protect migrants who enter Mexico and to manage ports of entry in a way that promoted the security and prosperity of the region (Presidencia de la República 2014b). The media and human rights defenders denounced *Programa Frontera Sur* as a "migrant hunting" program along Mexico's train tracks that pushed migrants toward even more perilous routes (OEA 2015). The implementation of the program extended the physical demarcation of the border, exemplifying the reference made by activists that border enforcement was vertical across the country as well as horizontal between nations.

Under President Andrés Manuel López Obrador (popularly known as AMLO), matters do not seem to have changed on the transit migration front. During 2019, he created a sixty thousand person National Guard the main task of which was to combat undocumented migration. Detentions rose that year, even if they dipped in 2020 during the COVID-19 pandemic (Meyer 2019). By 2021, they had surged to 274,000 and swelled in relation to deportations, which were 99,000 that year (Solano and Massey 2022). Currently, Mexico has one of the largest growing detention systems in the world, with sixty detention centers established by the year 2020 (Global Detention Project 2021). Detention centers have been argued to conceal human rights abuses and imprison asylum seekers (Cornelisse 2010; Mountz 2020).

In short, immigration policy in Mexico is double edged: it uses the discourse of human rights on paper but in practice presents a different reality. The horror stories of the "Highway of the Devil" (Urrea 2005) across the U.S.-Mexico border extend to the Beast (Martínez 2014), the cargo trains that Central Americans ride on, and now reach beyond the train tracks, into the mountains and less visible territories. Understanding the securitization of the border in Mexico goes beyond its physical demarcation to include other transit institutions, actors, and activities and how securitization is experienced and suffered by the migrant.

Beyond the Mexican context, structural violence linked to the criminalization of migration, securitized borders, insecurity, and humanitarian crises newly dubbed by civil society occurs around the world. Borders and boundaries are everywhere, and they construct irregular migrants socially and legally as criminals linked to movement, while multiple forms of suffering—up to death—have become grave concerns for humanitarian actors. Shelters mediate this conflict. Shelter exists in diverse architectural and humanitarian forms, from tents to cement structures, from church parishes to camps to the now-defunct Jungle of Calais to shelters (as *casas del migrante*)

Dignifying Transit and Liberal Humanitarianism in Shelters

The primary theme of this book is dignified and free transit migration: how it is constructed in the shelters on the journey of transit migrants, its productive nature from the perspective of actors that benefit from its use, and how its target group comes to be shown and taught through the shelter. Precarity in movement, the humanitarian crisis manifested across Mexico, displays a police mentality of persecution, exclusion, expulsion, and separation in which the shelter emerges and specializes in managing migrants as a group exposed to these practices.

In this book, beyond a focus on the solidarity that seeks dignity and free transit emerging in the tension between liberal humanitarianism and human rights activism in the humanitarian arena, I seek to situate *shelter on the journey* within the effects of "coloniality" (Quijano 1999, 2000). The coloniality of power is a historical world phenomenon that helps pin down disseminated colonial situations in late modernity and late capitalism (see, e.g., Grosfoguel and Georas 2001; Mignolo 2000). In using a coloniality lens, I especially consider three interconnected conceptual issues. The first is who assists as a humanitarian in the Global South; the second is what subject becomes classified as a humanitarian concern. And finally, I consider the specific political and capitalist conditions that construct those subjectivities.

In particular, humanitarian actors helping migrant subjects work to ensure their activity is seen through an "emergency imaginary" (coined by Calhoun 2008). This emergency imaginary is informed by movement-associated humanitarian work and is a useful heuristic device that frames the transit migrant situation as an emergency, thereby shifting its human consequences and ethical implications.

This book goes beyond mere critique of the limitations of the humanitarian project as not being able to change the emergency-like scenario and reveals both the potential and ambiguity manifested in the shelter's moments of solidarity, in the distributing of food and water as a subversive act and the activism that spins off these experiences within the humanitarian project in shelters nascent in the local Global South.

Dignifying Transit and Liberal Humanitarianism

Shelters stand at the heart of the mobility-driven humanitarian project in Mexico. These sites emerged in the 1980s along the U.S.-Mexico border and have proliferated across the country since then. When I conducted my fieldwork in Mexico, the principal shelter network, the Pastoral Dimension of Human Mobility (DPMH), had gathered sixty-three shelters, soup kitchens, and relief centers. At the time of my fieldwork, shelters had dormitories for migrants; there were *comedores* (soup kitchens) with health programs as well as programs linked to educational institutions, and six human rights centers were part of the DPMH (DPMH 2012:55). In the year 2020, BBVA (Banco Bilbao Vizcaya Argentaria) research published a map with shelters across the country. The number had risen to at least ninety-six. The map was compiled based on data from Médecins Sans Frontières (MSF), International Organisation for Migration (IOM), Network for the Documentation of Migrant Defense Organizations (REDODEM), the International Committee of the Red Cross (ICRC), news reports, and social media (BBVA 2020).

Shelters usually work with the church. The role of the church as advocate, in this case through the shelter, has to do with a broader development referred as the widespread de-privatization of religion, "that is, the increasingly public and active role played by churches and religious groups throughout the world in ways that sometimes challenge state institutions and their regulatory activities" (Hagan 2008:78). The role of the church and of priests acting as human rights defenders has particularities within most shelters. Some priests (often missionaries) working in shelters at times actually oppose church structures (Marchena 2016). Some represent their agenda as radical and emphasize their missionary conscience, the loss of fear that compels them to help those in need on the ground, even in a risk-filled environment. As noted by the main faith-based shelter network, the DPMH, "we went from providing humanitarian assistance to the responsibility to advocate for migrants as human rights defenders and promoters" (DPMH 2012:108). Shelters' main mission is to provide humanitarian assistance, and it is based on this humanitarian assistance that they bear witness to suffering, which then is used to share testimonies in political advocacy activities and reports.

As attention has been drawn to what is happening to Central American transit migrants, many actors have gravitated to the shelters, including national and international humanitarian actors and civil society. The key actors are diverse as the National Commission for Human Rights (CNDH), Mexico's ombudsman's office and an autonomous state-funded organization, and Grupo Beta, a patrol force of the INM established to rescue migrants transiting Mexico in dangerous situations. They include international humanitarian actors providing emergency assistance, such as the Red Cross and MSF. These international nongovernmental organizations (INGOs) have appeared on the scene, albeit only in certain locations, with projects of limited timeframes, and without joining the social movement. AI has drafted reports, issued urgent appeals for human rights defenders, and at times provided relief aid. The IOM is in an ambiguous position, providing relief aid but also serving states and lacking a human rights mandate. The United Nations Office of the High Commissioner for Human Rights (OHCHR) cautiously joins events to discuss the human rights of migrants. The United Nations High Commissioner for Refugees (UNHCR) has mostly engaged in indirect assistance (Hagan 2008:85). Shelters have joined in coalitions with other nongovernmental human rights organizations for human rights of migrants and established a network to seek support and unite as a social movement.

Given there is no official definition of humanitarian assistance, any actor can claim to be providing assistance as a humanitarian act. Shelters in Mexico refer to their distribution of material goods as humanitarian assistance as the main mission and style themselves as human rights defenders. Political advocacy is one part of the shelter's main work. As a social movement, the network of shelters (along with other civil society actors) seeks dignified free transit and justice for all migrants. It employs a counterhegemonic human rights discourse and an anticapitalist agenda. Thus, Hagan notes within this context, while civil society actors mediate between the state and migrants (2008:84), this book highlights they also actively work to denounce the state. In short, the shelter site reveals a morphing arrangement that includes multiple networks, authorities, struggles, social justice goals and moral drivers.

This might not be considered humanitarian work by international humanitarian actors (mostly from the Global North) precisely because it is political—they might classify shelter advocacy as human rights activism, which is also a distinction made by the *Dimensión Pastoral de la Movilidad Humana* (Pastoral Dimension of Human Mobility, DPMH) (DPMH 2012:108). Yet human rights activism in Mexico is part and parcel of humanitarian assistance.

At the heart of the shelter is the distribution of humanitarian assistance in the form of food, hygiene products, clothes, and more specialized services, such as helping with phone calls to family and friends, transferring money from family members to migrants, giving advice on the dangers and risks of the journey, and providing spiritual support.

No two shelters are alike when it comes to infrastructure, rules, staff, location, resources, implementing actors, donors, and so on. Therefore, it is impossible to provide a representative image of a shelter. However, shelters do share the common goals of providing humanitarian assistance and promoting the human rights of migrants. In *Humanitarian Reason* Fassin defines sets of responses to suffering as "humanitarian government." He argues that the vocabulary we use of "suffering, compassion, assistance and responsibility to protect forms part of our political life: it serves to qualify the issues involved and to reason about choices made." (2012:2). How humanitarian logics trickles down to transit communities has its particularities with its own set of potentials and limitations driven by other logics as will be detailed later.

Instead of following a single established path, shelters pick and choose from a variety of options to operate as humanitarian sites that go beyond conventional forms of bureaucratic authority and are governed by Christian logic to help those in need and express solidarity, hospitality, and—in the cases explored in this book—political advocacy based on bearing witness and sharing testimonies. This logic is informed by a long tradition of Catholic social teachings defending the right to migrate and the "church's view of itself as a 'pilgrim people in a pilgrim church' as well as on principles of Catholic social theology that emphasize that the causes of migration are embedded in structural injustices and must be resolved: poverty, market imbalances and political strife" (Hagan 2008:89). There are also documents from the Vatican on social teachings and pastoral work that use the concept of migration as a fundamental human right (ibid.).

In the shelters, this book focuses on how actors represent a diverse spectrum of authority informed by a liberal humanitarian agenda. This agenda supports liberal peace and respects the sovereign authority of the state to control its borders, an ethos that collides with the Christian concept of migration as a fundamental human right. Shelters must therefore navigate social and political dynamics in collaboration with other actors on the ground and operate within the territorial boundaries of the nation-state. International humanitarian actors enter the shelter site under the premise of apoliticism. Notwithstanding, scholars have pointed out that humanitarianism is unable to avoid politics (Barnett 2011:3–9; Ticktin 2011:19–20). Indeed, state actors use a humanitarian agenda to control migration and borders. All actors involved with shelters come together in this site to implement their services, donate, and cooperate.

Yet given that shelters bring together a plethora of humanitarian actors, contradictory political effects emerge within collaborations. Conflicts and tensions among the wide range of conceptualizations of humanitarianism become obvious. Therefore, attempting to create a clean division between distributing humanitarian assistance and human rights activism is challenging on the ground.

The confusion between humanitarianism and human rights activism is not an issue particular to shelters. Humanitarianism and human rights activism often are used as synonyms; they are not, though their definitions overlap. Scholars and human rights activists have added to the confusion, albeit unintentionally. For decades, the two concepts have been lumped together, hence the difficulty highlighted by Barnett (2011:16) in identifying the differences between them. The key differences, he notes, are that human rights activists deal with a legal, rights-based discourse, while humanitarianism deals with a discourse of needs that focuses on moral codes and sentiments. In other words, human rights activism deals with an instrument that serves to end suffering in the long term, and humanitarianism is about keeping people alive (ibid.). This demarcation, despite its usefulness, does not always materialize on the ground and is not obvious in shelters. The difficulty of sustaining these distinctions is mapped throughout this book. During fieldwork, I held assumptions of blurred distinctions; therefore, my quest was to find the politics of one humanitarian project for migrants in transit. What I found were many forms and many absences of humanitarian politics in the arena of irregular transit migration in Mexico.

Why the Shelter?

During my research, a prominent scholar asked me at a conference, Why study the shelter when there is still so much suffering and death in movement in the region? Why study the shelter if its impact is (perceived to be) so limited? These questions and assumptions are not misguided. Publications such as *The Land of Open Graves* by De León (2015) are much-needed reminders that the deadly effects of borders and migration controls are not stopping but increasing. In *Clandestine Routes*, Brigden (2018) evidences the tragedy of the clandestine journeys of those in transit. In *Transit Lives*, Vogt (2018) examines the commodification of the migrant in transit and the violent trepidations Central Americans are exposed to across Mexico—from the locality to the police and organized crime.

Literature on charity and humanitarian work argues that humanitarianism can be part of the problem rather than the solution, especially considering the kind of politics (or absence thereof) spinning off humanitarianism and the making of a subject of care. This body of literature does not intend to discard the value of humanitarian interventions but rather to tease out the issues that emerge in, for example, ethics and politics, how humanitarian interventions address needs, how interventions can be improved and whether they are needed, how humanitarian governance is contradictory, how it has created material hierarchies of humanity, the emerging militarization of the humanitarian helper, the constitution of the subject of need as humanitarian, and most recently, humanitarians themselves, their imaginations and motivations to help (Barnett 2011; Barnett and Gross Stein 2012; Barnett and Weiss 2008; Bornstein and Redfield 2011; Donnelly 1993; Fassin 2010, 2011, 2012; Fearon 2008; Feldman and Ticktin 2010; Malkki 2015; Ophir 2010; Petryna 2003; Ticktin 2011, 2014 among others).

The study of the shelter site makes a unique contribution to this body of knowledge, especially within the irregular transit context, concerning local actors and the Global South. Shelters do not only portray themselves as stops to find help on a journey; they seek to support free dignified transit migration as a matter of humanitarianism and human rights. They seek to provide such support along the way, distributing food, spiritual support, healthcare, and other basic needs and services and also lobbying for the human rights and free transit of migrants. In short, the act of dignifying movement in shelters reveals the value of supporting rather than controlling the movement of the suffering.

Notwithstanding, the shelter site is not problem-free and reveals the structures that bring migrants to its doors. Having a volition of its own, even if constrained, the shelter produces unique solutions to the issue of movement. By gathering diverse humanitarian actors, shelters reveal and contest the limits and potentials of alleviating suffering in movement through humanitarian intervention: legal status, persecution and abuse by authorities, xenophobia, poverty, risks, health and psychological ailments, destitution, uncertainty, and victimization by criminals. Looking closely at who is assisted reveals pervasive global inequalities linked to poverty, migration controls, and border enforcement. Finally, shelters reveal that irregular migration is not only a problem of state policies in receiving states (Castles 2004) nor only about death and violence. Unauthorized migration is also an activity of escape, survival, struggle, and resistance, of faith and great hope, of camaraderie and social relationships, of courage and resilience to violence, risk, and abuse. By shifting focus to local humanitarian solutions, this book does not seek to undermine awareness of strategic political plans that have resulted in systemic exclusion and grave human suffering. Instead, its aim is to provide further evidence of lived resistance to those plans, situated on the practices of the emerging humanitarian project locally and in the Global South.

As I noted earlier, shelters operate in collaboration with multiple other actors, many times with contradictory agendas concerning transit, borders, and migration controls yet able to cooperate within the same space. Shelters are developing outside the Western-dominated system of humanitarianism (Barnett 2011:16) but are awkwardly linked to it at a structural and practical level. Notwithstanding, other humanitarian actors often enter and leave shelters in an ad hoc manner. In shelters, humanitarian assistance emerges from the locality, the church, and civil society, as opposed to coming from across international borders (as is the case for example with the Red Cross and Médecins Sans Frontières, or MSF) with ostensibly apolitical agendas. International actors bring into play other political and moral dynamics. On the one hand, humanitarian agendas focus on saving lives and alleviating suffering, but on the other, an increasingly predominant liberal humanitarian agenda enmeshes the movement of a subject in a violent concern of criminal security rather than one of rights. To mediate this struggle, the shelter sees local human rights defenders unite in a social movement to demand acknowledgment of the lives disappeared, share testimonies, denounce states and criminal networks, and struggle to define and lobby for free transit as a matter of human rights.

The degree of enforcement of the U.S.-Mexico border has swelled, and so has the number of shelters across Mexico. Shelters, as local humanitarian sites in the Global South, have been much less studied than sites of violence such as the infamous U.S.-Mexico border. The heuristic value of shelters as humanitarian sites has attracted less political, media, and academic attention. Suffering pervades the conversation, and help is normally not seen as either the problem or the solution.

What is at stake here? Humanitarianism is known more broadly for being international and for alleviating suffering and saving lives threatened by war and natural disasters. It is also strongly imagined as apolitical. Within the realm of migration (including of refugees), humanitarianism has been denounced as contributing to managing immigration and asylum seeking—an issue of the highest political order—as antipolitical (see, e.g., Diken and Laustsen 2005; Muller 2004; Nyers 2006a, 2006b). Similar accusations have been made about human trafficking (Anderson and Andrijasevic 2008; Ticktin 2011:19–24). Humanitarianism has been criticized intellectually for not dealing with the structural causes of suffering—indeed, for facilitating their continuation.

Academics have highlighted how the framing of victimhood has depoliticized the subjects shaped by humanitarian help. Finally, lack of state legitimation of movement to escape suffering arising from poverty has framed this issue as developmental yet managed it as one of security. But there is a harsh reality, one that cannot be hidden behind demarcations of suffering and/or legitimate reasons to migrate: humans are increasingly dying not only while attempting to cross borders but also in transit across rivers, oceans, and landmasses to reach a better or safer place. Human rights defenders are demanding free transit through political advocacy on the basis of the humanitarian assistance they have distributed and the suffering to which they have borne witness while embedded in this national security framework.

The tendency to frame movement as opposed to security has destabilized the relationship of movement to freedom, especially since the turn of the twenty-first century. Local humanitarian assistance in shelters negotiates this abstract issue daily, showing how humanitarian work and activism manifests in the Global South and how this type of emergency safe haven is part of the ever-expanding landscape of border practices.

A Note on Methods Used at Shelters

The method used for the research underpinning this book is founded on a very traditional anthropological mode of knowing: fieldwork (Geertz 1973). I conducted my fieldwork in Mexico during 2012, when I volunteered and conducted participant observation in one soup kitchen and two shelters and lived in one shelter, which I refer to as La Esperanza.[4] The selection of these shelters and soup kitchen was informed by research before and during fieldwork and mediated through contacts in the field. The shelters were selected for their visibility in the humanitarian arena in Mexico and as key locations en route. La Esperanza, the protagonist shelter of this book, was identified as one of the leading shelters in the social movement—one of the most visible shelters in the movement in national and international media, attracting a wide and diverse group of humanitarian actors. Father Alberto, who founded La Esperanza, was seen as a moral leader in Mexico, leading civil society actors. He had won multiple human rights prizes and was a leader and key speaker for the movement. When volunteering and living in La Esperanza, I both participated in the everyday life of those studied and grasped their self-representations and practices. I also traveled across Mexico to visit other shelters.

Alongside my volunteering, I interviewed over one hundred migrants about their biographies in relation to the services they received and their understanding of human rights and assistance. I interviewed three key groups of migrants transiting Mexico: Mexicans, indigenous minorities (Tzotzils) in Mexico, and Central Americans. Most of my interviewees were male. Although most of the migrant interviews are not directly quoted in this book, they were invaluable in shaping my perceptions and interpretations of the field, shelter, and humanitarian actors.

The primary source for this book was ethnography in shelters and twenty-two interviews with actors with humanitarian agendas, including human rights defenders and actors from the IOM, medical humanitarian and human rights INGOs, NGOs, and the CNDH. Through unstructured and semistructured interviews, I sought to understand their institutional aims, agendas, experiences, understandings of humanitarianism and human rights, as well as their biographical trajectories.

In determining how the continuation of assistance is ensured and how subjects of this assistance fall between the cracks of the state, I considered how the state categorizes subjects for assistance, how other actors attempt to reshape, interpret, contest, and/or struggle against these categories (or lobby for other categories to be established), and how global observers of contested categorizations reinterpret those contests. What constitutes a correct classification in the context of crisis? Can state categories, human rights, and other institutional classifications be identical to the self-identification of the subject? What can academic analysis contribute to this challenging endeavor? How—and/or why—is that contribution desirable?

This book helps discover how the representation of assistance targeting high mobility is conceptualized and implemented as humanitarian, how representations and practices differ between humanitarian actors, and how these differences creates new acts and expectations of assisting migrants as humanitarian. The book relies on this social constructivist framework. If we consider the world as shaped by knowledge, then discourse and symbols construct the shelter world. Thus, discourse and symbols influence how we act, reason, socialize, create bonds, express affectivity and compassion, and participate in society. If we expect humanitarian work to accomplish its goals, we need to attend to how work succeeds in being viewed and legitimized as humanitarian and how its clients become viewed as humanitarian subjects.

During my time in the field, I quickly realized that separating "knowing" from "sensing" might not necessarily be valid for the subjects/objects of sociology studies. The idea of knowing versus sensing collided with the subjects I sought to study: migrants, human rights defenders, and their experiences of humanitarianism especially. Drawing on Durkheim's discussion of science and belief and Levi-Strauss's work on distinctions between magic and science, Hastrup highlights a valid recognition: "In human life, there is always both something that we know and something that we simply sense or feel" (2004:457).

This book represents my understanding of those I sought to research, shaped by the discourse from my academic background, which in turn incorporates and blends into my fieldwork. Anthropologists have noted that ethnographers and those they observe manipulate each other and the categories they use, producing new meaning (Solimene 2013:4). Reflexivity, knowing, feeling, and sensing all played important roles in the knowledge production of this book. My informants also observed me, talked about me, and had their own reaction to my presence as a female Central American academic. I did not attempt to interfere with the work being done in shelters nor with the perspectives of migrants, but I was aware that my presence, the way I talked, what I talked about, and my interpretations of daily experiences in the field were present in my data production and analytical journey.

Ethics

Given the nature of humanitarian interventions and the hierarchies of humanity this has implied, ethics have been at the heart of humanitarian research (see, e.g., Barnett 2011; Barnett and Gross Stein 2012; Bornstein and Redfield 2011; Barnett and Weiss 2008; Donnelly 1993; Fassin 2010, 2011, 2012; Feldman and Ticktin 2010; Malkki 2015; Ophir 2010; Petryna 2003; Ticktin 2011, 2014, among others). Within this context, from an ethical standpoint, there is vigorous debate over whether irregular migration should be researched at all (Düvell et al. 2010). The debate ranges from ethical issues to do with methodology to the type of knowledge produced on this topic.

Certainly, due to issues arising from constructed demarcations of legal categories, research on irregular migration is highly sensitive, and it is important to consider potential risks, understand where to draw ethical lines, and present findings in a morally responsible manner. Furthermore, this book follows research aiming to overcome "superstition and atrocities that characterise previous responses to a certain group, behaviour or phenomenon should be conducted" (Humphrys cited in Düvell et al. 2010:228).

This research deals with a pocket of irregular migration that falls within the realm of organizations, their representations, and practices. In relation to a "humanitarian reason," I follow Fassin (2012) and the need for much caution required, especially when studying those who assist marginalized groups. There is the challenge, as he notes, of how much distance the researcher should maintain to the subject so as to avoid accusations of both relativism and cynicism.

Based on the Swedish Research Council's ethical guidelines, I employed diverse strategies to make sure that I informed all participants clearly about my role, purpose, and research process, although I cannot, of course, guarantee their clarity on the information I provided. I volunteered in shelters, which gave me an insider/outsider role, raising ethical questions related both to access and to how the information I collected would be used. In making sense of this data, I refer at this point to "removal" as an allusion to what I have chosen to write about to sustain balance between human rights defenders, humanitarian actors, state actors, and migrants, to remain ethical, and to safeguard the safety of my informants and to not include any confidential information. All necessary anonymities have been made.

During my fieldwork, my informants and I moved between identities. I moved between being a researcher, a volunteer, a woman, a Central American, and so on. My informants moved between being volunteers, Central American, migrants, priests, men, human rights defenders, doctors, women, European and so on. These shifts are important to consider to delineate what it means to participate in the field and be an objective researcher.

Finally, a short note on language. All interviews, most reports, and the vast majority of information on transit migrants in the media were in Spanish. As a native Spanish speaker with a master's degree in bilingual translation (with merit), I am qualified to do the translations myself, though I must note that I am translating from my native language and not into it, which may reduce accuracy. This leads me to a final conceptual clarification regarding the term I translate as "shelters"—literally *casas del migrante* (migrant homes). Here I follow, for example, Missionari di San Carlo Scalabrini, a network of *casas del migrante*, which translates *casas del migrante* as shelter on its website. Other actors use the term interchangeably with *albergues* or *hogar-refugios*, both of which are also translated as shelter. Scholars may add to the confusion with some translating the term as houses (see, e.g., Díaz de León 2023). Yet most *casas del migrante* themselves translate these spaces as shelters on their websites as do other scholars (see, e.g., Brigden 2018; Hagan 2009; Vogt 2018). There are also soup kitchens (*comedores*), las Patronas (civilians), which distribute food along the train tracks, and other types of civil society organizations that join into networks. This book focuses on shelters (*casas del migrante, albergues,* and *refugios*) as civil society associations acting from the bottom up, which are faith-based and members of the Pastoral Dimension of Human Mobility (DPMH). Other actors that are not faith-based are also accounted for, and will be distinguished in the analysis.

Now, to this book's journey.

This Book's Journey

Chapter 1 sets the stage for this study by situating it in coloniality and in historical and theoretical considerations and by examining the politics, conditions, and operation of humanitarianism and human rights in general. I specify the particularities that arise when humanitarianism addresses issues of migration and forced migration, also considering conditions, instrumentalization, and politics. I build on previous critiques to delineate the vision of humanitarianism and human rights activists lobbying for free dignified transit in shelters in Mexico. I introduce the main groups involved in the distribution of humanitarian assistance in shelters, touching on key distinctions between groups and some of the ethical complexities that emerge in seeking to categorize humanitarian actors and their goals in relation to the interrelationship between dignity and freedom of movement explored in this book.

In Chapter 2, I review the social world of the shelter as an emerging humanitarian complex centered on hospitality. I begin with the social architecture of the shelter. Given that not all shelters are the same, I choose a highly visible shelter, which I refer to as La Esperanza, to illustrate the actors involved in assisting migrants across Mexico. I explore the open ethos of everyday life in the shelter, consider the role of rules and schedules, and uncover tensions manifested in the social dynamics of attempting to balance threat and support the migrant. The particularities of the shelter site begin to come to light.

In Chapter 3, I explore the political dynamics of charity and solidarity in shelters. This exploration implies examining two key humanitarian logics that manifest in shelters. One is based on a Christian logic of solidarity that supports the dignified transit of all humans. The other comes from a bureaucratic logic informed by liberal humanitarianism and seeks to shape a humanitarian subject that can be governed by specific humanitarian policies, also in the name of dignity. I begin the chapter by providing a comparative example of a site governed by international actors to identify key differences and similarities and the shelter and then explore the role of power behind different logics of distributing humanitarian assistance to irregular transit migrants. Finally, I examine the effects of these power plays on the ground by looking at the distribution of material goods and services. I argue that a fragmented humanitarian subject is emerging. The power struggles in the chain of distributing humanitarian assistance face contradictions regarding the issue of movement, yet collaboration is represented as necessary to trigger social change.

In Chapter 4, I delve into the conditions associated with humanitarian assistance and the potential political effects deriving from them. I begin by exploring the criminal business human rights defenders are confronting, business which preys on the irregular migrant. I then explore the impact of criminalizing migration on humanitarian assistance. I examine the politics of action taken by different actors in shelters and their loss of fear, concluding with a discussion of the politics of exposure implicit in assisting irregular migrants in Mexico that contributes to our broader understanding of how the humanitarian project is currently under threat.

In Chapter 5, I explore the complications around humanitarianizing precarious migration. I first look at the humanitarian visa as the only available humanitarian instrument of the state. I then consider two mechanisms for political advocacy: the production of data and the sharing of testimonies. I identify three potential political effects—postpolitical, antipolitical, and progressive politics—emerging from advocacy geared toward free transit. I ground my analysis in the identification of three mechanisms in creating these political effects: the use of extreme violence; the focus on violence and peace over freedom of movement; and the focus on violence at origin, transit, and destiny and the objectification of the migrant. On the other hand, human rights defenders demonstrated their progressive politics by denouncing the Mexican state and the INM, but with no clear conceptualization and practice of free transit (migration) as a human right. Research must continue to assess the knowledge and practices of humanitarianism and human rights and their role in producing social hierarchies and social struggles linked to the principle of freedom of movement.

Shelter on the Journey outlines how shelter sites challenge liberal democracies' need to control, restrict, regulate, punish, and securitize migration, focusing more specifically on the challenges the liberal humanitarian agenda poses on sites like the shelter. This book argues that these challenges are not only about notions of liberal peace and sovereignty but are also at the core of liberal principles of freedom of movement in relation to dignity, equality, and human worth. When we analyze migration in relation to the humanitarian project, we are often drawn to assumptions about sovereignty, peace, and security, but it is the very responses by states and liberal humanitarian actors that put these assumptions into question. How do ideas of freedom of movement, dignity, equality, and human worth fit within the restrictions set on mobility, especially targeting the poor in the Global South? The contradictions within liberal arguments concerning freedom of movement as embedded in human rights are not only a matter for the poor from the Global South but are also about the validity of the universality of human rights, extending a Western understanding of them.

1

"They Walk as Fugitives"

Situating Shelters and Transit Migration

"We were trying to find a place for them to hide as they were being persecuted everywhere," Father Paulino, a founder of one of the shelters better known in the North, tells me. He explains the vast range of challenges faced by migrants along their journeys—from difficulty finding a place to rest all the way to rape, kidnapping, and murder. There is concern over migrants' persecution, their experiences as fugitives. From this starting point, shelters' missions and visions have shifted across time toward political advocacy, Father Paulino continues to explain.

> Services such as lodging, health, the matter of giving services in regards to their rights—the team began to be perfected, little by little. When our work became known as organized, civil society shifted, social movements shifted [toward us], but this was after six years of work. In the first five years, we needed everything. We had only will and some very capable people. Later, we got support from everyone.

From those early days, the team became professionalized in his shelter: "Today it is not only a matter of food, lodging, and health. What we have today is humanitarian attention; we have professionalized the attention to victims of torture, healthcare matters, migration management, and political engagement." The shelters have shifted into being deeply political, and their leaders have clear, specific demands. "We are in it deep down, to the bone and flesh, for political change," expresses Father Paulino with passion.

Shelters are key sites for the construction of free dignified migration. Assistance and advocacy for people considered not entitled to protection (and whose movement has become a security concern) is a growing idea, practice, and politics in shelters. Assistance and advocacy are closely linked to the role of legitimation, recognition, and identity coming from receiving states, mainly located in the Global North. In places where migration happens, the law, policy, and practices cannot be separated into the legal categories used to classify individuals' reasons to move as the tool to recognize who is eligible for protection or not, whose movement is legitimate and whose movement needs to be controlled and/or policed. Suffering plays a pivotal role as the main device to categorize and pass political judgment over who to protect, expel, criminalize, detain, persecute, or keep waiting. Waiting has become an increasingly visible issue for irregular migrants. Scholars have looked at the temporal dimension of illegality both in terms of prolonged times waiting across borders and as embedded within sociohistorical contexts. In these contexts, they note the fluidity between "regular" and "irregular" and how both this status may overlap (Jacobsen et al. 2021). Menjívar (2006) coins this uncertain legal status in Salvadoran and Guatemalan immigrants as "liminal legality."

In the experience of shelters, a universalism in movement is assumed, and care necessitates a politics of solidarity that this book refers to as dignified transit. The dignifying of irregular transit migration is seen as highly relevant by shelters and other liberal humanitarian actors given the horror evoked from its violation. Therefore, unpacking dignified transit is not only about freedom of movement and human worth but also about identifying threat in these classifications. In the paradox of humans both threatening and giving worth to human lives, framed by Fassin (2007) as a politics of life, the role of power over the lives of those assisted or declared "illegal" situates the shelter within power struggles over protection, care, and giving worth to transit migrants' freedom of movement (in accordance to race, ethnicity, and economic privilege).

This chapter seeks to situate the shelter experience of threat and human worth in defining dignity and freedom in relation to mobility within the constitutive elements of global capitalist power. Global capitalist power is based on the imposition of the classification of the world's population in accordance with race, ethnicity, economic privilege (Quijano 1999:342), and, in this book, passport nationality.

In Mexico, migrant shelters have become specialized sites managing this threatened population of "others," which lacks the rights, documents, and/or visas to migrate. These shelters first emerged in the 1980s across the U.S.-Mexico border, anticipating increasing border controls in which irregular migrants, the vulnerable, were becoming "invisibilized" (their needs not acknowledged). Over the years, this humanitarian trail spread south across Mexico, ultimately reaching the southern border. These shelters are distinct from humanitarian spaces that have been denounced as sites of control of extraterritorial spaces targeting outsiders (Agier 2013; Diken and Laustsen 2005; Rajaram and Grundy-Warr 2004; Voutira and Harrell-Bond 1995). Rather than controlling movement, shelters seek to support movement. Yet this support is complex and occurs in the presence of multiple humanitarian actors, in an environment of violence and amid the global capitalist forces shelters seek to oppose.

The chapter begins by setting the stage, looking at precarious migration and its relationship to emergency conditions and humanitarian crisis. It briefly looks back to colonial times to trace the emergence of human rights discourse and humanitarianism in Mexico and then moves to looking at human rights and migration in Mexico. At the contours of this history lurks the figure of the (non)humanitarian subject being assisted as a matter of race, poverty, and criminality. The chapter looks at who is currently the subject of care and the issue of movement, from a liberal lens, beyond Mexico. Finally, shelter politics are outlined considering the insertion of liberal humanitarianism's (a)political nature into shelter life.

Beyond creating a new internationalism, the shelter site is primarily a local site of subversion, yet its power extends its boundaries and struggles with tensions latched to the agendas of liberal humanitarianism that reaffirm controlling movement. In the quest to dignify free transit, shelter on the journey confronts the instrumentalization of forced and voluntary migration based on where you come from and your economic assets. As this chapter argues, these distinctions have been pivotal to demarcating the (lack of) privilege to move and the subject of care as fugitive.

Setting the Stage: The Emergency Imaginary and Precarious Migration

Precarious migration has always been part of the history of the world. Beyond conquest, trade, and war, mobility has been about threat, risk, death, and, later on, slavery. Precarious mobilities today are also about emergencies, national security, and their relationship to immigration policy. Bridget Anderson, a renowned migration and citizenship scholar, writes in her book *Us and Them*: "All mobilities are by no means equivalent but are differentially constructed and experienced, forced, encouraged and prevented" (2013:12).

In Mexico, the shift toward denouncing and addressing precarious migration as an emergency occurred in the twenty-first century. The emergency imaginary, meaning how the human consequences of transit migration are understood, has rapidly morphed and been denounced a humanitarian crisis, mostly by civil society. Scholars have contributed in recent years to our understanding of transit migration in Mexico (see, e.g., Anguiano and Cruz Piñero 2014; Arriola Vega 2012; Basok et al. 2015; Brigden 2014, 2016, 2018; Casillas 2003, 2007; Nájera Aguirre 2016; Nyberg Sørensen 2013, among others) with considerations of issues around gender, unaccompanied minors, the securitization of migration, Mexican migration law, and the impact of U.S. border policies on transit migration and violence. The humanitarian crisis needs to be placed within this context. This chapter considers attempts to dignify irregular transit migration of the poor from the Global South within the emerging humanitarian space that is the shelter and what the emergency imaginary tells us about humanitarianism and human rights activism contemporarily.

In the Western-dominated system of humanitarianism, a humanitarian crisis is used to define an emergency. For United Nations (UN) agencies, a complex emergency is a sign of a conflict-related humanitarian disaster "involving a high degree of breakdown and social dislocation and, reflecting this condition, requiring a system-wide aid response from the international community" (Duffield 2001:12). The Red Cross understands complex emergencies to be a kind of humanitarian crisis (International Federation of Red Cross and Red Crescent Societies 2006).

The term "complex humanitarian emergency" gained currency from the 1980s (Duffield 2001:83) and was seen as successful in helping refugees and displaced persons by the UN at the time. The term suggests that some emergencies "have multiple causes, involve multiple local actors and compel an international response" (ibid. 84). The response from the international humanitarian community to complex humanitarian emergencies, namely the emergency imaginary, led to a shift in the global order on how we understand human consequences (Calhoun 2008:83–84).

Temporality also became a defining characteristic of the emergency imaginary. Even if the notion of emergency implies something sudden and unpredictable that requires immediate action, some emergencies develop over extended periods of time, even years, and take a long time to break into international consciousness or to be prioritized—or even acknowledged—in political agendas (ibid. 83). This temporal issue continues to be pervasive. The dire situation of Central Americans transiting Mexico has endured for several decades, even if not visible or acknowledged by the Mexican state or the international community.

In Mexico, the humanitarian crisis is mainly denounced along the lines of precarious migration linked to the impunity of authorities, criminal networks, and individuals and the violence this has implied. Precariousness should be accounted as multidimensional and "constructed by specific state policies, regulations and practices of policy implementation, activism, discourses and so forth" (Goldring et al. 2009:240). Precarious migration in Mexico is a complex matter informed by how irregular migrants deal with the alteration of their normal existence and negotiate precariousness when attempting to cross borders, transit, reside, and work in a place where they are not citizens. Human rights defenders also share depictions of this negotiation. As put by Father Amalio,

> Migration is clandestine and has many aspects. There are many migrants who do not go to shelters. They would not fit. Many migrants live in a psychological situation of war. For example, when they are persecuted, they do not follow the same route, nor will they seek the same resources. Migration spreads in many ways. Some stay, others continue their journey, others follow other paths. Many try to get busy here or in the capital.

Structural violence shaping precarious migration in Mexico is linked to an increase in deportations, detention centers, border patrolling, virtual fences, walls, and stricter (im)migration criteria in a country plagued with impunity. As put by Kotef: "State violence has its own movements, moreover, invasion, infiltration and conquest" (2015:7). In short, the situation in transit through countries like Mexico is appalling (Brigden 2018; Slack 2019; Solano and Massey 2022; Vogt 2018). Transit migrants travel in ever more perilous conditions and face additional risks linked to border enforcement across the country (Amnesty International 2010; DPMH 2012; Nyberg Sørensen 2013). In parts of the country, migrants are pushed to more dangerous routes or have no access to transportation and must walk for days. Rather than taking buses, many Central Americans must hitch a ride on the Beast, the cargo train, risking mutilation or death if they fall off or are thrown off by criminal gangs or train conductors. The cargo trains are sometimes abruptly brought to a halt with the purpose of shaking off migrants who refuse to pay a fare (Molina 2013).

Weather conditions and lack of appropriate clothing and protection have a serious impact on health: many migrants suffer from heatstroke, skin diseases, respiratory infections, and bee attacks, to name a few (see also MSF 2020).[1] Lack of water leads to severe dehydration; many suffer from exhaustion and lack of sleep or food. Laurelio, one of the many migrants I had the opportunity to meet, recounted, "I thought my blood was becoming thicker as I could not drink water for what seemed days. I found some orange trees, and that is how I stayed hydrated." There is also the psychological impact of the journey, which often goes unnoticed. Adding to the stress of transit through Mexican territory is family separation (Abrego 2014), fear of uncertainty, and confrontation with xenophobia and crime.

In Mexico, precarious migration is linked to other forms of direct and indirect violence, as in the case of impunity, corruption, and crime. Both at a national and international level, violence in Mexico is often perceived as a form of cultural, political, and/or institutional incompleteness that needs to be rectified by actors external to the country (Calderón et al. 2015; Legrás 2017; Sánchez Soler 2014). Violence in Mexico within the context of migration is also affected structurally and indirectly in the form of border enforcement outsourcing from receiving states such as the United States, which affects the violent landscape traversed by transit migrants through Mexico (see Introduction).

Other major concerns human rights defenders express are the crimes against humanity the Mexican state might be committing against transit migrants. A report titled *Confronting Crimes against Humanity*, issued in 2016 by the Open Society Justice Initiative, looks into this very issue. Border enforcement in Mexico has increasingly been linked to violations of human rights and abuse by border officials perpetrated against irregular migrants, especially those coming from the Northern Triangle: Guatemala, Honduras, and El Salvador (Basok et al. 2015; Huspek et al. 1998; Kuhner 2011; Marrujo Ruíz 2001; Nyberg Sørensen 2013; Solano and Massey 2022). The business of kidnappings, which is already widespread in the country, is growing (Amnesty International 2010; CNDH 2009, 2011; Ochoa 2012).

Both local authorities and criminal networks have been denounced by civil society as preying on migrants for economic purposes. Kidnapping especially is a profitable activity for organized crime and corrupt local authorities in Mexico. The CNDH reported that in 2008–2009 alone, 9,758 migrants were kidnapped in southern Mexico, most of them (55 percent) Central Americans. In 2010, this figure rose to 11,333 kidnappings in six months, from April to September (CNDH 2011:26)—and these are just the official figures. From 2011 to 2021 it was reported that kidnappings increased by 678 percent (CNDH 2021:7). These figures point to a democratization of kidnapping that has already affected the Mexican population for many years (Ochoa 2012). In the context of Mexico and the U.S.-Mexico border, there is also a denouncement of the proliferation of clandestine graves and lack of trace of those eaten by nature, perishing in the desert, devoured by vultures (Anderson and Reineke 2023; De León 2015; Falcon 2001; Huspek et al. 1998; Meneses 2003; MSF 2020; No More Deaths and Coalición de Derechos Humanos 2021). This is another form of violence demarcating precarious migration.

What is presented as a novelty is not exclusively new, yet there are shifts in both how migration has become framed in policy and law and, in turn, how migration is presented and addressed as a humanitarian crisis by some in Mexico. The definition of the situation as a humanitarian crisis is not shared by most actors nor by society at large. Precarious transit denounced as a humanitarian crisis that necessitates the need to dignify transit migration is as much about identifying threat as it is about human worth.

Tracing Dignity in Mexico

"Dignity" is one of the most controversial and used terms in relation to human life. Our worth as humans has been delineated in the Universal Declaration of Human Rights along the lines of dignity. Human dignity is tied to the recognition that humans have a special value linked to their humanity and are worthy of a certain respect simply because they are human beings. Dignity, in Article 1 of the Universal Declaration of Human Rights, is not only defined as a fundamental right but also as the basis of all fundamental rights. It is the value to be treated with respect for our own worth as humans (Stanford Encyclopedia of Philosophy 2023).

If we are all human, then do we not all possess the "Rights of Man"? In theory, we do, but history tells us that being a subject of human rights depends on war and colonialism and is closely linked to the construction of race (Grosfoguel 2011) and, this book argues, class. This is a history less considered in human rights studies and more presented by postcolonial and decolonial scholars who have focused on situating and showing how human rights have contributed to a capitalist system and logic that has helped to sustain a cheap labor force (Blackburn 2013; de Sousa Santos 2002, 2003, 2007). These criticisms have traced human rights at their inception as contributing to the establishment of a colonial order (Dussel 1999; Gott 2002; de Sousa Santos 2002).

The brief historical journey of this section seeks to situate the classifications that have come to demarcate the subject of human rights in the Americas. This history mostly considers the establishment of colonizers and human rights activists: the church and state, law and religion, constructions of race and the human condition, slavery and freedom, and the use of tools as criminalizing. It then traces the actors constituting caring institutions and solidarity in Mexico.

Who Has Human Worth?

From 1492 to 1500, around fifty thousand square kilometers and three million indigenous peoples were devastated through colonization in the Americas. By 1550, two million square kilometers had been colonized and twenty-five million indigenous peoples had been, integrated into a labor system as free labor producing profit (value) for Europe as the center. This marked Europe's advantage over the Muslim, Indian, and Chinese worlds. During the sixteenth century, in Dussel's words, Weber's "civilized," the supposed possessors of "cultural phenomena in a line of development and significance that had universal significance and value," had commenced a barbaric project characterized by violence, disciplining, and death (Dussel 1998:18). As this project of domination expanded, debates took place on whether indigenous peoples were even human.

The question *Is the indigenous person human?* Arguably arose from a racist imperial attitude at the heart of Eurocentric knowledge, emerging at the intersection between religion and the state and having as its target the "humanization" and "civilization" of indigenous peoples (Gordon 2006; Mignolo 2006; Suárez-Krabbe 2013; Wright-Carozza 2003). This question was debated in the realms of law and ethics in the famous Valladolid debate between the Dominican friar Bartolomé de Las Casas and the humanist scholar Juan Ginés de Sepulveda. The former saw "Indians" as free men in the natural order, while the latter saw them as natural slaves (Calhoun 2010:38). Given that, at this time, capitalist forces were not aligned with political power, the king supported the position of Las Casas because it helped strengthen central state power, while landowners supported Sepulveda so they could continue exploiting the indigenous population with autonomy (ibid. 38–39). But the king was far from the colonies, and his position was merely symbolic. Exploitation pervaded the colonies.

By framing justice in terms of rights, Las Casas became known as a precursor of social and political movements and human rights language in the Americas, such as the movement to end slavery (Wright-Carozza 2003: 292–293). Notwithstanding, Las Casas was denounced for furthering black slavery, a position he later rectified (ibid. 292–293).[2] Indubitably, the church furthered colonization, which threatened human worth through supporting enslavement but paradoxically worked on giving value to the indigenous people as humans. Christian rhetoric was used to justify the massacre and exploitation for profit of millions of indigenous people but also elevated the indigenous person to human during the "first modernity,"[3] a life-saving mechanism needed for "Indians" to survive. Human rights became embedded in struggles triggered by colonialist violence but paradoxically helped sustain this violence. The knowledge coming from the church was critical of colonialism but spoke out from within colonialism (Mignolo 2002:80), through unfounded rationalities of cultural superiority and of colonial powers to "civilize." The humanitarian project can therefore be identified as part of the "civilization" of people targeted by colonial powers to be exploited and conquered (Calhoun 2010:39) and as a form of solidarity seeking the elevation of the indigenous person to human.

In the short historical journey that follows, the legitimation of the indigenous person as free labor profit making and the elevation of human worth in the indigenous person is exemplified by two specific contextual accounts, especially relevant within the context of the shelter and transit migrants: the making of race and criminal bodies.

Situating Threat: The Making of Race and Criminal Bodies

Aníbal Quijano (2000), a Peruvian sociologist, traces the birth of race in its modern form to the Americas. He argues that "the idea of race is with all certainty the most efficient instrument of social domination invented in the last five hundred years" (Quijano 1999:1, translated by the author). Quijano describes that when colonizers first arrived, they began to demarcate themselves as different from those they colonized. These differences promptly were constructed as supposed biological differences between the groups. What followed was the production of completely new social identities: black, mestizo, *zambos mosquito* (given to the inhabitants of the Mosquito Coast), and Indian, among many others. Terms such as "Portuguese" and "Spanish," linked originally to geographical origin, now came to have racial connotations. The relationships established were of domination. And these newly constructed identities were associated with hierarchies and social roles as being constitutive of them. Race and racial identity became instruments not only of basic social classification of the population (ibid. 533) but also of universal social domination (ibid. 535). It is under this premise of racial differences, as "Indians," that (de)humanizing structures took force and questions of the humanity of indigenous populations were debated. As noted previously, the church participated in justifying the making of these racial hierarchies.

The criminalization of bodies was another instrument for domination that was brought by colonizers, linked to race, and involved the participation of the church and religion. Van Schendel and Abraham (2005) point out there are no clear lines between illicitness and laws of states. Law and criminalization emerge from ongoing historical struggles. Federici traces it back to the seventh century, where female bodies were criminalized as witches and punished. Such techniques were taken to America in colonial times to control, dominate, and enslave and were justified through the making of race. I use this example to provide a counter to the exceptionalism of criminalizing migration: from the witch body to today's "illegal," poor body. Federici shows that witches were used sociopolitically in the establishment of a capitalist society as a state initiative (2004:165)—they were made enemies of this state initiative and demarcated further patriarchal power relations. This process materialized with the criminalization of a practice; *maleficium* was introduced as a crime in the legal codes of Teutonic kingdoms in the seventh and eighth centuries. Initially, magical practices that damaged other persons or things were punished, but this punishment had changed by the fifteenth century. Witch trials emerged in the age of revolts, epidemics, and the feudal crisis, when sorcery was "declared a form of heresy and the highest crime against God, Nature, and the State" (ibid.). Twenty-eight treatises against witchcraft were written at the time, culminating with *Malleus Maleficarum* (The Hammer of Witches), published on the eve of Columbus's voyage.

During the early years of Spanish colonization of the Americas, witch trials escalated. The persecution of witches did not happen all of a sudden. Indoctrination was taking place; authorities would present their anxieties about the spread of witches, and people from the community would start denouncing each other. Methods for recognizing witches were shared in villages, and, most importantly, threats were made to "punish those who hid them or came to their assistance" (Federici 2004:166). As the witch hunt arrived in the New World, "Indians" shared a similar destiny with women in Europe. Witch-hunting and devil worshipping became part of the colonial project to break the resistance of the natives and justify colonization and the slave trade. "Everywhere the Spaniards saw the face of the devil . . . in the foods . . . (in) the 'primitive vices of the Indians' . . . in their barbaric languages" (de León 1985 I:33–34 cited in Federici 2004:198). In short, the subject of care from its inception in the Americas had much to do with the construction of race and the criminalizing of bodies.

Beyond conventional forms of territorial, juridical, and bureaucratic authority, the church, missionaries, state power, and landowners engaged the human rights discourse of civilization in the birth of humanitarianism and human rights discourse in the Americas. And even if the church sought to gear justice toward rights, the effect was domination and labor exploitation.

Situating Solidarity and "Civilizing" Powers

In the Mexican case, beyond struggling for the humanization of the "Indian," the church was given the responsibility of taking over institutions that cared for the neediest in society. Starting with the opening of Jesús Hospital by Hernán Cortés in 1524 in Mexico, the church took charge of social assistance in institutions such as hospices and orphanages. It also had an important role in shaping the social fabric during the colonial period. As the colonial period ended, the liberal state acquired the responsibility for administering social needs but was unable to fill the vacuum left by the clergy.

The president, Porfirio Díaz, during the end of the nineteenth century, allowed the church to continue with its social work (Butcher 2010:3–5), a role it continues to fulfill to this day. In short, "civilizing" powers not only took lives and brought salvation but also brought education, medical care, and spiritual (Calhoun 2010:39) and social services to the colonies.

Social and spiritual services have been important spaces for opposing the state. In Mexico, the church has been crucial for both helping the neediest and constituting the main form of solidarity and civil society itself. Religious institutions became vehicles for those who had the time to volunteer and could provide charitable donations, and Butcher (2010) thus argues that they are the basis of Mexican social solidarity and civil society. Seen from this historical perspective, current volunteer activity—and civil society more broadly—comes from ecclesiastical rather than civil structures (ibid. 5). In other words, "civilizing" and "humanizing" powers have constituted important social movements, opposing racist and imperial attitudes while also contributing to them.

One aspect omitted in this targeted history of human rights and humanitarianism in the Americas relates to native cultural and social beliefs and how they intersect with the Christian religion in charitable institutions, volunteer action, and civil society. Certainly, other important manifestations of solidarity and charity emerge within a society constituted by many cultures, where impulses to do good are not specifically linked to religion and are missed in this account. The sheer plurality of indigenous cultures before colonization makes it an impossible task for this book to address this gap. However, even with this important limitation in mind, seeing the emergence of humanitarianism through an institutional lens has its own value, and considering the role of the church and religion in Mexico in relation to understanding freedom of movement and the humanitarian project provides an important contribution to the puzzle of this book. We now transport ourselves to the links between human rights and migration in contemporary Mexico.

The Issue of Human Rights and Irregular Migration in Mexico

The subject in need of care, rights, and freedom to transit Mexico is heavily informed by liberal forces that have instrumentalized forced and voluntary migration, which by default inform our understanding of human rights and undocumented migration in Mexico, yet with some particularities. Immigration policy often rests on the distinction between asylum and immigration (Anderson 2013:54). In the following section, the instrumentalization of forced and voluntary migration as centered in suffering is considered.

Then the role of citizenship (and the noncitizen) within the context of Mexico is situated and there is consideration on how human rights are territorially bounded by nation-state structures with implications within the Mexican context.

As O'Connell Davidson notes, suffering occupies a key place within refugee and forced migration studies (2014:142), by default informing migration studies in general and indeed humanitarianism and human rights. The selection of suffering in migration is up to each state's criteria. In accordance with international refugee and human rights law, those who are understood as having suffered are identified with a status that grants them certain rights and protections. In the absence of an objective measure to determine who suffers, states use selective processes legitimating certain types of suffering that have forced a person to move. For example, suffering from poverty is not considered a legitimate cause to move in the refugee protection regime (ibid.). Thus, the suffering of some becomes invisible in the protection categories implemented by states.

Indeed undocumented migration triggered by suffering from poverty is identified as illegal migration. Illegality and smuggling struggle with fitting in/accessing a protection regime and seeking asylum. The human rights of those identified as illegal are vaguely defined, if defined at all, in relation to policing activities within borders, detention centers, and deportation mechanisms.

Scholars researching the refugee protection regime have also noted the dehistoricization and derooting of the body so it can be recognized as universal (Diken and Laustsen 2005; Malkki 2015). The literature on refugees tells us something about how the tortured body is the ultimate symbol of the refugee, but it has to be tortured *there* not *here*, or not even *on the way*. This has resulted in the depoliticization of noncitizen bodies (Diken and Laustsen 2005; Nyers 2003), which seldom accounts for suffering incurred en route and at the destination. As Ticktin notes, "bare life" provides the political tools used to create the conditions of care (2011:14), and it is also used to explain the body in need of care that falls between the cracks of the state and is excluded/included from the polis (Diken and Laustsen 2005; Rajaram and Grundy-Warr 2004; Ticktin 2010:14).

Flaws in the definitions used to design tools for the state and international community to identify a subject in need of protection mean that the humanitarian body is mostly *invisible* (in the words of this book), unreachable, and/or challenging to identify (Anderson 2008; Yun 2004). Denouncements on the "medicalization" of the suffering body have been made (Fassin 2012:83–108; Ticktin 2011) and, in the case of human trafficking, of the management of suffering from exploitation as a crime rather than an issue of rights (Agustín 2007; Andrijasevic 2003; Berman 2003; Boontinand 2005:177; Capous Desyllas 2007; Doezema 1999; Flynn 2007; Kempadoo 2005; Kempadoo and Doezema 1999). Criticisms of migration and border controls have helped shed light on how the politics of suffering[4] based on state criteria of identification give or take away access to protection and rights from noncitizens. This politics of suffering has also implied a desire for (im)mobility driven by poverty.

Within the debate of suffering, human rights have become the resource used to instrumentalize assistance and protection to noncitizens. This naturally leads us to consider the pitfalls and exclusionary/inclusionary role of human rights when contrasted with citizenship structures as the path for protection (Balibar 2003; Rancière 2004). Yet, as outlined, in the Mexican context race, criminality and a cheap labor force have also played an important role for both citizens and noncitizens. This role for both citizens and noncitizens is not altogether unique to migration.

Within the context of nation-building in Latin America and the formation of the subject of the Rights of Man, there were (i) modern institutions of citizenship; and (ii) political democracy, which implied a democratization of the control of work, the production of resources, and the governance and establishment of institutions. In theory, citizenship can ensure legal, civil, and political equality for people who are socially unequal. However, for modern Latin American nation-states, whose populations are mostly indigenous, mestizo, and black, this Eurocentric trajectory has been impossible to replicate. This has been the case even in Mexico, despite its long struggle for social decolonization through revolutionary processes (Quijano 2000).

When Latin American countries achieved independence in the beginning of the nineteenth century, 90 percent of the population was indigenous, mestizo, or black as socially constructed by colonial authorities. In the new states, these peoples were denied participation in decisions over social and political organization. It is questionable whether states built on such conditions can be considered nations at all, unless one can prove that the minority of colonizers were representative of the colonized population (Quijano 2000:556–559). Beyond debate on whether nations were actually constituted, even if citizenship structures appeared to eliminate racial inequalities, their consequences seemed unavoidably racist. This context needs to be considered when contrasting human rights to citizenship rights in the region. The former has been recourse for many citizens in Mexico to demand rights.

When it comes to the undocumented, we find yet another difficulty with accessing human rights entrenched in the structures of the nation-state and established forms of citizenship. The binding character of liberal democracies, which are territorial, sets limits on their jurisdiction, and undocumented migrants are practically and conceptually excluded (Dembour and Kelly 2011:6–9). The pervasive nature of exclusion based on territorial jurisdiction in reality rarely guarantees citizens access to rights. As far as irregular migrants are concerned, the only morally legitimate policy goal identified has been to reduce vulnerability and to contest their exclusion from the political community (Carens 2008:163).

Access to human rights by migrants and, in this case, the promotion and defense of these rights is problematic not only because of the status of migrants as noncitizens but also because they often come from indigenous and ethnic groups that have historically suffered from economic and political exploitation. The denial of their rights might have more to do with political and social status (Dembour and Kelly 2011:9)—and, I add, economic status—than with the actual act of crossing an international border. Beyond the nation-state and citizenship structures, migrants have faced blocked pathways to sanctuary from wealthy nations that either have not signed multilateral agreements upholding humanitarian principles or have simply not adhered to the agreements signed (Betts 2010).

Human rights in Mexico have origins in the making of race, criminal bodies, cheap (free) labor and human worth, yet the four have different emphasis and relationships to freedom. The issue of human rights and freedom in transit is therefore not really about movement itself but about the wrong group of persons doing it in the wrong place. The problem of suffering from poverty, in contrast, is related to movement and the making of these kinds of movement a threat, not an issue of rights. The issue of movement, as discussed later, is often about undermining the security of those who already face multiple threats and highlighting the need for security for those who already have it.

The Issue of Freedom and Movement and the Liberal Subject

Unpacking the issue of movement is pivotal to this book. Movement and how we understand it today are linked to liberal notions of freedom, which derive from receiving states, mostly located in the Global North. Across time, the meaning of freedom of movement has become destabilized in this context. Yet the matter-of-fact reality that mobility has been pivotal to survival, adventure, seeking a better life, and generating change for humans is undeniable. Liberal notions of freedom belong to the Global North but have impacted the Global South. The physical enforcement of borders is a clear example of the weight given to control versus freedom. Most nations in the Global South have been tardier in developing any form of border enforcement. Borders are known to still be very porous in many parts of the Global South.

The trend of destabilizing freedom of movement has been traced by Kotef (2015) to the nineteenth century. At this time, the liberal subject's liberties located in the moving body were displaced by reason: "The will emerges as the substance to freedom" (Green 1986 in Kotef 2011:6). It is not this shift itself that is relevant, but rather that for many later liberals, "man's will is himself" (ibid.). Today, the Universal Declaration also defines freedom within "freedom of expression" in Articles 18 and 19 (United Nations General Assembly 1948). Kotef highlights freedom is noted in Arendt's claim that "freedom of movement is the materialization of the liberal concept of liberty," while tracing Hobbes attributes this freedom to mobility of bodies exclusively, and that Locke sees movement as central to freedom (2011:5).

Accompanying liberal notions of freedom was the challenge that liberalism faced in crafting order reconciled with the concept of freedom. The idea was presented that in order for freedom to have political value, it had to be regulated. This regulation, in the Foucauldian sense, meant self-regulation—internalizing in the subject that, in order for freedom to reconcile, the subject had to be self-restrained. However, the ability to self-regulate was not assumed for all subjects. Temporal, racial, class, and gender lines "dissected the regulated and ordered movement of able and masculine European bodies" (Kotef 2011:8). In other words, the freedom of the liberal subject moves in and out of visibility in accordance with privilege and in and out of invisibility in accordance with nonprivilege. The freedom of the liberal subject becomes a matter of reason and not mobility—more specifically, a matter of reason ascribed on temporal, racial, class, and gender lines.

Slavery, on the other hand, presents the first example of constructed social inequality migration produced by colonial powers. Anderson ties the need to control movement of the poor body as the main threat back to fourteenth century England. The law on vagrancy, which sought to control the movement of the poor, actually predates the British state. At this time the passport was used as the main method to control the movement of the vagrant (Anderson 2013:20).

Chomsky frames freedom of movement as being much more about privilege, situating the privilege of movement in the citizens of former colonial powers and postcolonial elites who can travel freely but routinely deny entry to people from their former colonies, especially the poor (2014:28). This process has involved religion, race, and national, class, socioeconomic, and political inequalities between the Global North and South. In this, she argues, European reason is legitimized, and with this reason, mobility, while the mobility of the unprivileged is not only controlled but criminalized (Chomsky 2014).

The current trend is toward the securitization of borders and criminalization of migration (see Introduction). Currently, there are two notable recent historical trends affecting liberal notions of freedom and movement in Mexico. The first occurred during the 1980s when there was a movement toward security within Europe linked to development geared toward the Global South. Wæver (2004:72) points out that during the 1980s, much of the research aiming for peace, especially in Europe, was a movement for security. Meanwhile, the concept of security was transformed and gained proximity with risk. This movement was initially linked to development and focused on the Global South (ibid. 88–92). The second trend came about after the 9/11 attacks in 2001, when the "Axis of Evil" was identified as a threat to peace. Peace then became the more prevalent concept, overtaking security. It is implicitly in the name of liberal peace that migration is criminalized and borders are securitized concerning—or with concern for—certain subjects, especially from the Global South.

The merging social movement in Mexico and beyond advocating for irregular migrants is lobbying for dignified, free transit, or more radically, for no borders at all and the dismantling of the INM. Yet "shelter on the journey" has emerged with important limitations and collisions with liberal notions of security, peace, and freedom outlined previously. The issue of (un)privilege and the precarity it implies to movement sits at the center of this book.

In practice, liberal notions of freedom and movement trickle down to migration policy through the framing of migration as a threat or problem to be solved. Receiving states have dominated this debate (de Haas 2009). It has since been addressed in policy in two predominant ways: in a conservative, repressive variant (policy geared toward strengthening borders) and a more liberal one (addressing root causes that are normally framed as related to violence and poverty). Regardless, migration has been framed by receiving states as dysfunctional and harmful, in need of being addressed and, ideally, stopped (Castles et al. 2013).

The issue of freedom and movement presents particularities in the Mexican context, in the confrontation shelters have with liberal notions of freedom, and in how, through everyday life, these sites reimagine what freedom and movement means. Throughout this book, the politics of freedom of movement and the emerging shelters on the journey are used to unpack this liberal conundrum, making us consider what can be revealed by looking at solidarity to freedom of movement versus controlling precarious migration within the institutional hierarchies of humanitarian actors and the migration regime.

The issue of freedom of movement today is inextricably linked to the making of the liberal subject. Yet, as noted, specific subjects are excluded in this formation. Who is the subject of care in shelters? Which characteristics count? The answers have to do with the vexed question of the relation between the controllers and the controlled by migration and border regimes as part of the same fractured and contradictory liberal formation.

The (Un)identifiable Humanitarian Subject

Who is the subject of care in shelters today? Many researchers have turned to Giorgio Agamben to understand the state's role in the making of "bare life," a life stripped of all rights. Others have turned to institutions like the UNHCR to understand the response to bare life or, in the words of Arendt, "being only human" and its relationship to the making of a subject of care (Agier 2013; Arendt 1967; Fassin 2012; Rancière 2004; Ticktin 2011). Most migrants transiting Mexico fall into the cracks between the state and the protection regime.

Central Americans transiting Mexico are swamped with multiple other problems that make them invisible, such as poverty, violence, and climate change. Not only are their human rights rejected, politicized, and criminalized—irregular migrants are often missed by the radar of statistics gathered by state institutions, seldom denounce the crimes or abuses committed against them, and often attempt to pass unnoticed to avoid detention and deportation. The mobility-driven humanitarian crisis is indeed a politics of "invisible journeys" in a "visible geography" (Brigden 2018) across Mexico. More extremely, some end in clandestine graves or turn to dust in nature. The intersection of poverty, migration, and border regimes make of those fleeing not survivors or fighters but fugitives and invisibles. As invisibles, they provide the political tools to create the subject in need of care in shelters facing the unsurmountable challenge of reframing voluntary and forced migrants. No matter the reason behind the decision to migrate, migrating without documents implies significant threats to human rights in the region (Menjívar 2006).

Across time, those who reach the doors of shelters have mainly been linked to voluntary and labor migration, produced as illegal noncitizens, and had the issues of their movement linked to development issues. Between the United States and Mexico, there has been a recognized, institutionalized revolving-door policy, where mass deportations take place simultaneously with mass importations of undocumented Mexican (and other Latin American) migrant workers (Boehm 2011; De Genova 2004:163). It must be noted that Massey (2020) evidenced Mexican migration had come to an end (although the pandemic has shifted this scenario), and migrations from the Northern Triangle (Guatemala, Honduras, and El Salvador), with many expelled from violence, face both the remnants of the revolving-door policy and the wall of violence. Scholars like Vogt have traced men and boys from Central America as the children of the Cold War (Solano and Massey 2022; Vogt 2018), distinguishing them from Mexican migratory flows.

44 / Chapter 1

To complicate matters, dignified movement in Mexico does not exclusively affect noncitizens; it is linked to citizens, the deported (including deported criminals), and indigenous Mexican minorities. As Father Amalio confirmed,

> And also, for example, Mexicans who are deported—some were deported because they (INM officials) thought they (Mexican minorities) were from Guatemala or El Salvador and they send them to Central America, so when they come back, they go to seek help at the municipalities. Some say they went to the consulates and were not helped. They say, I went to the Mexican consulate in Guatemala, and they did not help me. And then they go to the municipalities in Tapachula and along the way, and nobody helps them, so they have to traverse Mexico like all other migrants and come to us. We also receive Mexican migrants here.

This story was confirmed by a civil society actor I met in Chiapas. He presented the issue of Mexicans being deported from Mexico because they could not properly speak Spanish or sing the Mexican national anthem when asked by authorities (see also Egremy 2002).

Even if Mexicans have different motivations to migrate, the production of illegality in the United States has impacted Central Americans in similar ways. As with the construction of race in the colonial project, in this case, the process of producing illegality has been argued as racialized in the case of Mexicans and also of other Latin Americans today (De Genova 2004:161). This production of illegality has materialized in a restrictionist policy, which is being perfected and has led to policing across time that has also led to pervasive grave human rights abuses by border officials.[5]

To complicate matters, the calamity of the rightless in the context of irregular migration is vested in their movement being made into a security threat. More generally, "undocumented immigrants are desired precisely because they can be denied all rights" (Ticktin 2011:43). The law has not only been instrumental in producing a cheap, vulnerable workforce but also in justifying social inequalities and different legal treatments of different groups (Chomsky 2014:23). When status is inscribed in the law, the justification for inequality is legitimated—"it is the law!" (ibid. 28).

Although less considered, the role of poverty has been necessary in the making of illegality and a cheap vulnerable workforce (Wong 2005). Receiving states have long focused on poverty as linked to violence and as something to be prevented from infiltrating the border, making invisible our understandings of demand for labor migration (Cornelius 1989). Connectedly, domestic conditions such as poverty have been framed as urgent and potential breeders of terrorism (Barnett 2011:31; Harvey 2014). These concerns have been presented through a one-sided focus on poverty in isolation rather than as emerging from a growing gap between the Global North and South.

In a postcolonial/decolonial vein, de Sousa Santos reprises the dynamics of economic migratory routes of black slavery; in modern times, these dynamics follow the logic of economic accumulation. Even if criminal networks are not central in global transnational markets, he identifies inequalities between the Global North and South "as promoting clandestine logics that lead to subhumanity" (de Sousa Santos et al. 2009:71, translated by the author) that is exploitable.

Alongside the development of a system that produces and sustains a cheap, vulnerable workforce, questions have become louder on whether a noncitizen criminal is the subject of rights. As Arendt points out, the subject of human rights is that who has no other right than being human, and the calamity of the rightless is that they do not belong to any community whatsoever (Arendt 1976 [1968, 1966]:295). To sustain and morally legitimize the paradoxes necessary to produce dehumanizing institutions and nonhumanitarian subjects, Stevens argues, states have undertaken the task of shaping subjects as enemies of the nation-state—as, for example, in the case of slavery (Stevens 2010)—also used to perpetuate the power of rulers. I noted previously how this was accomplished through the criminalization of the witch body predating colonial times. Today, poor migrants have come to reaffirm security-driven hierarchies in which safety is the priority that helps sustain a status quo in the perpetuation of power of some groups over others. Sociopolitical processes have reaffirmed the poor body as criminal and victim. Whether for witches or illegal migrants, this process is linked to the production of enemies. In the case of slavery, it was not only about increasing a nation's productivity but, more importantly, a way for rulers to control their enemies (Stevens 2010:16–18). In the Americas, led by the United States, migrants have been constructed as enemies of the nation-state by the media and pundits (Chávez 2001, 2013). More specifically in Mexico, the neoliberal experiment has been disastrous; securitization has been used not only to profit from the poor but also to frame them as threats in what Gledhill (2015) has called "the new war on the poor."

Producing enemies to consummate hostile relationships is a way for rulers to control their subjects within the social system. Today, nation-states have taken active steps to foster hostile environments for migrants and refugees by staging them as threats, criminals, and enemies in order to justify punitive policing and, at times, extreme dehumanization, to not only control but also put on the spectacle of the deterrence of movement. This was the case with President Donald Trump's zero tolerance policy, which separated hundreds of children from their parents (Congressional Research Service 2021).

In Mexico, the majority of migrants transiting the country are Central Americans from the Northern Triangle. The origins of mobility from the Northern Triangle are not new, although they have changed in volume. Though not exhaustively or comprehensively, and with important limitations, I outline several factors that should be added to the considerations shaping the (un)identifiable humanitarian subject in shelters (see also Solano and Massey 2022). The first factor is violence and its history: migrations from Central America to the United States date back to the 1980s as part of the U.S. Soviet containment strategy (Chomsky 2021). Later on, Honduras entered the magnet of violence during the Reagan administration. Before the 1980s, Central American migration to the United States was barely graspable. Even if the civil wars ended in the late 1980s, migration from the region never returned to its previous state. Why? There were other forms of violence fueling these flows. Issues of gang violence proliferated, and the economies of these countries never recovered from the destruction undergone in the 1980s (Massey et al. 2014). Women also left the region to escape feminicide, rape and threats by gangs. There is also widespread impunity for these crimes (Menjívar and Walsh 2019).

The second factor is the role of expansion of the informal proletariat and the liberalization of markets. In Latin America, this class expanded in the 1990s as a result of neoliberal adjustments and an influx of cheap imports under the "new open market" doctrine and shrinking of the public sector, which ended in the reduction of formal employment (Portes and Hoffman 2003:50). This class lacked social security and other legal protections. Rodgers (2009) links this informal proletariat to gangs and "slum dwellers" in Central America, especially in Nicaragua, and argues the issue of violence can be better visualized from rural to urban transitions. He characterizes the brutality in the region as "urban wars of the 21st century." Moreover, in the 1990s the liberalization of markets caused the abandonment of crops and the Central American region continued to be characterized by stark inequalities and poverty in rural areas (Siegel 2005).

The third factor is social: now with established networks, some Central American migrants from this region attempt more pervasively to draw on these networks and escape the violence and poverty that plague their everyday lives (see, e.g., Abrego 2014). The fourth factor is global climate change, which has also affected migration from the region. Also referred to as the "dry corridor," the Central American region, has suffered from multiple climate disasters and disruptions, from El Niño phenomenon to aridity that impacts agriculture. Among the estimated 380,000 Central Americans making their way to the United States every year, many are agricultural workers and peasants (Álvarez Velasco and De Genova 2023:30–31). There is also the issue of extractive projects especially affecting Honduras. Many rural communities live with the uncertainty of mining, deforestation, and dams infiltrating their communities (ibid. 35). Moreover, Honduras suffered category 4 hurricanes that devastated the country in 2020 (Americares 2020).

The characteristics aforementioned are insufficient to outline the profile of the transit migrant but are important to consider when unpacking the subject of care being shaped in shelters. I must alert and highlight that in this book, the focus relies on the subject shaped by the humanitarian project.

Human rights, and humanitarian interventions, claim to be classless and raceless, yet the issue of movement and of who is the subject of rights in shelters is unavoidably about race and poverty. To base this debate on uncontested notions of universalisms of the liberties of humanity coming from Enlightenment ideas rather than on the colonial history of human rights, liberal principles of freedom and movement, and the neutrality of the law risks underestimating the power behind institutions that have excluded and targeted specific groups through the demarcation of the liberal subject. This very much concerns the politics of dignifying free transit and their confrontation with liberal humanitarian politics and the identification of a humanitarian subject in relation to freedom of movement.

Shelters and Liberal Humanitarian Politics

Shelters in Mexico emerged long before international humanitarian actors entered the scene, long before precarious movement was denounced as a humanitarian crisis, and before migration along the southern border of Mexico was securitized, criminalized, and became a human rights concern.

As noted earlier, many of the structures for the instrumentalization of humanitarianism and human rights today relate to the nation-state and democratization processes. Within the modern maximalist state, civil society redefines itself based on laws and regulations coming from the state, presenting a tension that strikes at the core of human rights. In the words of de Sousa Santos, "while the first generation of human rights was designed as a struggle of civil society against the state, considered to be the sole violator of human rights, the second [social and economic] and third [group] generations of human rights resort to the state as the guarantor of human rights" (2002:40). By default, attempting to dignify transit raises questions around social constructions such as law, citizenship, and sovereignty situated within geopolitical power asymmetries and the making of a subject of care, as noted previously. This is a matter not only of illegal status produced by the state but also of who the subject produced as illegal is. What characteristics are desirable to make legal status and, in turn, illegal status in relation to migration?

In this mapping of geopolitical power asymmetries that affect especially the mobile from the Global South, we find not only shelters but also aid and humanitarian action organizations. There are several distinctions that are noteworthy in this context. The first is that "a clear-cut distinction between international development and global humanitarianism is . . . difficult to sustain" (Emerson 2011:71). Diverse humanitarian actors work, donate, and/or cooperate with shelters. This set of actors brings to the table different, and at times colliding, politics to the issue of movement.

To this politics conundrum, I add that we must consider that the distinction between human rights activism and humanitarianism continues to be both contested and used (as discussed in the Introduction). In Mexico, charity from the church has also been constituent of civil society and solidarity. Humanitarianism and human rights activism are difficult to separate on the ground, and delineating a boundary between alleviating suffering and transforming institutions becomes more ambiguous in the context of shelters. For this reason, the effort of assistance is complicated; even providing food and water in shelters is represented as a pure act of subversion. Scholars such as della Porta and Steinhilper (2021) have argued that when we explore social movements, civil society, and humanitarian studies in a disconnected manner, we ignore that, in practice, their activities intersect. Humanitarian practices can manifest in a form of contentious politics and vice versa.

On the other hand, liberal humanitarian organizations routinely represent themselves as apolitical (Barnett and Weiss 2008:36)—an assumption accompanying the widespread claim from aid organizations that when politics fail, humanitarianism appears. Barnett and Weiss argue that this boundary is socially constructed and depends on the criteria and segregation created and presented by knowledgeable actors. Within this apolitical nature, there is tension between a consequentialist effort that links the project to seeking social transformation and a minimalist approach that is reduced to care and protection (Calhoun 2008:75). Aid agencies themselves operate, at times, with contradictory conceptualizations of humanitarianism. It is therefore more productive to assess their relationships based on these conceptualizations (Barnett and Weiss 2008:37–38).

Another challenge faced by shelter politics is the problematic trend of linking humanitarianism and security. Presently, many countries, especially the United States, view counterterrorism and humanitarianism as crime-fighting partners (ibid. 2008). When security is merged with humanitarian goals, humanitarian organizations can end up participating in convincing local populations of the goodness of armies that invade in the name of freedom—in this case, of the border police raiding cities. States may also resort to a "humanitarian alibi" to avoid costly political decisions (ibid. 25). This is problematic at two levels: first, humanitarian organizations, which once sought to use states for intervention, become tools for states' political and strategic objectives through the former's aim to extend the "responsibility to protect" (Barnett 2011:32; see also Rieff 2003). Second, states use humanitarian organizations to further human rights discourse and fulfill their own objectives, paradoxically threatening the humanitarian project itself. In this case, the most visible overarching issue has been strengthening the border.

There is further nuance as to how we understand shelters and liberal humanitarian politics. Drawing on the Spanish terms *política* and *incidencia política*, I want to clarify from the outset the distinction between what can be translated as "political" and "politics" in Mexico. *Política*, politics, means what normally is referred as policy or political activity—a process designed to create guidelines with the purpose of governance of a person or issue, normally involving activities from those who aspire (usually within the government) to administer public affairs. *Incidencia política*, political, in this context, is interlocked with advocacy. It means that there is an attempt to influence the created order with the purpose of social change. Social change therefore normally comes from political advocacy. Politics normally involve control and order.

In short, three political effects identified within the politics of dignifying irregular transit migration are accounted for in this book: antipolitics, postpolitics, and progressive politics. Brown (2006:15) defines antipolitics through depoliticization processes: "construing inequality, subordination, marginalization, and social conflict, which all require political analysis and political solutions, as personal and individual, on the one hand, or as natural, religious, or cultural on the other." In this case, depoliticization happens when poor migrants are criminalized, exposed to violence, and have their movement restricted through the portrayal of their choice to migrate without documents as an individual decision. Depoliticization also happens in attempts to constitute the criminalized subject as humanitarian, used to infiltrate politics under a humanitarian agenda that gears assistance and protection toward strengthening border enforcement and migration controls as opposed to upholding human rights and freedom of movement.

Postpolitics take place in the politics of dignifying transit not by "'repressing' politics but by 'foreclosing' it" (Diken and Lausten 2005:86). Politics are repressed when resorting to metaphorical instruments such as the universalization of particular demands; these instruments aim to restructure the social space. This process serves as preemptive risk management, so that nothing really disturbing happens, thereby ensuring that "politics" does not take place (ibid.). In this context, postpolitics manifest when all

50 / Chapter 1

actors unite for the universalization of demands disavowing politics—for example, discarding the need to consider freedom of movement in order for liberal peace to prevail.

Finally, progressive politics in the humanitarian agenda are accounted for in this book despite their structural limitations—human rights continue to be key mobilizers for social justice (de Sousa Santos 2002) in Latin America. As de Sousa Santos has pointed out, it is as if human rights are being called on because of the voids left by socialist politics (ibid. 39). Are they, or can they, become the language of progressive politics? The answer is yes. The definition of progressive politics, drawing from de Sousa Santos (2002), happens within the politics of dignifying transit: when producing collective and participatory knowledge on the structural conditions criminalizing movement of poor noncitizens with the purpose of control and regulation and using this knowledge for mobilizing emancipation (i.e., dignity and freedom of movement) rather than regulation and control.

Thus, the conditions in which shelter politics geared toward free, dignified transit are shaped and reshaped are inherently political. Many humanitarian actors claim an apolitical agenda based on their own assessment and make the decision to separate themselves from those they assess as making politics—yet they cannot avoid being political. On the other hand, human rights activists in the Global South often distribute similar assistance to relief and aid. Today, the humanitarian debate in shelters regarding the legitimation of dignified free transit is embedded in an exclusionary politics of suffering based on the entitlement and privilege to be mobile or not.

Conclusion

The framework presented in this chapter is designed to serve as a guide to situate, understand, and analyze the shelter site as an emerging humanitarian complex. The chapter goes beyond mere critique, seeking to explore the potential for social consciousness and transformation within humanitarianism and human rights discourse. In the first part of this chapter, the emergency imaginary is linked to precarious migration in order to set the stage. In the Mexican context, the role of the church and civil society in the birth of human rights discourse and assistance is identified. Conceptual notes on the subject of care being reshaped in shelters are outlined considering how the transit migrant is predominantly identified and framed through fractured distinctions between citizens and noncitizens, voluntary and forced migration, through selective suffering within the currently established protection regime and the making of the migrant into a security threat. The chapter ultimately argues that the humanitarian subject in shelters is embedded in inequalities between the Global North and South over how the migrant has been framed within still-pervasive civilizing and humanizing powers over the "other": the noncitizen, based on race, poverty, and criminality in the Americas. This book needs to be placed within this context.

This book departs from the theoretical premise that humanitarianism and human rights thinking and practices addressing irregular transit migration are inextricably associated with liberal principles of freedom of movement, social construction, and exclusion of race and the poor. The shelter site provides a lens to go beyond the nation-state and consider other geopolitical structures that promote social hierarchies and the social struggles (re)produced around migration in our world today. These social hierarchies and struggles are well exemplified in who enters the shelter. The subject of care, for example, does not belong to the rankings of powerful passports according to the Henley Passport Index, which is based on the number of destinations a person can enter without a visa. How this subject is framed informs the implications of dignifying irregular transit migration. Shelters confront both immigration and border controls and liberal principles of security, freedom, and peace that are not neutral; they are productive and are having disastrous effects, currently denounced as a humanitarian crisis. In the following two chapters, the shelter is presented as an emerging humanitarian complex.

2

"I Was a Migrant and You Gave Me Shelter"

The Open Ethos and Social World of the Shelter

The proliferation of shelter sites marked the end of an era in Mexico—that of uncontested, precarious transit migration across the country—and the beginning of a new era, one of a growing presence of humanitarian actors and humanitarian-based transit restrictions. Father Alberto explained to me that, before setting up the shelter, he conducted a kind of exploratory mission. He spent a year observing and following police and officials from the INM on raids. During the year, he saw how not only criminals but also the authorities abused migrants: how they raped, threatened, tortured, and attacked them. Father Paulino confirmed this state of affairs in an interview in Mexico City:

> When migration comes, it is highly criminalized, and there is a rejection even from Catholics, thinking—imagine what a stupid thing!—that they could not help migrants because they were "illegal," and if they helped them they would be committing a sin, because we would be helping enemies of the *patria* [homeland]. The thought is so silly. There is a prejudice; that is why I talk so much about changing cultural patterns. Because of this, nobody supported migrants—they walked as fugitives, as ghosts, being victims of everything. There were many rapes of women, mutilations [of migrants] because they were thrown from the train. But the worst thing in that short time was that they started killing them. They killed Delmer, Alexander, David, Juan—they shot them. Six months later

"I Was a Migrant and You Gave Me Shelter" / 53

they stoned Ismael to death, the guards of the train; they killed him like a dog.

These dangers came not only from individual criminals and criminal networks, as Father Paulino noted, but also from corrupt authorities and xenophobia in transit communities. Dangers were enmeshed in blurred and obscure social relationships, in a world of rumors and diverse representations of the transit migrant situation. Sometimes, official versions of incidents from civil society and local authorities appeared in the media, but often even these versions were inconsistent or inaccurately reported (see Brigden 2018). Authorities colluded with criminals; criminals pretended to be migrants or volunteers. Fathers were defamed and called smugglers by communities and the authorities. Some migrants saw smugglers as saviors. Civilians helped one day and threatened the next. Transit communities did most of the helping but also housed significant threats to migrants. Government humanitarian actors, such as Grupo Beta, were there to rescue migrants but were denounced for working with criminal networks, handing migrants over to kidnappers, and extorting and abusing migrants. Father Paulino continued,

> The shelter was urgently needed. I was not there; I was at the border. We had to start immediately, *fíjese usted* [just imagine], so that they would stop killing them, with nothing, just with a lot of courage, of course. With a very broad vision, we started the work in the shelter and our civil association.

From an eagle-eye view, the open ethos of shelters makes these sites the epitome of unconditional hospitality. Yet several factors complicated this apparent openness. By looking at shelters, I consider how social spaces are set in modern state-building, between citizens and noncitizens (Friese 2010:324), and how this represented openness had certain boundaries. Through this lens of the state, Derrida (2000) has pinned down an unresolvable tension between unconditional openness to the foreigner and protectionism of the sovereign from foreigners. As Father Paulino described in the previous quote, in the shelters this unconditional openness and protectionism was linked to the criminalization of migration, which trickled down to communities and religious beliefs.

Hospitality in shelters had other limits: as Father Alberto put it, the shelter blossomed like "a garden in an oil mine." By this, he meant that the shelter, especially, was set in a context of violence where both authorities and criminals profited from irregularity, and this profit was linked to the vulnerability produced from migratory status. There were the markers used to classify the subject of (il)legal mobility entering shelters. This goes beyond only looking through a migrant-centric lens at the tension between humanitarianism and security, but markers such as race, poverty, and economic inequality based on income (Picketty 2014) carry as much weight as migratory status (see Chap. 1).

This chapter suggests a tentative outline of the social world, constraints, and potentials of the hospitality practices of the shelter geared toward supporting mobility. This and Chapter 3 are mainly guided by ethnography conducted in La Esperanza, where I volunteered and lived for the most extended period of time. The chapter examines the shelter's unique governance emerging from the presence of a wide diversity of operating actors inclusive of local, national, and international humanitarian actors. The chapter also looks at the everyday life, schedule, and rules of the shelter. Looking closely at the diverse missions, roles, social relationships, and shared risks in the "open door" nature of everyday shelter life, this chapter sheds light on the complexities inherent in trying to identify clear perpetrators on one hand and deserving humanitarian subjects on the other, especially in relation to supporting free transit. As this chapter reveals, the hospitality of the shelter mattered greatly in reimagining dignified transit as concerning human worth in relation to freedom of movement rather than as a threat in need of control or for profit. Finally, this chapter reveals that shelters emerged in a complex environment: constituting a welcoming space and a refuge from threat while exposed to threat and sometimes housing liberal humanitarian actors that worked with the issue of movement as a risk and/or threat with short-term alleviation goals and a neutral stance to the issue of controlling movement.

In contrast, and in spite of its context of crime, violence, and insecurity, the shelter supported migrants' decision to move, be it for survival or to seek a better life. This chapter reveals how shelter hospitality even with its limitations and microcosmic nature, contested a liberal political order where movement is controlled—where freedom of movement is not a right but a privilege granted to those deemed fit by nation-states. For this reason, the shelter did not stand free of threat or attacks from transit communities, authorities, or criminals. It was a site of subversion of border sites, checkpoints, and detention centers but was limited by them. In this chapter, the particularities of the shelter site begin to come to light.

The Social World of the Shelter

Looking at the social organization and management of humanitarian assistance, focusing particularly on shelter staff, means looking at the system of actors and roles in relation to the mission of the shelter: to cater to the population defined as being in need—in this case, poor, criminalized transit migrants from Central America. The stereotypical picture within the governance of assistance and serving those in need involves the polarity of intergroup behavior of "us" and "them" (Voutira and Harrell-Bond 1995). "Us," in this case, is the humanitarian project forming in shelters, while "them" refers to the group in need. In fact, the whole reason for the existence of the shelter related to the displacement of a population in need of assistance outside assistance structures of the state but also made by state structures. The "new" proliferating presence of humanitarian actors and volunteers addressing irregular transit migration in shelters was strongly linked to the growing presence of surveillance and border posts.

The reality of the shelter was therefore far more complicated than that of other social architectures of assistance, like that of development aid and the refugee protection regime, set up by more straightforward bureaucracies. Complications were mainly manifested in the paradox of politics of inequality and solidarity in relation to freedom of movement present in shelters. In general, one can assert that moral sentiments are geared toward the poor and their vulnerability (Fassin 2012:3), yet how this sentiment was framed in relation to movement was often contradictory. Migration as a risk and threat solicited control, and migration as a universal activity to seek survival or a better life solicited support.

A defining characteristic of the social architecture was its open-door policy to helpers. At first glance, La Esperanza seemed open not only to those who needed help but also to all who wanted to help under their own humanitarian agendas, free from restrictions. Another way of viewing this is that there was a dependence on those who offered to help, no way of choosing among those who did, and no staff stability due to the high turnover of volunteers. Therefore, at times, both volunteers and other humanitarian actors entered the shelter with contradicting roles in relation to supporting movement.

Before exploring the composition of workers in the shelter, I present the other protagonist of this book: Father Alberto.

Father Alberto

At the time I conducted my fieldwork, Father Alberto was an important protagonist of the shelter movement. He was seen as a moral leader of the whole country and had been nominated and won multiple human rights prizes. His voice circulated often in political circles and the media from the main newspapers to the main news channels of Mexico. Many other human rights defenders followed him. Notwithstanding, he also gathered opponents, even within the social movement. He guided the expansion of this movement and nurtured collective activity in the country geared toward the human rights of migrants.

His charisma was palpable. When he talked, everyone listened. He had the power to inject his views into the public and political domain—whether they were later absorbed or not was another matter. I followed him around the shelter when he spoke to migrants; we traveled together to human rights events and went to meetings at the municipality, to civilian homes, and to television and radio interviews. This proximity provided a full circle view of the work that human rights defenders engage in from the bottom up.

The actions of shelter protagonists like Father Alberto are inscribed in a long story of social struggles in Mexico and the repeated question not only of the relationship of the individual to the state (citizenship) but also of the church to the state (politics), human rights and humanitarianism to the state (guarantor), and individuals (not collective groups) to human rights and humanitarianism.

Shelter Staff and Humanitarian Workers

In La Esperanza, there were striking visuals at times of the day when multiple actors entered the shelter to offer their services, from doctors to Grupo Beta and the CNDH. The space housed multiple institutional presences, even if it was not structured as such. This fragile balance was possible given that La Esperanza mainly operated as a transit site for migrants. Doctors normally huddled in the parish, and Grupo Beta and the CNDH often approached migrants individually to offer their services.

From the outset, this fluidity of actors evoked immediate confusion in my attempt to unpack one humanitarian project within the shelter. I often asked humanitarian actors to map out the humanitarian organizations they worked with on the issue of transit migration on the ground, the networks they joined, and the events where cooperation took place. Nobody could provide a clear mapping, inclusive of all actors, of the humanitarian community spread out in shelters across Mexico. This indeterminacy is not unique to the Mexican context. Humanitarianism and human right activism projects are often morphing and seen as ambivalent (Fassin 2012; Ticktin 2011).

Even for actors who had worked in the field for years, it was a nearly impossible task to map, with exactitude, a unified discourse, goals, missions, visions, workings, and outcomes of humanitarian-geared work toward transit migration given the fluctuation of actors and contradicting, opposing, and vague agendas entering shelter sites. On one hand, the scenario was indicative of the confusion, contradiction, opposition, and precarious conditions that defined humanitarian governance targeting irregular migrants in Mexico. On the other hand, it would be farfetched to claim that humanitarianism and human rights operated in a vacuum in the country.

Focus in this book is given to exploring how actors under a liberal humanitarian agenda within the shelter operated with contradictory conceptualizations of humanitarianism and human rights regarding how to assist those in transit and how to assess these actors' relationships and authority beyond the actual shelter site. Even if what was happening on the ground carried important weight in the transit migrant situation, what extended the physical boundaries of the shelter was also of relevance. Many organizations published reports based on data gathered in shelters on the situation of transit migrants. For example, MSF published the report *No Way Out* in 2020 on the situation of transit migration as a humanitarian crisis. AI published the report *The Invisibles* in 2010, outlining the risks, threats, and human rights abuses Central Americans endured across Mexico.

Therefore, based on the roles that emerged in the shelter, a discourse and representation of the transit migrant situation extended to the general humanitarian arena outside Mexico. The roles of humanitarian workers have different designations. In the Introduction, a clarification between human rights activism and humanitarianism and the challenges in differentiating the two on the ground was given. The challenges of dissecting human rights activism and humanitarianism also pertain to clarifications needed regarding humanitarian workers. In shelters, it had to do with those operating under the Western-dominated system of humanitarianism as well as those operating on the margins of this system.

When it comes to the Western-dominated system of humanitarianism, two prominent types of workers enter shelters referred by Barnett (2011) as: emergency and alchemical. Emergency workers are concerned with relieving suffering and saving lives in an immediate, neutral, impartial, and independent manner (ibid. 37–39). Examples of agencies engaged in emergency humanitarianism in Mexico include MSF and the Red Cross. Alchemical humanitarianism, on the other hand, is concerned with saving lives but seeks to address the root causes of suffering. Alchemists attempt to "harness the science of the day to transform social, political, economic, and cultural relations so that individuals can lead more productive, healthy and dignified lives" (ibid. 39). An example of an alchemical actor cooperating with shelters is AI. Alchemical agencies' relationship to politics is more complicated, as they attempt to maintain an apolitical stance by presenting their activities as technical rather than political (ibid. 40). Most volunteers as well as aid workers from the Global North assisting migrants, refugees, victims of trafficking, and the irregular count themselves among these two groups. Many of the actors approaching the shelter operated within the Western-dominated system of humanitarianism.

There is considerable literature that looks at actors outside these margins and contributes to our understanding of the emergence of humanitarian efforts outside the Western-dominated system (Brković 2020; Horstman 2017; McGee and Pelham 2018; Sandri 2018). These authors address alternatives to humanitarianism by looking at volunteer work, alternatives to professionalized forms of aid, and intersections in everyday life of humanitarianism among actors at a local, grassroots, and international level, situating humanitarianism socio-historically in order to unpack specific ideas of humaneness. All the aforementioned literature is focused on developing paths to understand help as humanitarian, following a universal humanitarian logic, based on providing help under the premise of shared humanity. Dignifying transit in shelters shifts the focus from a universalizing notion of humanity to a universalizing notion of free movement based on our humanity.

Dignifying transit refers in this book to assistance provided by local actors in shelters in line with specific ideas of movement as a response to a need emerging from state structures that cannot be addressed by a humanitarian machine that stands by neutrality and being apolitical. It follows universal humanitarian logic but in a political form, in contrast to international humanitarianism.

Shelters form part of a growing social movement supporting and lobbying for the human rights of transit migrants. Shelter workers were, at the time of my fieldwork, designated predominately as human rights defenders (and were also widely identified as religious workers; see, e.g., Hagan 2008). The term "human rights defender" needs clarification, as it is absent from most of the literature on humanitarianism.

The UN uses the term "human rights defender" to describe those who, individually or with others, act to promote or protect human rights. Human rights defenders are identified above all by what they do, and it is through a description of their actions (see Section A in UN definition in UNHROHC 2016) and some of the contexts in which they work (see Section B in UN definition in UNHROHC 2016) that the term can best be explained. The examples given of the activities of human rights defenders are not exhaustive (UNHROHC 2016). In a nutshell, human rights defenders can be anyone from journalists to professors to missionaries, from lawyers defending political prisoners and their right to a free trial to the mothers of disappeared persons demanding to know the fate of their children, from union workers fighting for economic rights to organizations fighting against those committing human rights violations with impunity.

In Mexico, the community of human rights defenders was not homogeneous and represented a variety of social, political, and local issues. Human rights organizations were defined through the defense of human rights across the country and as producers of knowledge and information. As stipulated in the Declaration on Human Rights Defenders, adopted in 1998, it was not only organizations that were human rights defenders but also a host of individuals and loosely organized groups. Tallying the number of human rights defenders in Mexico is, for this reason, challenging. A CNDH census in 2004 captured over six hundred registered organizations (CNDH et al. 2004). The list did not include, for example, defenders at the community level (UNHROHC 2016). Most importantly in the context of shelters, pastoral and religious workers were designated as human rights defenders (DPMH 2012:72).

Finally, there was the prominent role of volunteers in shelters. Volunteerism was the beating heart of the shelter. Without volunteers, there would have been no humanitarian trail in Mexico and no humanitarian-distributed assistance. La Esperanza had depended on volunteers from its inception. They were, and continued to be, to some extent, migrants themselves, especially migrants who had been injured or had had an incident that made them linger or stay permanently at the shelter and take leadership roles. In general, the length of stay of the volunteer staff fluctuated greatly. In La Esperanza, as in other shelters, volunteerism expanded vastly and became more professionalized over the years, attracting Mexican and some international students and professionals. In most shelters, volunteer staff could be divided into five main groups: religious volunteers, university students, international students, professionals, and migrants themselves. In one of our conversations, Father Alberto told me he had a "super team." He saw it as a super team in relation to having many professionals volunteering in the shelter at the same time.

Volunteers performed all the key activities of the shelter, including administering and distributing donations, cooking, cleaning, registering, coordinating with other implementing actors, and fundraising. The population of the shelter was mostly from the same region, and most volunteers were either Central American or Mexican. Very few volunteers were truly "international," that is, from outside the region. Volunteers from Europe and the United States came at random times, and none arrived during my time there.

All humanitarian workers in shelters had different roles in relation to transit migration, working at times conjointly with a national security framework and at times against this security framework. Many were migrants themselves. Humanitarian workers in shelters presented a confrontation and interrelation between what Ticktin (2011) has defined as "new humanitarianism"—referring to the shift toward a moral imperative rather than making politics—and human rights defenders' highly political activism and bottom-up solidarity with migrants in relation to movement. The result was a unique microcosm of humanitarian assistance that supported transit, yet not without limitations.

Shelter Governance

If we examine the structure of governance and authority in shelters from the top down, we see that shelters were usually founded by priests acting as

60 / Chapter 2

human rights defenders and were highly dependent on volunteer work. In La Esperanza, authority had its own set of particularities given the presence of multiple humanitarian actors, yet the backbone of authority and power over such sites were the human rights defenders who founded shelters, who were in their vast majority priests and missionaries. Some shelters, including La Esperanza, defined themselves as "horizontal" institutions. Father Alberto reminded me in a conversation that the shelter was not his, that he might not be there forever and might end up going elsewhere to help others. He saw La Esperanza as belonging to the migrants and open to being administered by whomever wanted to help. The complexity of this assertion is further considered in Chapter 3. It was clear that it was not migrants or volunteers who made decisions on needs, assistance, and lobbying issues. Priests working as human rights defenders were the leaders and had ultimate authority to decide what was done in the shelter. They also had a role of moral leadership in the shelter and community, and some, like Father Alberto, were important moral leaders at a national level. This influence was confirmed by most civil society leaders in Mexico.[1]

Power in shelters also involved those working directly with the shelter and those using the shelter to implement services and projects. Power therefore had to do with how other actors made the shelter do something the shelter would not normally do and with how the relations between different actors allowed for the shelter to take its own path. The power of some of the actors entering the shelter was prominent and protagonist in the Western-dominated system. Some, like the Red Cross, have historically been considered the patriarchs and founders of humanitarianism (Barnett and Weiss 2008). In short, beyond the shelter site, the role of authority involved considering both politics and practices.

Shelter governance was also based on local life and a universal notion of movement. Most shelters had as their mission to be organizations that distributed humanitarian assistance and provided guidance to all migrants in transit in Mexico, with the vision of offering a spirited defense of all migrants' human rights. In this way, shelters invited everyone to express hospitality and live in solidarity with migrants. They also gathered in a network. By 2012, many shelters had joined the DPMH network. The DPMH was highly decentralized, meaning it did not interfere in the administration of member shelters; each shelter was independent, yet the DPMH was available to support pastoral work in shelters and gathered these sites in the most prominent network in Mexico that united shelters to lobby for the human rights of migrants.

The DPMH laid out its vision in 2012 (2012:72, my emphasis).

We share with the Social Ministry the mission to: a) Contribute to the animation of the new evangelization fostering participation of the secular in the transformation of Mexico; and b) Try to make Christ Alive present, giving testimony of *Christian charity* fostering a culture of *solidarity* with all men and women, *especially the poorest*, most marginalized and excluded. The purpose of the Social Pastoral is to build, in harmony with the creation, a society, just, fraternal, with solidarity and sign of the Kingdom of God.

The struggles circling hospitality and the nonrecognition of undocumented migrants therefore manifested not only in migrants' irregular status but also on their poverty and on rejection of protection based on the former and latter. When I interviewed Jorge, a key actor in the DPMH network who had been working with migrant issues for over a decade, he explained in more detail the vision behind the focus on migrants and their mobility.

> There is a part, this dimension is part of an area that exists in the whole world. In fact, in the Vatican, there is a special name for it. It is not pastoral; it is of migrants, nomads, refugees, and asylum seekers . . . because in the Bible, there is a part that talks about the need or obligation or solidarity of the person to help his neighbor. This part of I was hungry, I was thirsty, and you quenched my thirst. It is under this logic that the church obliges itself to assist . . . the migrants.

The Catholic Church had already played a significant role in demanding protection and policies of assistance for migrants in Mexico through its ministries. Initially, the church addressed the issues of Mexican migrants through the Mexican diaspora. It had a significant role in "organizing the flock"; for example, both the church and the state opposed and supported emigration at different moments (Fitzgerald 2008:98–99). It is noteworthy that religious discourse historically played an important role in demarcating conquest, colonization, and territory in the Americas (see Chap. 1). Later on, religion was instrumental in the demarcation of the U.S.-Mexico border through the ideology of Manifest Destiny, which held that God favored the conquest of Western lands by the United States (mainly white American settlers) and was eventually used to justify territorial aggression against Mexico (Martínez 2006:9).

The role of the Catholic Church was visible in shelters, which often followed the logic of Matthew 25:35 and quoted it on their websites, replacing the word "stranger" with "migrant": "I was hungry and they fed me, I was thirsty and they quenched my thirst, I was a migrant and they gave me shelter" (see, e.g., Casa del Migrante 2016; Frank-Vitale 2015).

In a context of extreme violence in which the authorities also colluded, shelters redirected their Christian mission to become human rights defenders, as stated specifically in a DPMH report, *Activities 2006–2012*. This included giving assistance to victims of crime and meant that pastoral workers, acting as human rights defenders, needed protection and defense of their own rights, given that their work became the object of threats and infiltration by smugglers and kidnappers (DPMH 2012:58). Threats also came from nation-states themselves. For example, the United States coordinated with the government of Mexico to develop a joint database used to target journalists, attorneys, and human rights defenders who attempted to cross the border to access asylum seekers and/or provide material forms of support, going as far as to formally deport and exclude these actors from Mexican territory (Devereaux and Ramos 2019).

Notably, DPMH joined other civil society organizations as part of a growing social movement advocating for the human rights of migrants collectively framed around transit. It sought protections for migrants who were prey to abuse and exploitation on their journey toward the United States. Civil society actors that joined this growing social movement included faith-based and secular organizations, churches, community groups from local to national, regional, and transnational organizations, and advocacy networks. In 2012, seventy-one organizations were registered in *Todos los derechos para todos y todas* (All Rights for All), the national network of human rights civil organizations (EG 2012), in addition to the members of DPMH. By 2020, the mapping included 286 organizations (GTPM 2023). In short, a very significant humanitarian project had been established and continues to grow exponentially in Mexico. The majority of these organizations monitor the state's migration laws, policy, and implementation, while others do the same work for the state.

This book focuses mainly on shelters and actors who collaborated directly and indirectly to provide services and distribute humanitarian assistance; their political advocacy was informed by the shelter site.

Moreover, within this context, some human rights defenders (such as missionaries) expressly went against the church structure (see, e.g., Martínez 2012) given its trajectory of supporting the border and the state in different moments historically. Thus, there were conflicting missions, even within the Christian logic that emerged in the shelter site, that guided how each actor operated under a humanitarian agenda and how they assessed their own and others' work regarding humanitarian assistance, human rights, migration controls, border enforcement, and violence.

As noted previously, in this context of violence, priests were compelled to become human rights defenders, seek their own rights and protection, and function as mediators with criminal networks. Thus, the problematic relationship between security, humanitarianism, and human rights in relation to migration framed not only poor migrants but also, at times, humanitarian workers as part of the migration problem rather than the solution. In contrast, the shelter's mission included a politics of care that sought to welcome migrants, feed them, and accompany them in the journey as part of a vision that mobilized free transit with dignity. This mission was not homogeneous and interacted with other missions that entered the shelter. I now consider other missions that intersected the shelter's mission and inevitably suffused into the humanitarian debate in Mexico.

Institutional Hospitality and Other Missions

As noted previously, the particular origins and collective activity of humanitarian governance in shelters offer insights into the politics of inequality and solidarity that define contemporary precarious migration. La Esperanza stood for institutional hospitality, defined here as: being open and giving access without restrictions, not only to migrants but also to those who sought to help or learn about the shelter and the migrants. This was not necessarily true of all shelters but was a characteristic shared by most. La Puerta, another shelter where I volunteered, had the most restrictions, but this I accounted to individual decisions. In La Esperanza, Father Alberto affirmed,

> I have not set any restrictions on this shelter. They can come in and talk with whomever they want; they can investigate what they want. I have a critical attitude toward the outside—why cannot they have a critical one toward the inside? Why not? They can look at my finances; they can investigate what we have inside. I tell you there are no restrictions.

The shelter was presented as a transparent, open space; La Esperanza was open to being scrutinized. Certainly, human rights defenders were very aware of the contradictions in the work of their counterparts and the issues arising from volunteer work. They also understood that social transformation does not come about in isolation and that these problematic codependencies were necessary for the survival of the shelter. La Esperanza represented a unique microcosm of assistance among the shelter network, one that gathered local, international, and national humanitarian actors. Some shelters more than others attracted different humanitarian actors. In general, the humanitarian actors entering La Esperanza could be classified in five categories: emergency organizations, INGOs, international organizations, governmental actors, and civil society.

Even if La Esperanza was unique in this context, it was this very gathering of diverse humanitarian actors that situated the shelter as a key analytical unit in understanding dignifying movement as a humanitarian endeavor. At the time of my fieldwork, there was the direct and indirect presence of an emergency organization distributing health care services; the IOM, an international organization donating earmarked funding, shared campaigns, and emergency relief in the form of, for example, blankets; the CNDH, which distributed legal advice and human rights information and also sporadically donated emergency relief; Grupo Beta, a government actor that entered the shelter mainly to offer repatriation services; and AI, an INGO that donated, for example, cameras and computers and was an important counterpart of shelters in producing reports and urgent actions. The presence of this myriad of actors made of the open ethos of the shelter an act of access rather than welcome and manifested a different selective process than that of access to the shelter.

It is noted that beyond the shelter site, these workers as humanitarian are not operating under an equal playing field in the humanitarian arena. Power relations and authority extend beyond the shelter site and need to be accounted for at a local, national, and international level. The missions to alleviate suffering in transit through caring rather than resolving the long-term issues that affect the irregular transit migrant situation involve different levels of authority and power within and outside the shelter site.

In shelters as in other humanitarian architectures, power ultimately rested on authority that also concerned other humanitarian actors that entered the shelter. Authority and power are especially challenging to explore within the humanitarian field given the premise that humanitarianism's value is meant to rest in its neutrality and apolitical stance. Scholars have pointed out that humanitarianism is not devoid of power and that different types of power hierarchies emerge at a level of authority (other hierarchies of humanity are explored in Chap. 4). One way to understand authority is as "the ability of one actor to use institutional and discursive resources to induce deference from others" (Barnett and Weiss 2008:38).

Authority within the Western-dominated humanitarian project manifests at different levels. In general, Barnett and Weiss (2008) have identified four kinds of authority within the Western-dominated humanitarian project: rational-legal, delegated, expert, and moral. Expert authority, for example, is claimed by MSF, which acquires practical and specialized knowledge assisting victims and bearing witness to what is happening on the ground. Moral authority is claimed through maintaining that work is sustained by values of independence and neutrality, not special interests (Barnett and Weiss 2008:39–40). The actors that entered the shelter had different positions in this spectrum of authority in the humanitarian arena in general. This evaluation is out of scope of this book, although this book does draw on how authority entered and engaged in shelter life by looking at the missions of organizations that entered the shelter and in relation to how shelter staff engaged with these collateral missions.

A key actor of the emergency organization explained the specificities of his organization in Mexico: "There is no network especially here in Mexico. We are not human rights activists; we are an organization of humanitarian medical action. Our main objective is to improve the state of health or situation of health of this population. . . . We are not a development organization; we are an organization more of emergency."

As with other emergency organizations, medical humanitarian organizations have come to provide new brands of humanitarianism and reinvented the concept of emergency aid. As noted earlier, Ticktin (2011) refers to it as "new humanitarianism" and characterizes it as impregnated with antipolitics, manifested through a shift to the moral imperative when the social, political, religious, and medical become conflated. In this case, the mission behind medical logic was meant to make visible physical and psychological abuse and had as its goal to treat rather than cure. More specifically, in relation to migration, the emergency organization staff member in the shelter said,

> We are not pro migrants, and we are not against migrants. We just see that at a level of migratory processes, in some cases, a situation of crisis is generated, with an extremely vulnerable position, generally victims of violence, of all types of aggression with problems of access to health, because they are undocumented. This is the position we assume in what we see at the level of medical and psychological consultations or in water and hygiene activities, we try to demonstrate the situation of the population, how to reduce vulnerability or reduce aggressions to facilitate access to health.

At La Esperanza, the emergency organization also catered to the local community to avoid tensions, xenophobia, and attacks on their offices (although the organization did not specifically include migrants living by the train tracks). The logic behind this strategy was that catering exclusively to migrants in this already very poor community might fuel more tension. This decision came from the top down rather than the bottom up. One of the doctors from the emergency organization said that they were rarely approached by people from the community. In short, the mission of this organization differed from that of the shelter, but close cooperation existed between the two. Indeed, this emergency organization had an office in one of the main entrances of the shelter.

Meanwhile, IOM was in an ambiguous position, claiming to be neutral but working as a service-oriented organization for the government at the time. In 2016, after the conclusion of my fieldwork, IOM became a UN agency. The implications of this institutional shift were not apparent during my fieldwork but are important to consider when examining IOM's continued work with the shelter. At the time, an IOM staff member said, "We are an organization with no human rights mandate." Despite this assertion, in the 1990s IOM expanded its operations to include humanitarian work. It set up its first Emergency Relief Unit in 1992 when, "according to IOM legal adviser Richard Perruchoud, there were more diverse and complex causes interacting to create population movements. There was also increased funding from the international community for humanitarian operations" (Hall 2016:91). The establishment of IOM as a provider of emergency relief and its involvement in humanitarian crises had not been problem-free and had been criticized by other humanitarian organizations (ibid.). As IOM staff recounted,

> We are always in cooperation with local authorities, federals, with the National Institute for Migration [INM], which is our natural counterpart to develop these activities. . . . It was an initiative of the state government to launch [anti]kidnapping projects, so then it was coordinated [for the state].

Thus, concerns around IOM interventions emerged from the fact that it worked with some of the same actors denounced by civil society as embedded in the wall of violence, such as the INM and other state authorities, and functioned as a secondary intermediary within the shelter and the state (see OIM 2016). Moreover, the IOM often engaged in campaigns to prevent migration as a risk, including state-funded antikidnapping projects mentioned by IOM staff, which went against the shelter's mission to provide guidance for migrants to continue rather than abandon their journeys.

AI also cooperated with La Esperanza. The organization self-defines as a global movement (Amnesty International 2016). My interviewee affiliated with the organization explained that the organization, which had a prominent presence in Mexico, was politically neutral to avoid accusations of corruption in its field offices. It denounced abuse but took no political position to support, observe, or criticize the government, only the violations the authorities committed. Impartiality was important to the organization and to protect the safety of its membership. As the interviewee explained, if it campaigned against the INM in Mexico, it did so through other countries so that the local membership would not be threatened or faced with retaliation.

Government-affiliated actors in the shelter included the CNDH, the Mexican ombudsman's office and an autonomous state-funded organization. CNDH is accredited with the UN and became fully independent from the government after constitutional reform in 1990. However, it remained reliant on funding from the Mexican government. Its program to assist migrants included disseminating information on human rights, issuing recommendations, receiving and following up on complaints, visiting migrant holding centers (MHC) to provide assistance on human rights, collaborating with NGOs to collect information and detect human rights abuses, and conducting research on migration as a phenomenon (CNDH 2016). "We are like the IFE, by which I mean we are an autonomous organ that is financed by the state. We attempt to keep a close relationship with the defenders, with the priests and volunteers in the shelters, and that includes sometimes doing extraordinary things," said a CNDH official. The official clarified that "doing extraordinary things" meant, for example, gathering blankets.

Ultimately, CNDH was limited to submitting recommendations to the Mexican state. How these recommendations materialized might be problematic and disjointed from their inception. For example, on the recommendation of the CNDH, the INM established Grupo Beta as a patrol force to rescue migrants transiting Mexico in dangerous situations. Grupo Beta launched its first projects along the U.S.-Mexico border in Baja California in the 1990s. The defined purpose then was to assist victims of crime in their transit through Mexico; this group later became known as Grupo Beta Tijuana. Grupo Beta Nogales was established in 1994, and by 2016 there were twenty-two Grupos Beta in nine Mexican states. In 2011, the state formalized the creation of the Grupo Beta through Article 71 of the Migration Law (INM 2016), which stipulates that

> the Secretariat will create groups of protection for migrants in national territory, which will have as an objective the protection and defense of their rights, independent of their nationality or migratory situation.
>
> The Secretariat will establish agreements and collaboration and concertation with dependencies and entities of the Public Federal Administration, of federative or municipal entities, with organizations of civil society or particulars, with the objective that they participate in the establishment and operation of groups for protection of migrants.

The mandate of this patrol force was to provide humanitarian and migratory assistance, first aid, and orientation and information to migrants on their human rights. Grupo Beta's stated mission approximated that of shelters: to protect and defend the human rights of migrants, providing humanitarian assistance and legal advice. The government website noted that Grupo Beta was trained in migration law, human trafficking, and human rights (INM 2016)—though paradoxically, and perhaps predictably, not on

68 / Chapter 2

abuse by INM officials. From this, one may gather that Grupo Beta was defined by the Mexican state as an organization of human rights defenders, yet its role on the ground was problematic. It was state-funded and worked for the INM. As Father Alberto clarified,

> In Mexico, because of the situation with infiltration with PAN taking power, which is the official party of the Yunque, the organization of the ultra-Right, Grupo Beta cannot be expected to fulfill a function that is 100 percent humanitarian. With one hand they give the tuna cans and, with the other, intelligence. With one hand they give water, and with the other, they give direct information to the government on migration. And it is a security context, that is why Grupo Beta is there; we know that perfectly well.

To conclude, actors that entered the space of the shelter represented a diverse set of humanitarian missions in relation to movement. They focused on the health vulnerabilities of migrants but not on their causes and ranged from collaboration with the INM to political neutrality and caution, from projects directed at human rights defenders and the emerging humanitarian crisis plaguing migrants to international organizations cooperating with shelters without a human rights mandate and launching projects under the aegis of the state. The shelter as an unrestricted open space to a plethora of other hosts gathered a form of "ambivalent hospitality" (Fassin 2012) that complicated even further the host-guest/enemy binary between the shelter, migrant, and state.

Yet what is most striking in the Mexican case is that shelters gathered this diverse range of actors and collaborated within the site despite differences in missions and humanitarian logics concerning movement. Shelters also extended humanitarian assistance and participated in political advocacy, which did not involve most of the aforementioned actors. Thus, shelters like La Esperanza functioned as a social movement in the promotion and defense of human rights and to lobby for free transit (as further explored in Chap. 5). Actors adhered independently to life in the shelter and had other agendas, power variables, bureaucratic constraints, and funding dependencies, which this book does not address. Shelters represented a unique—often paradoxical—microcosm of missions of humanitarian assistance concerning transit migration. On the ground, the limitations of the agendas brought in by other actors were less relevant, and the support for migrants to move forward dominated. Yet in the bigger picture of shifting the way transit was managed, there was no consensus nor unified effect. In general, the shelter's mission focused on denouncing the profit being made out of migrants and the poverty of those affected—a valuable contribution to the debate and unpacking of the transit migrant situation.

Hospitality Rules and Everyday Life

"Hospitality rules" were made for the protection and humanitarian assistance of a targeted group but rather than universal access, bring to light inclusionary and exclusionary mechanisms within them. As noted by Fassin (2012), humanitarian reasons can legitimize help but can also legitimize not helping under certain conditions.

In contrast to refugee camps, where identification is a prerequisite (Agier 2013; Rajaram and Grundy-Warr 2004; Voutira and Harrell-Bond 1995), everyone in need was, in theory, welcome in the shelter. Yet although there were no identification criteria to access shelter services, assistance was implicitly unavailable to certain groups, such as local residents, the homeless, and permanent migrants on the tracks. However, this rule was left to the discretion of the father or the volunteer in charge and was not strictly followed. Even during my time at La Esperanza, exceptions were made. Shelter staff decided who entered the shelter; other organizations had no say in the matter. In this, there was no collaboration between actors. On the other hand, other organizations influenced how long a migrant stayed if they needed further assistance.

In La Esperanza, as in other shelters, migrants could come and go as they pleased. Even if some shelters had lockdown schedules, they let migrants in and out on a daily basis. Anyone who wanted to leave the shelter could do so whenever. After registration at La Esperanza, migrants received a card that functioned as a permit to stay in the shelter. On this card, volunteers wrote down the date and the number of days migrants could reside in the *casa*—two to four nights. Most left before the expiration date.

The shelter was not designed to provide indefinite housing. As Father Horacio put it: "Here in Mexico it is common to say that the dead and *el arrimado* [uninvited guest] stink after three days. And the migrant is a bit like that." He explained that on the first day migrants are welcome; on the second they are provided further support, and if on the third day they are still there, they are asked why. In shelters in the north of Mexico, for example, if migrants did not move on when they were expected to, they were not fed. On this level, the shelter defined assistance as humanitarian for the highly mobile. Put another way, it facilitated continuous movement. One of my informants explained,

> There are different types of shelters; there are shelters that are very well organized and more structured physically because they are completed projects. This project is five years old, and it has been constituted little by little. There are more structured shelters as, for example, x shelter, which is more organized, and there is more control, and in x shelter, they ask for a document so the migrant shows they

are in that shelter. In this way, they give access without cost and also food, but once they leave, they do not let them in again.

This is in contrast to refugee camps, where inhabitants may be stuck for years (Harrell-Bond 1985), and shelters for victims of trafficking, where victims can be imprisoned (Gallagher and Pearson 2008:5). The temporary nature of the help is indicative of how the shelter site emerged beyond a protection regime and how it provided a new way to assess the humanitarian project in relation to (im)mobility, freedoms, and restrictions.

Beyond access, the first rule at La Esperanza was that there were no rules. This is not representative of all shelters; indeed, within the migration aid paradigm, this rule made it a unique space. The no-rules rule was a complex one, and Father Alberto discussed it with staff while I was in the shelter. For example, smoking was not allowed in the food hall, and the group brainstormed how to frame this in a sign without using the word "no." Likewise, drinking and weapons were prohibited, and registration was compulsory in order to receive services, while the length of stay was regulated (although it fluctuated from week to week between two to four nights). Men and women were divided into separate dormitories, though there was no dormitory for children. There were issues with this in practice, as most migrants traveled without identification and lied about their age, and a separated male child who appeared older than eighteen would not be allowed in the female dormitory. Families often slept outside on flattened cardboard so they could stay together, and this was allowed.

As mentioned, Father Alberto saw volunteers as gathering in a "super team." He had never had so many professionals volunteering in the shelter at the same time. There was an implicit demarcation among hierarchies of volunteer staff that had to do with the professionalization of volunteer work. This manifested in practice. Authority and rules were organized along lines of dominated/dominating or givers/recipients based on professionalized versus nonprofessionalized assistance. In La Esperanza, at first impression, authority seemed rather scrambled, but markers between professionalized and nonprofessionalized assistance were evident. Other shelters, as La Puerta, staffed with student volunteers, had stronger hierarchies. In La Esperanza, time working at the shelter played a role in authority. Volunteers who had been there longer took on the authority to tell others what to do.

There were unwritten rules around chores and what needed to be done. Meetings were held to assign tasks to each volunteer and to recruit help from migrants. While there was an effort to assign people to different tasks, this was difficult as staff rotated often. The father did not want migrants to do chores, as he argued that they were tired and needed to be taken care of. However, volunteer staff understood that help was necessary to get things done. Chores included cooking, collecting wood, going to the market, getting tortillas and chickens, sorting fruit and vegetables donated from the market, cleaning the toilets, and so on. In most shelters, such volunteer work was expected from the migrants. Rules emerged on an ad hoc basis for volunteers, for example around which tasks they were in charge of, but these were never strict and seemed inconsistently applied.

The work schedule was divided into office work, chores, meals, and other services, including leading mass and providing advice on the onward journey. The office had daytime opening hours, although these were not strictly adhered to, and some volunteers stayed around in the evenings to use the computers. Office work included organizing visits from potential donors, agreeing or declining to participate in campaigns, organizing visits from other civil society actors or documentary makers, getting help for migrants from legal counsels, doctors, or hospitals, and organizing visits for humanitarian visas. There were activities with the police, NGOs, and teenagers from the local high school who came to do volunteer work.

The shelter's schedule and rules fluctuated, and it was up to the designated volunteers to understand what needed to get done, when, and under what conditions to welcome migrants. No two days were alike. Issues surrounding rules or the absence thereof were part of ongoing struggles in the everyday life of shelter hospitality within an absent bureaucratic structure. Ultimately, the no-rules rule was part of an agenda in the shelter that deprioritized security over supporting the migrant—making the shelter site unique. Shelters got their core job done no matter what: they provided food and a place to sleep to all migrants who approached the site and thus could be seen as filling the void of, and produced by, the state and in opposition to the violence spilling from migration and border control political decisions, especially affecting the poor. This type of hospitality trickled down to everyday life in the shelter and manifested in the tensions confronted between humanitarianism and security in relation to transit migration.

Hosts, Guests, Enemies, and Everyday Life

When I entered shelter life for the first time, I was taken to the volunteer ranch, where I shared a small room with two other volunteers: a nun and a former university student. I met Luis, a migrant with a disability caused by a fall from the train. He could walk a few steps with difficulty but mainly used a wheelchair. A tattoo on his hand with three dots forming the shape of a triangle told me he was once a member of a gang. I had learned months before that each dot represented a valid reason to leave the gang: hospital, jail, or death. No other reason was acceptable. Luis fell off the train, the Beast, around one o'clock in the morning and was found along the train tracks by

72 / Chapter 2

volunteers the next morning, around seven thirty. He immediately told me he did not like to be photographed or for people to make money out of his face, his life. He showed me an article about him cut out of the local newspaper, which he kept in his wallet paradoxically, given his expressed dislike to being in the public spotlight. Luis had started traveling at age eleven and was now forty-five.

I also met Carlos, a boy from Guatemala who had lived on the streets since he was twelve and now claimed to be twenty-one. Oscar, from Nicaragua, still had a mark on his face from the beating he received when he was assaulted during his journey north. He now worked as the shelter cook and was dating one of the Mexican volunteers. We were a diverse group in the volunteer ranch: Mexican volunteers, a master's graduate, a nun, Carlos, Luis, Oscar, and me. Many other volunteers came and went during my stay at the shelter.

A couple of weeks after I arrived, Luis, the injured migrant, was looking out from the door of the ranch. He normally did not leave the ranch. As I approached him, he told me: "I have been watching you. I can see everything from here. I also know everything that is going on in this place. I am not in the office, but I know what is happening in the office. I have informants everywhere." I look at him, perplexed.

"Come, stand here, you see that man over there?" He pointed at a migrant. "He is a *pollero* [human smuggler]. I know him, and the shelter staff knows that he is a *pollero*, and they still let him in. You know the Mexican girl volunteer who was a migrant? She is also a *pollera*." Luis continued: "In fact, most of the volunteers are involved in some kind of business. The same with the INGO that works here—they are all corrupted."

Luis was filled with distrust and paranoia despite all the assistance he received, which, even if extreme in his case, was not altogether rare in this context. Structural issues resonated with his perceptions: those of violence, corruption, impunity, and widespread crime in Mexico. Staff were greatly concerned about his well-being. There were often discussions about who should bring his food to the ranch, take him into town for a distraction, or take him to physiotherapy so he could recover and move on. Ultimately, Luis and the staff's relationship involved dealing with a common place that housed hospitality and hostility, manifested in the confrontations of hosts, guests, and enemies as interchangeable.

In fact, hospitality is linked etymologically to hostility. "Hospitality" derives from *hospes*, guest, which stems from *hostis*, enemy. And it is attested that both derive from "stranger" (Fassin 2012:135). Within a context of criminalization and violence, it is expected for meaningful hostile relationships to emerge. Conflict theory shows how hostile relationships make both "us" and the "other" enemy composites of the same social system (Schlee

2010:11). In shelters, this has to do with tensions between humanity and security linked to movement. This type of social system has made of everyday life in transit a matter of profit from its criminalization and part of a social system of vulnerability, domination, and help that makes it difficult to dissect who is a perpetrator or a helper, who is the enemy, guest, or the host.

The issue of movement in shelters in fact contradicts Simmel's (1911/1997) account of the traveler, the stranger, as one who arrives and remains; transit migrants arrive one day and are gone the next. Ultimately, the issue of transit has to do instead with exclusion and recognition. In transit specifically, it has to do not only with legal differentiation but also with poverty and multiple forms of suffering endured en route—including criminal victimization. As discussed in Chapter 1, Stevens (2010) argues that the making of enemies is more about domination than profit. On the ground, most of the issues experienced at a local level were driven by criminal profit. In the bigger picture, this state-made problem helped justify the problem's reification and the domination of one group over another.

It is worth noting that the context of violence and threat was not static in Mexico. As noted in a report by AI (2010), the nature of the threat in shelters changed over time. A shelter staff member told me,

> It was not like that in 2010, but there were increasing *enganchadores* [persons who try to get migrants to accept their services] infiltrating the shelter from the Zetas. For example, in x town they try to get as much security as possible. [The year] 2011 was the last time they received help from an international organization and from a European country. They had been receiving this help since 2005, but in 2011 a European volunteer was threatened with a gun, and since then, they stopped going to the shelter.

Manuel, Father Alberto's right hand, who had first entered the shelter as a migrant victim of robbery, recounted how he was threatened in the shelter by one of the heads of a gang who used to come to the shelter to sell gum.

La Esperanza was indeed open to anyone who wanted to help, but it was not itself immune to this openness. There were random incidents where criminals preyed on its openness, and other civilians and authorities threatened the shelter. During my own time in the shelter, I interviewed a visiting "volunteer" who claimed to work in a shelter up north. He described his history with the shelter, enumerating actors and chronological events, explaining that he was a psychologist, and sharing his personal experience.

> For me, [this work] is not unsafe, in fact it is the work where I feel the safest. . . . It leaves me satisfaction, it leaves me a great feeling, it

leaves me a sense of value, it leaves me a sense of respect for myself, it leaves me loving my family more, it leaves me respect, it leaves me the admiration I feel for others, in other words it leaves me great things.

The day after I conducted this interview, I was on a bus with Father Alberto and his assistant headed toward Mexico City. I was joining them for a series of events and meetings on human rights for migrants. Manuel received a call during our bus ride. He looked concerned. As he hung up, he asked me, "Do you have a picture of the volunteer you interviewed yesterday?" I stared back at him, perplexed. He explained that the volunteer had stolen the shelter's petty-cash box, a camera, and other small goods. The lengths this man had gone to pass as a volunteer were remarkable. He had seemed more knowledgeable about human rights actors and debates around assistance to migrants than many other volunteers and human rights defenders I had met. Yet he had come to the shelter to steal.

This event was not altogether unique. From the time I arrived in Mexico, I heard rumors and testimonies of robberies in shelters and transit communities where I conducted fieldwork. Incidents happened, some more serious than others. A rumor spread during my time concerning a volunteer and robbery. This volunteer had been in charge of helping migrants withdraw their money transfers. It was rumored he was taking part of the money. This was never confirmed, yet he left the shelter shortly after the rumors were spread. Even if deception, distrust, and rumors were deprioritized, they emerged as real obstacles in the everyday life of the shelter. Father Alberto pointed out that theft had been an issue with some volunteers. "If they betray me, I never trust again and never forgive them," he said.

Poverty was endemic in the country and affected many transit communities. This was the starting point of assisting migrants in Mexico: a transforming landscape of threat and hospitality fueled by the criminalization of migration, border enforcement, poverty, and authorities and criminal syndicates triangulating these into a business. The setting was presented in a grotesque picture of violence but could be more accurately characterized as a grotesque picture of an extreme absence of rights. The heterogeneous amalgamation of subjects entering the shelter made it difficult to distinguish who was a volunteer, a migrant, or a criminal.

But the picture was not only a dark one. From the outset, people shared their desire to help those in most need and "do good," to do the Christian thing. In the words of shelter staff, to give human dignity to all who seek a better life or escape for survival. This intention also marked my time in Mexico. Assistance in Mexico was about losing fear and learning to manage rumors as much as actual threats. At this level, shelters represented a window for progressive politics as sites of hospitality open to all migrants and all who wanted to help—contesting the control of movement and its dehumanizing effects along the way.

In the end, the truth was difficult to unpack in most shelters where I volunteered. In Christian logic, focus remained on serving those in greatest need with dignity irrespective of who they were. Yet there was a great challenge: gossip or banal stories, lies or truth, the tension in attempting to not judge others but not being able to escape judging, and the attempt to go beyond control, security, and punishment as a way to handle the circumstances, represented in the hierarchies of authority of the shelter.

These were uncomplicated, minor situations when one looks at the larger picture of grotesque abuse and suffering, unimaginable torture, and psychological destruction endured by migrants. But these were the realities faced by shelter governance and should not be completely cast aside in trying to understand the practical realities of managing threats and upholding human worth for those in movement. They are indicative of the effects of migration and border controls and of global inequalities between the Global North and South that trickled down to transit communities and La Esperanza, where camaraderie, support, and an openness to receive those who approached the shelter gates prevailed.

Conclusion: Shelter Hospitality as Subversion

Concerns about the humanitarian act, what it should stand for, and who it should be geared toward engaged an ethics of hospitality in shelters that had much to do with threating and universalizing free movement. The open ethos of hospitality coming from the shelter to serve those in need revealed that shelters, known to be the only sites for respite, food, and other services for migrants on their perilous journey north, were also subject to threats of criminals infiltrating to prey on migrants. This type of threat to movement was often the most visible and used in consensus by all humanitarian actors gathering in shelters. The side effect (also unwanted) of this consensus has often been an agenda that supports the strengthening of borders at a policy level. Everyone agrees that crime should be stamped out. This social dynamic of hospitality and hostility partially configured the socialization of precarious migration in shelters. Shelters attracted a wide spectrum of actors wishing to volunteer, study, document, prey, and profit. Thus, the social dynamics of the shelter as an emerging humanitarian complex presented a series of tensions at the level of social setup and rules. The spiritual value of welcoming all was the most immediate measure of support along the journey that set the shelter site apart, yet the missions of alleviation of suffering and provision of protection were often not aligned concerning the issue of free transit among all humanitarian actors working within the shelter.

The social dynamics explored in this chapter tell a story of hope, refuge, and openness intersected by threat and criminal activity that inform the emergency imaginary. These challenged the shelter's desire to maintain a wholly open environment, free of restrictions, and highlight tensions between the explicit and implicit goals of freedom and control in relation to movement and human worth. Rules and restrictions emerged on an ad hoc basis, adjusting to situations as they arose, mostly as a result of threat or criminal activity. Beyond the altruistic image we are presented with, shelter life faced a series of challenges, from infiltrating bad actors to lack of human resources. Still, despite the difficulties in the social reality of shelters, they continued to cope and opted to remain open as an act of subversion to an increasingly restrictive policy landscape driven by a national security agenda in Mexico.

For migrants, this choice ultimately meant access to a site of support along the way, which was at times lifesaving or provided appreciated support. The setup of the shelter, with multiple humanitarian actors with different missions, provided an alternative to how movement should (not) be managed. The shelter reveals that mobility is a human activity that can be practiced beyond control and punishment yet is constrained by this relationship. Most importantly, the hospitality of shelters reveals the critical consequences that can spin off border enforcement and migration controls and that account for not only the suffering of migrants but also the proliferation of an industry that profits from these approaches to mobility. Even if obvious, there was no straightforward consideration of the poverty of the migrant by other humanitarian actors entering the shelter. The missions of (im)mobility within shelters that made of the guest an enemy at times or vice versa showed a small window of possibility to imagine mobility as a universal right rather than a privilege or problem to be solved.

Helping the poor on their journey is a particularity of local humanitarianism in the Global South, yet it is seldom framed along these lines, as are the human consequences of transit. The humanitarian trail across Mexico is also a reminder of how precarious migration is an issue that affects the Global South on a much greater scale. La Esperanza shows that shelter hospitality is ultimately the integration of an unauthorized underclass that has as a unique destination of respite—the shelter—underscoring the importance of *shelter on the journey* on the ground. In the next chapter, I explore in detail the distribution of humanitarian assistance and the politics behind this assistance to complete the exploration of the shelter as an emerging humanitarian complex that seeks to dignify transit.

3

"Of Course There Is a Difference between Charity and Solidarity"

The Power of Giving

During a bus ride to Mexico City, Father Alberto advised me to get in touch with an organization I refer to as Helping Home to better understand how the humanitarian project, with the involvement of international humanitarian actors, had emerged for irregular migrants. Just a few days later, I managed to arrange a meeting with Roberto, a former key staff member from Helping Home who promptly agreed to meet me at a *cafeteria* (a café or diner). Roberto had worked many years with international organizations and knew their ins and outs, strategies and goals. As we sipped our coffee, he explained that UNHCR had started the project as a consultancy to raise awareness about human rights, peace, and the violence to which refugees are subjected. This move was a clear example of the infiltration of humanitarian organizations into issues of human rights, peace, and security (Barnett 2011), revealing the liberal humanitarian agenda led by UNHCR since the 1990s. Roberto explained that at the time, UNHCR conducted awareness-raising activities in schools and churches. UNHCR had identified the refugee issue as apparently very distant for Mexicans, although many persons have been displaced by violence throughout Mexican history. This project could not continue as a consultancy and needed to function under the aegis of an organization; therefore, Helping Home was delegated to an INGO.

Helping Home later was set up as a documentation center, a library of refugee issues, he explained. After the INGO took over the project, it collaborated with an NGO to expand its function, turning the physical space

78 / Chapter 3

into a place for meeting, attending to both refugees and migrants with the involvement of diverse actors. At that time, there was a desire to use the space for raising awareness and mobilizing Mexican society to promote the rights of refugees, but the project moved toward humanitarian advocacy. Many persons, groups, and churches expressed solidarity through donating medicines and food.

The INGO only worked on activities directly related to its mission regarding refugee rights and did not deal with migrant issues. In Helping Home, there was exposure to the issues faced by refugees and migrants who came to ask for help or food. Those who approached expressed issues of discrimination, housing, access to work, and health. Then the organization became interested in getting involved with migrants. Thus, those approaching Helping Home, in this case, migrants, also informed the service. There was pressure from UNHCR to cater to refugees, but supporting the local population had a big impact. Roberto explained that UNHCR's role had become conflicted, as their mandate was to work for refugees. "As Helping Home, we started to confront many situations with UNHCR," he said. UNHCR started to put considerable pressure to have an impact on the local integration of refugees and make visible the refugee issue. He added that UNHCR was "super creative" and saw the migrant issues as competition for them. Working on migrant issues took away visibility from UNHCR and the refugee issue, he explained.

For the INGO, there was pressure to be linked to Helping Home. At the time, the INGO was showing more interest in migrant issues, but the funding was coming from UNHCR, which focused only on refugees. As a program, Helping Home was linked in matters that went beyond educational work and the INGO's mission and politics, giving food and other type of advice regarding work and health. At this point, the project and the involvement of UNHCR started to be questioned by the Secretariat. There were questions regarding the use of intergovernmental funding beyond educational activities.

The INGO and UNHCR agreed to the creation of an independent organization. "Within the INGO, it [Helping Home] always had a peculiar profile; we were and we were not the INGO. When it was convenient, yes, and when not, no." But, Roberto said, Helping Home also had the possibility and flexibility of developing its own profile. "We started to have impact with finding people who were under threat, moving them to temporary places, and then there was a mutual agreement to make it [Helping Home] into an independent organization." It ended up being registered as a civil association. "This is why I tell you that the position reflects the INGO but goes beyond. I would rather put it as [the position of] Helping Home." Thus, the UNHCR project was delegated to the INGO due to bureaucratic constraints with which it was assisting, and this was, ultimately, linked to its funding. As the project changed direction away from education and advocacy toward providing medicine, food, and a space to hang out, the INGO delegated it to Helping Home. And as it began providing other services, Helping Home was transformed into a civil society organization. After this conversation, I understood that funding ultimately was linked to politics, not needs.

Today, Helping Home has as its mission to promote the rights of migrants, and its vision is to work in networks that allow persons to develop in an environment of peace, human rights, and respect for their surroundings.

Chapter 1 described how the shelter was situated in the paradox of threatening and giving worth to humans, where the church both supported and opposed the colonial project and civil society became the fabric of social solidarity in Mexico. The shelter existed in a context of liberal forces within the humanitarian project moving from security toward peace and the manifestation of peace within the issue of movement. Chapter 2 presented shelter hospitality and the social world behind its doors. The open ethos of the shelter, embedded within hospitality and liberal notions of security in relation to movement, presented challenges in shelters in distinguishing who is a migrant, a criminal, or a humanitarian worker. Notwithstanding, La Esperanza, as a local actor in the Global South, remained open and supported and was a site of subversion to migration and border controls.

This chapter is guided by Helping Home's example, which reveals the important role of the webs of power behind how assistance is funded, organized, named, and targeted. The humanitarian project is well known for being established on the premise that there is a population in need of assistance. This premise is guided by a unique "humanitarian reason" (Fassin 2012), a logic in this case fed by both Christian and bureaucratic logic in shelters.

This chapter examines the politics of distributing humanitarian assistance, which builds on what I refer to as "warm and dry" logic, with diverse humanitarian agendas that include charity, donations, earmarked funding, and professionalized services and volunteerism geared toward the transit migrant situation. By warm logic, I mean one nurtured by Christianity that goes beyond the material, legal, and territorial and focuses on solidarity to not only the migrant but especially the *poor* migrant. This warm logic in shelters comes from a moral imperative that goes beyond the material to the spiritual. The biblical passage "I was a stranger and you gave me shelter" (Matthew 25:35) lay at the heart of most shelters. Dry logic is the bureaucratic logic of the state and other international humanitarian actors that enter the shelter site. This is a category governed by specific policy and often heavily informed by a liberal humanitarian logic, which prioritizes security and peace in relation to mobility across and within borders.

Within shelters, help was traditionally charity driven yet solicited as a form of solidarity to the migrant and presented as humanitarian assistance. I therefore asked Father Alberto if there was a difference between charity and solidarity in the shelter. He replied, "Of course there is; you cannot do charity without seeking transformation, without seeking justice, without seeking that the poor and the abused by the capitalist system become a subject. They have to be a subject, of course." He affirmed, as noted in Chapter 2: "The shelter is theirs; the migrants own it." If the migrants theoretically owned the shelter, they should be the ones defining what humanitarian assistance is, but obviously, the distribution of humanitarian assistance did not function in this manner—nor did migrants own the shelter in reality or decide what they should receive.

As noted in the previous chapter, shelters were set up without an identification process in place as a prerequisite to accessing services. Yet diverse needs—from persecution, abuse, violence, crime, and poverty to health, legal, and repatriation services—were accommodated by the shelter. The chain of giving was an essential element in the social process of helping transit migrants and establishing what a humanitarian agenda really implied. The "gift," a term coined by Marcel Mauss (2000 [1924])—in this case, the humanitarian gift as a cultural universe of giving and receiving—was complex in shelters. Malkki argues that humanitarianism cannot be easily inserted into the world of gift giving as it is part of an "uneven kula ring" (2015:109). Those who receive humanitarian aid cannot pay it back. Yet in this chapter the chain of giving is a useful heuristic device to explore the role of the givers, including a variety of factors affecting power relationships between givers of assistance, such as differing agendas, distance and proximity, time, physical presence or absence, freedoms and restrictions, dependence and independence, and spirituality and secularism. Givers, both inside and outside the shelter, were bound by these webs of power, vertically and horizontally, directly and indirectly. An analysis of this chain of giving is one more piece of a puzzle that attempts to understand the impact of *shelter on the journey* on the migrant's situation.

Beyond assistance intended for transit migrants, or framed as "theirs," the reality of the shelter was complicated by other webs of power that emerged between the givers: those who cooperated to support the migrant within the shelter space. This chain of distribution involved webs of power that defined what humanitarian assistance meant for each giving actor—there was no consensus on this matter. One way to more concretely understand the power relations between the giver and receiver in shelters is to consider the role of universal reciprocity. In this principle of exchange, reciprocity is not only about "giving while receiving but a series of disguised strategies of power relations," which Weiner describes as "keeping while giving" (Weiner quoted in Voutira and Harrell-Bond 1995:211). In humanitarianism: "The claim that the very act of giving to distant strangers is driven as much by our needs as by the needs of others is not to damn humanitarianism but merely to underscore the intrinsic ambiguities of the humanitarian act and the ever-present possibility that our needs may in fact be driving actions that (presumably) benefit others" (Barnett 2011:15). On the other hand, doing charity has been explored by scholars as both a power over the receiver, happening out of self-interest, and as an act of solidarity (Komter 2005). In shelters, despite a distinction made by the priest between charity and solidarity, both self-interest and solidarity were manifested in the chain of giving.

The goal of this chapter is not to scrutinize what was given and received but rather to unveil the webs of power that lay behind making freedom of movement a matter of support to continue the journey with dignity or to return. It is in line with the goal of this book to unpack the emergency imaginary—as a matter of solidarity rather than charity or vice versa. This chain of giving ultimately presented a subject in need of care and defined the political reality of each shelter, which went beyond merely focusing on this problem as migrant-centric but as one actually nested in inequalities and power asymmetries between the Global North and South. This chapter grounds this argument on power asymmetries on the case of La Esperanza through looking at the chain of giving on three levels: (i) the infrastructure of the shelter and material distribution of assistance; (ii) the power asymmetries between external humanitarian actors and the shelter staff; and (iii) the actual services distributed that ultimately shaped a (non)humanitarian subject.

Infrastructure: Space and Sociopolitical Action

Father Alberto told me that La Esperanza had come a long way by the time of my fieldwork in 2012. When he had arrived in 2006, there was nothing in comparison to what could now be observed—there was not even a proper floor. As he shared,

> In regards to the shelter, we had nothing; we had nothing but land and sky. Later, with time, we accomplished things. A woman helped us to build the food hall, but first the chapel and then the food hall. And then I achieved things slowly. Slowly they have been helping us [donors] with the southern part of the men's dormitory, for the women's dormitory, but also, donations from a very important person. Today we can claim we have 80 percent of the shelter built—that if they are going to come, we have a roof; if the rain comes, we have somewhere to put them.

82 / Chapter 3

Most shelters started with nothing more than land, sky, and courage. In other words, they were established without official aid and were dependent on ad hoc donations from the local community, the church, and miscellaneous funding from other humanitarian actors. In general, funding for helping unauthorized migrants suffering from lack of basic needs or from abuse during the migratory process were scant or invisible.

Here, I note a distinction between human trafficking and irregular migration. The rescue industry for combating human trafficking, though obviously ineffectual, has proliferated and received millions of dollars despite being heavily criticized for only having identified a handful of victims throughout the years. Investments of up to $150 million were made between 2000 and 2007 by the Bush administration in the United States, even as it was claimed that fifty thousand persons were trafficked into the United States every year. In 2010 alone, the Office to Monitor and Combat Human Trafficking (G/TIP) made ninety-seven grant awards in fifty-one countries across all regions of the world (U.S. Department of State 2010), totaling over $33 million. Only 3,619 convictions took place (U.S. Department of State 2011b:38), although millions of victims were estimated to be trafficked across the globe. These figures call into question how much of this funding ends up in practical protection, highlighting issues of identification and the politics behind classifying human suffering and choosing who receives the funding to help and under what agenda.

In Mexico, a rapidly proliferating humanitarian trail has been buffering most of the cost of the humanitarian crisis experienced by transit migrants. Notwithstanding, there is a growing community of solidarity with the migrant and the shelter networks. Funding, donations, and relief reach the shelters daily, even if in a disjointed manner. Some shelters receive more donations, funding, and food than others. Most shelters struggle to make ends meet. The funding in shelters is unavoidably linked to how state and humanitarian actors in the Global North perceive the movement conundrum in Mexico as will be explored later.

From an eagle-eye view, La Esperanza was spread out, like an archipelago emerging from the ground. All buildings were separate. This spatial distribution might have been the outcome of the founder's planning vision but was likely also influenced by the shelter's dependence on funding to expand and improve buildings. Ultimately, the layout of the shelter had to do with negotiations and compromises made over time between institutional funders, philanthropists, and the shelter's founder.

Donor influence on the shelter was evident. The female dormitory, which had received more funding, was painted and had two bathrooms and two showers with curtains for privacy. It had only fourteen bunkbeds (half the number for men) in a larger building and was thus much more spacious than the male dormitory. Most of the time, it was half empty. According to a 2013 report by REDODEM, on access to shelters in 2012 only 256 women accessed shelters versus 2,979 men. This discrepancy between what was needed and what was donated to the shelter is an example of the collisions and contradictions between bottom-up and top-down interactions in the space. The male dormitory had been set up with funding from a German Catholic organization, while the improvement of the female dormitory had been possible with funding from IOM. It was evident that what was donated was not dictated by migrants.

"Space and environment can be seen as rationalities of government" (Huxley 2007:186). It is therefore important to consider funding in relation to organizational rationalities, social and political action, and vice versa. How much remained to be fixed, built, added, or improved at the site was also open to interpretation. La Esperanza was primarily founded on a belief in helping others, with a strong Christian basis that prioritized hospitality toward the poor over material things, as explored in Chapter 2. Indeed, the infrastructure of the dormitories was simple, with cement walls and roof. The male dormitory had five toilets and showers (one was not working), all in the same room, with no curtains or divisions. In the dormitory itself, there were twenty-eight bunkbeds (fifty-six beds). One afternoon, Father Horacio, a visiting priest in the shelter, pulled me by the hand and said: "You need to look at this now that there are no migrants around. There is no dignity in this." He said this in reference to the state of the bathrooms. After we left the bathroom and shower area, he listed other practical issues, such as sewer cleaning, and multiple infrastructure issues he thought needed urgent fixing. On the other hand, Father Alberto pointed out to me one day, "We are not trying to build a Hilton hotel." This statement was indicative of the ideology of the priest and other helpers that permeated the shelter: it stood against the material world and had an implicit anticapitalistic agenda. At the same time, it was indicative of the fact that the shelter was not catering to the wealthy and suffered precarious economic conditions. Therefore, social and political action also affected the space (see Augé 1995) of the shelter. Even with debates on infrastructure and the financial situation, La Esperanza was one of the better-established shelters and had more space available than most. In other shelters I visited, migrants were often crammed in one room.

Another example of funding and socio-spatial dynamics was the lack of a physical wall surrounding the shelter; Manuel, the assistant to Father Alberto, told me that certain unspecified funders had proposed building one, but it was never really clear whether the shelter staff or the funders came up with this plan. Instead, at the time, there was a "virtual wall" of surveillance cameras donated by AI, but I was told that nobody was available to monitor them regularly, nor were there human resources available to attend to any emergency. I must note the layout of most shelters is not open, and they usually have gates adhering to lockdown schedules.

At La Esperanza, some volunteers expressed concern at not being able to close the doors to their rooms. Walls and a sense of safety, through the donation of cameras and a wall surrounding the shelter, are examples of the rationalities of government that infiltrated the shelter through earmarked funding. The establishment of the virtual wall can be seen as mirroring the (in)security context in which shelters are embedded and/or simply, as was the case of La Esperanza, are donated but not used. Walls might be erected just because funding was earmarked for them, or they might be seen as necessary given the interactions taking place in the shelter. They might be erected without having much meaning other than in the funders' agendas. At the time I was in the shelter in 2012, there was a fence built on one side of the shelter. Father Alberto said the funding for that had come from *Obras Pontificias del Papa Benedicto XVI* from the Vatican. "This at least protects the northern part of the shelter, so we do not need to be guarding it, to at least have one section closed." By 2015, there was a wall surrounding the shelter.

The shelter site ultimately housed diverse interpretations, stories, and struggles of humanizing and supporting transit among diverse social and political actors. In La Esperanza, the infrastructure prioritized (to a small extent) women and children, allocating them a better dormitory. This priority goes in line with how the humanitarian subject has suffered from gender essentialisms. Advocates for protection often focus on women and children (Carpenter 2003, 2005). Notwithstanding in shelters it was mainly men and boys who accessed the space (see Chap. 5). Beyond raw infrastructure, the priority was to support migrants in their transit, yet this support meant the entry of other humanitarian actors' agendas and priorities for the space. Two priorities emerged from this example: what was prioritized in the everyday life of the shelter and by whom, manifested in the space, and how the space itself told of the actual situation. Herein, funders' priorities entered shelter life, but on the ground, their goals were not actual priorities in shelter life. Migrants came, slept, and ate regardless of whether there were beds or not, space or not; some slept on cardboard boxes. These socio-spatial interactions tell us something exercised in the case of refugee camps as "states of exception" (Agamben 2005), where the rule of law is transcended for the common good. Shelters, in contrast, emerge as oasis-like spaces, where the law as violence is contested. Spatially, one can see the state of exception across the transit trails of Mexico, and side by side along the way, shelters emerge not only to help but also in solidarity, to contest and bear witness to the abuse traversing Mexico implies.

El Taquito: The Distribution of Food and Water as Subversion

It is almost dinnertime. As migrants wait to receive their cards permitting them to stay in La Esperanza, Father Horacio welcomes them. He asks them to queue up, to give a place to women and children first. "You are going to receive food here, a place to sleep; we know you are tired," he says. "We are here to help you and give you advice. The journey is difficult, and there are many precautions you should take. Do not fall asleep on the train, and if you do, tie yourself with a belt. Try to take a shower; take off your migrant uniform [sneakers, cap, and backpack]. Rest as much as you can."

Depending on the day, the line for food lengthens or shrinks. If there is no space in the dining room, migrants find a place in the surroundings to slump down and eat. Most are tired: they slurp up the chicken soup and go to bed. Others share their experiences and give each other advice.

The next day, volunteers try to recruit help with preparing breakfast and lunch. A handful of migrants normally agree to help with the peeling, chopping, cleaning pots, or whatever else needs to be done. The office opens to make phone calls, text families, provide assistance with money transfers, accompany doctor visits, coordinate with lawyers to put in claims, support applications for humanitarian visas, provide advice for the rest of the journey, coordinate with other cooperating actors, provide spiritual support—the list goes on. No day is the same, and the actors entering the shelter especially fluctuate, as does the volunteer cohort.

The issue of poor nations as responsible for the aid of humanitarian subjects is not exclusive to the Mexican state, although it remains unaddressed and unacknowledged by it. Historically, most refugees in Africa have been hosted by some of the poorest nations in the world (Harrell-Bond 1985), and it is the local community that gives the most. In fact, Voutira and Harrell-Bond point out that international aid historically always arrives late, and those who find refuge in poor host countries live among the host population; many refugees end up never receiving official assistance in refugee camps (1995:217).

Giving charity, as in the words of the priest, can also be geared toward seeking social transformation. Doing good as a humanitarian act might take many different forms. In shelters, those who gave the most were not those from far away. Beyond the undocumented, the shelter catered to those traveling in economic precarity.

When I asked Father Alberto about funding, donations, and the practicalities of feeding migrants every day, he said,

> We are very free in that. I do not recall one donation or something that has been given to us that has conditioned our conscience, at least mine and not that of the shelter. Also, not in that sense, we do not accept nor can receive money that is conditional. You cannot take everything; everything can be negotiated except our conscience. And the conscience is part of that closeness with the migrant—we live with them. We see what happens to them, and then we share all the information with the team. In other words, our work is totally from the bottom up. It comes from them [the migrants]; we cannot take another vision nor put another voice that is not theirs [the migrants']. I say this with all freedom; we are very free from money.

Shelters operated under precarious economic conditions, and many founders stated that they lacked everything. In shelters, uncertainty was the *pan de todos los días* (daily reality). Funding was scarce, and many shelters struggled to pay their bills at the end of the month. It was not unusual for founders to resort to funding the shelter themselves. Even as Father Alberto spoke of the shelter's freedom from money, he admitted: "We have had months where I have had to pay for the tortillas to feed the migrants from my own pocket." This was not unique to La Esperanza, and similar examples were documented in the media at the time. The issue of the electricity being cut was one example that was an issue in 2012 and still was present in 2022 (see, e.g., León 2022).

The backbone of the shelter was the distribution of food. Human rights defenders often called on people from the community to express solidarity with migrants through charitable donations. Those who supported the shelter were not those with the most economic means. As Priest Horacio told me, "There are people, mostly well off, who look down on the migrant." He explained that they had the knowledge to reason themselves out of helping. He added, "We discovered a huge mine of solidarity, with people being so poor." He said that the majority of donations came from the communities— "We do a *colecta* [a religious collection]," he said, but clarified, "It is not enough." This established trail of charity was rooted, as detailed in Chapter 1, in the role of the church as a pivotal actor in civil society structures and solidarity in the country.

Help was not only altruistic but also utilitarian for the giver. Markets and bakeries were important sources for sustaining food resources. Some shelters had close relationships with locals. In other areas, where there was more tension with the locals running the market, shelter staff traveled to markets in neighboring communities. At La Esperanza, I first went to the market with Carlos. Despite his young age, he was in charge of collecting donated fruit and vegetables. He was savvy and already knew which vendors would have some for him and under which conditions they would be gifted. We entered the first stand, and the vendor pointed at several boxes of vegetables. It was obvious that these vegetables were unsellable. I began to pick out what seemed edible, but Carlos quickly told me we had to take everything, otherwise we would not get anything. And so we went stand by stand, picking up boxes. Most of the contents were not fit to be sold, though some of what was donated was in good condition. To some of the vendors—though not all—Carlos explained, donating to the shelter served as a garbage disposal service. When we returned to the shelter, the process of selecting what was still edible began. The more sensitive volunteers had to put a handkerchief to their mouths to bear the smells exuded by some of the boxes. Other shelters reported similar experiences. One human rights defender speaking at a university event mentioned that they had to select from hundreds of bread rolls to find the few fit to give to migrants. Shelters took a great deal of care to make the best of the situation. They selected from what they were given carefully and laboriously and, most importantly, sought to ensure that migrants got a hot plate of food. La Esperanza also received donations of chicken, and money (out of pocket) was always spent on giving the migrants fresh tortillas.

Food relief still had not reached the shelters on an ongoing basis and came through ad hoc donations in moments of "extreme" emergency. Many migrants perceived their humanitarian predicaments in Mexico as not merely an issue of charity but also of solidarity, continuously expressing their need and gratitude for food contributions and their dependence on the goodwill of people who gave them "a taquito" to eat on the journey. Some migrants, on the other hand, refused to enter shelters and took pride in not taking *limosnas* (handouts). In shelters, support was often locality and charity driven. The distribution of food became an act of solidarity and a form of witnessing, even if migrants' suffering could not be ended. This idea of charity resonated with how emergencies came to be understood and how help for the poor in the community came to encompass strangers. It also reflected the biblical parable of the Good Samaritan: "members of the sufferer's own group refuse to help but an outsider does" (Calhoun 2010:35–37). In transit communities, the realities of those who gave were not that distant from the realities of those who received.

Shelters themselves struggled daily to make ends meet. Rather than merely interpreting this help as sustaining the status quo of emergency, as humanitarian literature would argue (Barnett 2011; Calhoun 2010; Fassin 2011; Ticktin 2011), migrants and shelters in the Mexican context experienced the situation of crisis in a shared territory and experiences, which manifested as bottom-up support and subversion of the state's attempts to regulate, control, and stop migration. Expressions of solidarity and charity through food, *un taquito*, sought to promote social cohesion and a more humane reception of migrants within these communities.

Webs of Power between Donors and the Shelter

The disjointed character of humanitarian assistance has been noted by academics, and issues like efficiency, collaboration, competition, bureaucracy, and accountability have been considered (Escobar 1995, 2011; Kovács and Tatham 2009; Stephenson 2005; Stephenson and Schnitzer 2006). Beyond this denunciation regarding collaboration between actors with contradictory aims, we can consider that "giving and taking are elementary activities upon which the building of communities still rests" (Komter 2005:4). Personal relationships based on giving and receiving assistance were essential for building a humanitarian community within La Esperanza. This strategy enabled collaboration, bartering with earmarked funding, and adjusting to needs on the ground for shelters across the country.

Earmarked funding entering the shelter under the definition of humanitarian assistance was diverse, and most of it fell into the categories of indirect assistance, direct assistance, or infrastructure support. A major donor to shelters was the church, which, as discussed in Chapter 2, presented itself as accompanying migrants on their journey. The church, apostolic groups, and other religious actors were important donors in the more prominent shelters. By donating to infrastructure, the presence of the church became visible to the community, migrants, and society at large. Alonso, a key human rights defender in the shelter network, shared that "the church in the United States was the DPMH's main source of funding," which meant that funding also went to other activities of the network, not only to infrastructure.

Other donors included international organizations, such as IOM, which contributed to shelters using earmarked funding. For example, at La Esperanza, IOM donated to the women's dormitory (as noted previously). It is difficult to dissect how allocation actually worked out in every case, but organizations were obliged to report to their donors whether funding was directed toward something specific, for example the female dorm at La Esperanza. As noted, the majority of migrants were male: on average, only about 10 percent of migrants in shelters were female (REDODEM 2013). Thus, one could easily assume the priority of the donor rather than the needs of the shelter was the primary consideration. Although this priority was also manifested by most human rights defenders I spoke with during my field-work. They all saw the vulnerability of women as essential to address. In the words of Priest Paulino,

> We separate women. . . . We even exaggerate around women. They have their own dormitory, apart, very clean and well set up. Because we know they are the most humiliated . . . we want somehow to give them back their image of dignity in the shelter, their tenderness, their delicacy that no woman should be separated from because she is a woman. So yes, they have special treatment.

IOM had asked shelters to join programs giving direct assistance to victims of trafficking or kidnapping. State-funded at the time, IOM functioned as an intermediary—the shelter, for which it funded earmarked projects, thus became a second-hand intermediary. In Mexico, IOM's main activities were programs of assisted voluntary return for migrants in situations of high vulnerability and assistance to victims of trafficking and migrants who had been the victims of kidnappings. Priest Federico explained his perception on the negotiations before setting up the campaign.

> With regards to the campaign that they are going to make with the government, a consensus is achieved, and it is found good as a common denominator, like a fifty-fifty of the governments and the migrants. It is kind of like that. What they do is with the governments, and they bring the project when it has already reached a consensus. They ask how we see it, and then we say it is ok. We try to see if it is profitable to the interests of migrants, and we adhere consciously, taking that into account.

The poster of one campaign (Fig. 3.1), joined by several shelters, read as follows:

> Information is your best luggage to walk safely. Every year, there are thousands of persons traveling irregularly across borders. When you migrate, you expose yourself to constant risks, grave crimes such as kidnapping, human trafficking, slavery in the form of labor or sexual, to assaults, robbery, sexual rape, and even death. Inform yourself on the dangers that you might encounter on the way to your destiny. Come to [name of] shelter. Address given and phone number. Your queries are confidential. IOM and x state actor.

In contrast, in another shelter, there was a map of Mexico painted on the walls with markings warning of places to avoid in order to *facilitate* a safer

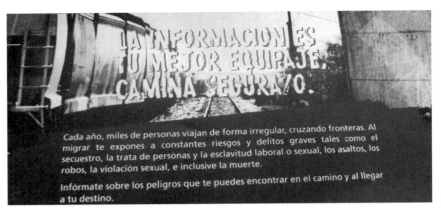

Figure 3.1 IOM campaign poster, March 2012.

journey. The map marked the locations of where the authorities were charging fees, risk zones, and areas of kidnappings and robberies (Gatti et al. 2020:8). There were other prominent messages painted on the walls of shelters, such as "Jesus was a migrant," "There is no such identity as nationality, only Christianity" (Hagan 2008:98), and "Dreams cannot be walled." As argued in Chapter 2, this Christian logic guided the charity and solidarity practices of shelters beyond only focusing on threats in movement.

In contrast, in the case of IOM, with a convoluted message between institutionalization and individual decisions at an organizational level, a staff member of the IOM shared,

> Of IOM we can expect assistance because IOM is of governmental character and it is an organization of all affiliated governments, partners. This is why, because of their institutionalization of helping them [the governments], they are not going to create any progress for questioning structures. They are not going to protest—it is not their style; they do not set up a fight [*no se van a patadas al pecebre*]. But to us especially, x [a high-ranking officer] supported us and took personal care and even came here [to their offices] and helped us economically.

Importantly, on the ground and in relation to IOM, human rights defenders expressed that there was some space to maneuver with what was donated or offered to the shelter. Priest Federico noted: "The only condition we have when those organizations approach us, such as IOM, is that they do not impose conditions on us. If they want to donate attention to migrant victims of kidnappings, I tell them do not come demanding from me a semester report of kidnappings. We try to have an institutional relationship but without conditions." In the case of IOM, the role of individual relationships was also relevant and made of each context unique.

These negotiations were never clear cut to me, and I found myself revisiting this issue with most human rights defenders and humanitarian actors I met and/or interviewed. Father Alberto specified further how this worked in his shelter. In some cases, shelter staff got what they actually needed through a type of barter.

> One day, they gave us a lot of money for medicines. Very well, they bought them and gave them to us. But we did not have use for them; there were no doctors. Who was going to prescribe them? So we ended up donating them to the health center where they assisted the poorest people, and in exchange, we asked that migrants be assisted. It was kind of like that.

There was little scrutiny of funding from organizations that might have contradictory understandings of how assistance as humanitarian related to free or dignified transit, as was the case of IOM. Father Alberto explained to me that instead,

> In this regard, we have created a network of friendship and solidarity, of care. I can choose to see it like this: that we have created a community. For example, that the shelter is open but also my relationships and those of the team with others, with institutions—that it is open, warm, and not judgmental with fear. We, for example, have my friends from IOM, from the chief of mission. I love him and his wife. . . . I have many homes to go to. I can go to them and feel very loved. We have gone beyond the institutional level. We have dealt with personal things, and it has been my privilege to talk face to face, beyond privileges, beyond formalities, beyond everything. Do you understand?

Another example was with the medical INGO. As Father Alberto said, "We are now working with [INGO]; I was also in x city with them. And I saw the care they have for me, and I also expressed our care for them. And we have such an affinity that we are now neighbors [they have offices within the shelter]."

Of CNDH, Father Alberto said: "We have had a good relationship, but unfortunately everything in this country is corrupt and politicized. And also, in a certain way, they have unfortunately received pressure. Of our allies, they have been the best allies. It has not been as free as one would have wanted."

Regarding state actors and cooperation with the shelter, Father Alberto noted that there was openness even with members of parliament: "The same, same, same, even if they are from different parties, we can talk; we can understand each other and have a common language. There can be a common denominator of solidarity with migrants. I think that is nice." What was prioritized was keeping dialogues and cooperation open, which in itself, even if open to many pitfalls, limitations, and critiques, allowed for the migrant situation to at least be present in the debate.

The matter of personal relationships beyond the institutional remains ambiguous to outsiders of the individual relationships themselves. Yet personal relationships and "making of community" was critical to Father Alberto. As was confirmed by the IOM staff member quoted earlier, situations differed depending on the person in office. This limitation at a structural level may be seen as hindering long-term solutions, yet it was often such forms of cooperation that actually triggered change, like getting access for migrants to the health care center.

Even if seldom happening, Father Alberto mentioned monetary offers from suspected criminals or corrupt officials to close the shelter or move it elsewhere in return for a donation. This is a noteworthy point to summate to monetary donations offered to the shelter. But Father Alberto affirmed that they had stood strong and rejected offers of land and large sums of money.

> We have had two occasions. One very intense, I recall a money offer, and even if it was true, they were not imposing conditions on us, but they were putting conditions on the quantities and how to give, and we did not want that. They wanted to give us a lot of money, but we said no, we do not want that, and we do not need it. We do not need a hotel. We need the basics, the essentials from people so that they fulfill; another thing does not interest us. They also wanted to give me a house. They tried to convince me and the risks I take, we have to take care of you. You are an old person, and you need a house so that you can work better, and I said no, I do not need a house, just put up a hammock in any corner and I am happy. I looked into it, and I had to say no to a large sum of dollars. We thought about it; among other things, we realized it might be money from the *narco*. . . . We turned it down, and they said we were crazy and that no one had ever turned down so much money.

To sum it up, with the exception of the attempt to make illicit donations—which in itself is indicative of the complex environment in which shelters are embedded—humanitarianism could easily be assessed as serving the needs of other actors that help the shelter, putting up IOM posters, distributing pamphlets for Central American governments, and so on, also exemplified in the disposing of unsellable produce for markets. Yet in most cases, donations, services, and campaigns were more importantly represented as a bridge of solidarity between cooperating actors that, as in the case of the health center, focused on solutions from the bottom up.

The Politics of Toothbrushes: Chain of Distribution Representations

The webs of power described, which highlighted the role of reciprocity of "keeping while giving," also transpired the issue of representing aid organizations as apolitical and devoid of power. Beyond what was given, I assess the politics that emerged based on the representation of the distribution of material goods by different humanitarian actors. Acts of donation, in the form of emergency relief, aid, and/or charity, carried an agenda and implications for how humanitarian acts were framed in relation to the transit migrant situation. Ultimately it is argued that this chain of giving created hierarchies of morality that were defined by differing representations of human worth as universal yet based on moral merit. Hierarchies of lives and who is worth of protection also were manifest. To illustrate this point, I look at the representations of distribution of basic items such as toothbrushes. In this chain of distribution, items came to represent human rights, seen as saving lives, alleviating suffering, and/or being used by migrants for monetary gains.

A handful of toothbrushes was donated one day to La Esperanza. As rumors spread that toothbrushes were available, some migrants swarmed in to demand one. Volunteers were very cautious in handing them out, as there were not enough for everyone. A volunteer shared his perception that some migrants took such goods to sell them. Between the shelter door and the office, a struggle erupted. A migrant shouted at the volunteer: "It is my human right to have a toothbrush!" This representation of the toothbrush as a human right extended the shelter to carrying a different meaning. A DPMH report criticized the manipulation of human rights discourse in relation to material goods like toothbrushes. It pointed out that, for example, the former commissioner of migration had reduced respect for human rights to giving migrants toothbrushes and soap in MHCs even as police work against migrants intensified (DPMH 2012:33). What seemed a simple battle over a toothbrush was taken to represent power struggles infiltrating transit migration politics and, ultimately, highlighted the fragility and strength of calling for solidarity and human rights alongside simple gestures of giving under the humanitarian flag. Anyone can claim to provide humanitarian assistance by giving a toothbrush. Ultimately, even if giving a toothbrush in acute situations can make a big difference, how the humanitarian act is conceptualized has different implications in the long and short term. In the context of transit migration, it cannot be equated to a human right, as did the migration commissioner mentioned in the DPMH report, especially when police action was being simultaneously intensified. Nor can it be used to assess who is worthy of legitimately showing need and getting a toothbrush.

Other sporadic awareness-raising campaigns brought in waves of specific donations with different loaded meanings. One awareness-raising activity undertaken by AI called for donations of socks. A representative of the organization told the media that when migrants were asked what they needed most, they said socks. Another official, quoting a migrant, said to a media outlet that "in a journey that can be of hundreds of kilometers, blisters without treatment can be life-threatening and a pair of clean socks can make a fundamental difference" (Noticias Terra 2012). In this way, socks morphed into emergency relief aid. This type of campaign on socks geared toward an emergency imaginary was not altogether unique. Socks form part of collecting campaigns across different parts of the world and are often highlighted as the most important clothing need (see, e.g., organizations like Sock It to 'Em, Socks and Soup, Socks for Refugees, Wool Socks for Refugees).

Staff from the Mexican ombudsman organization, CNDH, noted, "Despite it not being part of its mandate, CNDH has coordinated donations of necessities to shelters." CNDH donated for humanitarian relief in the most acute situations, such as when a train derailed with lots of people on it, the CNDH actor explained. However, these donations were rare or one-offs, shedding light on assessments made of what to consider an acute situation and why to help in certain peaks of crisis or not. IOM also contributed with rare one-off items such as blankets for shelters, as noted by the staff member I interviewed. There were many one-off donations, such as the security cameras from AI that no one could monitor. During my time at the shelter, AI also donated a box of soap. This time, Father Alberto decided the soap should go to the women, whom he saw as more delicate, and to those who faced the greatest hardship.

Ultimately what was donated had less weight than why it was donated and when: organizations typically used donations to depict themselves as expert authorities in the field and hence took the authority to designate the donation, be it as a human right, emergency relief, humanitarian assistance, or a simple donation in accordance with the agenda of the donor—not necessarily the shelter's needs. At this level, how external agendas affected the daily life of shelters was less relevant; what was prioritized morally was supporting movement, and donations in small ways provided one-off alleviation of suffering for some at the time they were donated, even if inconsistent. As highlighted by Father Alberto, it was about sustaining cooperation with multiple actors, yet material hierarchies demarcating human worth emerged. La Esperanza is unique in this way, given the wide range of actors it attracted.

The Chain of Making the (Non)humanitarian Subject

It is late. Most migrants are tired and just want to eat up their soup with tortillas and go to sleep, but a handful are filled with adrenaline from recently having gone through some ordeal like robbery or coercion. A few are eagerly waiting for dinner to be over so they can approach staff to receive further help. A young couple share how they were robbed; the young woman is pregnant and not feeling well. She is nauseous and tired, and her boyfriend is frazzled and debating whether they should return home. That same night, a migrant arrives with many severe bee stings from when the train passed a hive.

During dinner, I meet three sisters traveling together. One, with two children aged eight and twelve, describes what can only be understood as their moral destruction as a family. The youngest child is kicking the chair where he is asked to sit. His mother looks very tired and can barely talk to him. His aunts ask him to please sit down. As I bring over some soup, his mother apologizes for his behavior: "I am sorry," she says. "We have been through a lot; we all were raped down by La Arrocera, and the kids had to watch."

After dinner, some gather to listen to the priest. Others go to sleep. By the time dawn breaks, a few suffering from insomnia are still chatting and smoking. Beyond the spectrum of suffering, the priority for most migrants is to move on even if they are physically and mentally exhausted, destroyed; have not eaten or slept properly for days, weeks, or months; or have been raped, abused, humiliated, or kidnapped.

As morning breaks, the first actors to come in are INGOs. They always arrive as a team and gather people in the parish to describe the services they offer. Later in the day, a staff member from CNDH comes to give out pamphlets with information on human rights and migration to a few migrants, while Grupo Beta shows up to ask if any migrant has requested to be repatriated. As the day passes, other visitors and actors come. But these actors fluctuate significantly, as do the services they offer.

Actors such as international organizations, INGOs, civil society, CNDH, and state actors such as Grupo Beta approached shelters to donate and/ or offer their services in accordance with their own agendas, not the other way around. Therefore, they were not constituent actors of the shelter itself but adhered independently to the site. The shelter opened its doors to all

96 / Chapter 3

these actors, both to gather information and to provide services. Struggles, collaboration, and contradictions were expressed regarding the humanitarian assistance offered depending on the organization that entered the shelter to implement services. Moreover, this kind of assistance as humanitarian was tailored to shape specific subjects depending on the organization.

Volunteer Support as Solidarity

As noted in Chapter 2, most shelter staff were volunteers. The *Oxford English Dictionary* defines a volunteer as "a person who freely offers to take part in an enterprise or undertake a task," yet this freedom to help in the volunteer has been contested academically. At a bureaucratic level, humanitarian actors are often framed as motivated by feelings of power and superiority, guilt, religious redemption, salvation, or the desire to simply demonstrate that one is good to others and oneself (see Barnett 2011:15). Malkki's anthropological commitment in the book *The Need to Help* turns the eye toward humanitarian workers and their individual motivations to help. She pins down the neediness of aid workers to be part of something greater in the world, to fight loneliness, and also the neediness as a part of their personhood. This overview focuses on helpers coming from the Global North. Helping out in general may be motivated by the self-soothing afforded our conscience by volunteer work or charitable giving or by understanding gratitude as a reward (Komter 2005:124). In the shelter, the freedom to help was constrained by motivations of volunteers to assist and concerned mainly volunteers from Mexico and migrants themselves.

The nuns who offered services or were connected through their congregations to a shelter were there because of a decision by their congregations and/or what they believed awaited them in the afterlife. Volunteers from local schools were there as part of compulsory community service. Volunteer work also came from university students, both Mexican and international, looking to advance their research (such as myself) or contribute their knowledge, with its own academic bias. And volunteer work coming from migrants themselves took a position at times. Beyond general motivations, volunteerism as mutual support between volunteers and migrants, be it linked to academia, school, the church, or among migrants themselves, was a key constituent of shelter solidarity in Mexico. All volunteers gathered behind an ideology—in most, warm logic—that supported the need to transit the country.

The services of volunteers were essential to keeping the doors of shelters open. This type of emerging local volunteerism fulfilled important needs not addressed by the Mexican state or by other humanitarian actors. This grass-roots distribution of humanitarian assistance, also referred to as "volunteer humanitarianism," can be a powerful symbol against borders (Sandri 2018).

It was not a straightforward form of solidarity, however. Solidarity in transit meant confronting the very diverse perceptions of migrants held by both nonmigrant and migrant volunteers: from deceiver to victim, ignorant to savvy, and so on. Migrant volunteers themselves often spoke of *justos pagan por pecadores* (the just pay for the sinners), a Spanish saying meaning that those who have done nothing have to pay the price for those who do wrong. In this context, the saying was often meant in reference to migrants' belief that they were being punished for those who had committed crimes. Beyond actual criminals, states had set up visa systems that made the journey legally impossible for most, given the economic requirements (Menjívar 2010).

Many small but varied debates took place on needs and the help provided. Some included passing moral judgment on migrant behavior. This included the politics of toothbrushes described earlier. Should we give them a toothbrush? No, because they might sell it. Should we let this migrant back in? He was here just a few weeks ago. While most volunteers perceived the migrants' needs as acute, this view was not homogeneous. Such questions arose on a daily basis. Ultimately, most migrants were allowed in the shelter, fed, and given a space to sleep. In short, the need to move on was supported.

Anticapitalist Spiritual Support

All shelters with religious actors were able to provide spiritual support. In the context of spirituality and religiosity, the priest confirmed to me that he wanted to provide migrants with a home, not just a shelter, placing value on mental well-being. He prioritized the role of self-esteem and empowerment while contesting capitalist goals: "We learn to trust in people and discover the richness of the poor and to trust in their strength, but also, from history, we learn to fight for them and with them but not for them; each has their own task. It is a very long story. . . . I know that is a cause that we will win; we have won it, but it will take a lot of time."

Father Alberto also spoke of the commercialization of humans. When he described the mission of the shelter in one of our talks, he referred to the commercializing and merchandizing of the migrant, linking the story of one of the apostles, John, and how "he dismantled a system of oppression that denies men and makes man into a thing and commercializes him, and that very system is not only in history. In a moment it is inside us, and we can reproduce it. That is why you can see humans as merchandise two thousand years ago." He connected this to current forms of exploitation: "The forms have changed . . . but today they torture them, and ultimately, they disappear them and kill them; they squeeze them as merchandise."

98 / Chapter 3

Within this context of exploitation, he pinned down the value of the shelter as a space to give worth to the migrant.

> So the shelter is a space where the migrant can recover, even if only quickly. And at least it plants the seed in their conscience of their own worth. This is why we plant self-esteem. We tell them they should not tolerate humiliations or other abuses to their rights. They are persons with rights, so no one should ignore this. We tell them that if this happens to them, they should defend themselves—that there are institutions that defend them and that we are with them.

During a sermon at the shelter, the priest reminded migrants not to believe that they were going to a paradise; they were going to a hell where they would become slaves, and he advised against idolizing money. This view was not altogether unique. The Catholic Church has historically distanced itself from capitalist ideology and held it responsible for social inequalities. Catholic social theology that emphasizes that the causes of migration are embedded in structural injustices like poverty and market imbalances has also been identified by Hagan (2008:89). In this case, the message could lead to supporting the immobility of the poor.

The spiritual guidance in La Esperanza was accompanied by three kinds of awareness raising: about the exploitation that migrants might endure in their search for the American dream and their low human value. But this advice was presented along the lines of their capacity to migrate and change the system.

> We can tell them they [migrants] have a mission. They do not go for dollars, and the mission they bring is to change the capitalist heart of the United States. A materialist heart, that although very religious, it is atheist because it does not obey God, the real God, and it has beautified money, and that is why everything is privatized. It is not easy because you [the poor] take values with you. You are poor; you are the spiritual reserve of the world but could be at risk of being turned into one of them and also materialize and go to the other side. We tell them that.

When I asked the founding priest his thoughts on the support migrants receive when transiting Mexico, he said: "Have you asked them about God?" In fact, most migrants spoke about God and how he accompanied and protected them in their transit. The actual value of this spiritual support to the migrant is beyond the scope of this book, but it should not be underestimated or used in a simplistic analysis that makes of migrants' faith a form of cultural incompleteness in a colonized society framed by missionaries. Important values and issues should be further scrutinized in this context. Ultimately, the priests provided spiritual support as a form of solidarity and even subversion, at times conveying a message contradictory to supporting movement based on goals. Mobility for material goals was not directly supported yet was not an actual prerequisite to not have material goals to receive help, nor something inquired. Spiritual support was encapsulated mainly in a Christian logic of serving others, especially the poor, along the lines of giving worth by supporting transit.

Healthcare: The Medicalization of Transit Migration?

In general, immigration has been identified as a social determinant of health (Castañeda et al. 2015). Notwithstanding, the grueling circumstances of the journey affected migrants' health in multiple ways. Humanitarian assistance in the form of healthcare was generally limited. Very few shelters had the support of medical INGOs. La Esperanza was the only shelter at the time of my fieldwork to house one particular INGO, the reach of which was thus very limited. For more acute health issues, migrants were referred or taken directly to the community hospital. Other actors, such as the Red Cross, could be found in some locations and had mobile stations but faced similar limitations.

The immediate mission of the INGO, with some European staff, was to give medical and psychological assistance, and it had the long-term objective of contributing to improving living conditions at the shelter by promoting hygiene practices and renovating the kitchen, for example. At the time of my fieldwork, it attempted to remain on the sidelines and not interfere much, focusing on collaborating with the shelter. Within the Global South, academics have pointed out that aid workers can leave mixed results (Duffield 2012; Escobar 2011) and evoke impressions of neocolonialism. However, in the context of the shelter, on-the-ground collaboration was achieved and adjusted at different levels, even if agendas were not aligned. Most human rights defenders valued interventions and knowledge shared by international actors.

The INGO's interventions were cautious, and its staff was aware that interfering could be highly problematic. The most obvious problem was that if an organization meddled in the shelter and made recommendations, these may be challenging to follow practically in the long term for various reasons, like funding and staff training, and also it was important to give value to what was made available. Fassin (2012) provides the example of the Sangatte refugee and migrant camp in Calais run by the French Red Cross, which was constantly denounced by immigration and human rights campaigners for its material conditions. Yet the material conditions were themselves used to justify closing, on humanitarian grounds, a shelter that had originally been opened for humanitarian purposes (ibid. 133–135). In La Esperanza, medical staff often expressed concern over the sanitary conditions of the kitchen yet opted to not interfere. In this case, the judgment made, when expressed to me, was mainly based on the presence of cats, which might not be deemed an issue in other circumstances.

There were two services beyond primary healthcare that the INGO staff took special attention in describing to migrants when offering their services at the shelter: preventive medication for sexually transmitted diseases (STDs) for the sexually abused, especially women, and psychological attention, especially for men. These were indicators of what shaped assistance as humanitarian. If STDs and psychological assistance were the focus, then it was migrants with STDs and psychological issues who accessed services, shaping the irregular migrant especially as a victim of STDs and male psychological distress. Other primary healthcare services were, of course, provided.

This emergency organization specifically shaped a subject of care based on healthcare needs, which in turn could lead to the medicalization of migrants in order to be granted services, having to use their body to barter for assistance and rights (see Fassin 2012; Ticktin 2011).

Repatriation Schemes as Humanitarian Assistance

Grupo Beta, the human rights division of the INM, offered repatriation services in the shelter on a weekly basis. It represented its services as protection and defense of human rights through rescue, humanitarian help, and legal orientation (INM 2016). These repatriations were, in many ways, identical to those of migrants apprehended by the INM; the difference was that through Grupo Beta, the repatriation was "voluntary." Migrants described to me how they had accepted Grupo Beta's services on other occasions without realizing that they would end up in MHCs—detention centers. This was cautiously confirmed by Grupo Beta staff at the shelter. They said there was nowhere else to house migrants at the time. Hagan (2008) gives examples such as the provision of a bus ticket to a rescued migrant abandoned by a *coyote* confirming the activities by the Grupo Beta as a "humanitarian" act. The question remains, is assisting return a humanitarian act?

On the one hand, one can consider Grupo Beta as representing the institutionalization of the production of a rightless subject. The state takes away rights by not granting legal mobility and administers human rights discourse by renaming humanitarian acts as repatriation schemes through Grupo Beta, where deportation become a humanitarian act framed as repatriation. On the other hand, this does not mean that there were no migrants who wanted to return. This specific act, whether framed as humanitarian or as a security measure, meant not supporting the decision of the transit irregular migrant to move. Grupo Beta has also been denounced for corruption, collaborating with criminal groups in kidnapping migrants, and other abuses. Migrants in the shelter mentioned being robbed and coerced by Grupo Beta agents. Again, this does not mean that Grupo Beta does not assist migrants, yet how this is done and the heterogeneity of how actors in these institutions are presented in the Mexican case is problematic and of concern.

An ex-member of Grupo Beta, whom I will call Rolando, described how "given the context of national security, everything is obscured, and there is no access to statistics on who is committing violations to whom." He explained that migrants were sometimes told they could spend up to four months waiting for their claim to process. So migrants would decide to withdraw their claim to leave, and all such claims were simply archived. But he said that regretfully, no statistics were kept. Access or not to repatriation schemes shows a sociohistorical context of corruption and the temporal dimension that guides the transmigrant into making decisions on denouncing abuse outweighed their mobility.

Human Rights and Migration as a Security Concern

The CNDH often entered the shelter to raise awareness among migrants on their human rights. In La Esperanza, the CNDH was especially concerned with kidnappings. The organization gave migrants pamphlets on human rights, instructions on what to do in case of crime, phone numbers of institutions throughout the country, and information on their rights in MHCs. There was also information on shelters they could find along the route. They told migrants that shelters were the safest spaces to be and that they should not stay on the tracks, where it was more dangerous, especially for women. A CNDH official shared in an interview: "We ask women and children to be more careful as they are more vulnerable. We accompany them to process the visa so that migration does not mistreat them. We accompany them until they have processed their claim or obtained the visa."

Within the multiple dialogues human rights defenders engaged in, the CNDH had a heavy focus on crime and human rights abuses that were, at times, indistinguishable, as they were mostly linked to robbery and kidnapping (CNDH 2013). In a conversation between CNDH and shelter staff, for example, there was talk about La Arrocera (a location on a major migrant trail) being the most critical point of the journey. Migrants were raped, assaulted, and kidnapped there all the time, staff said; the police chief there colluded with gangs. Even in 2022, the media was still reporting on atrocities in La Arrocera (Diario del Sur 2022).

102 / Chapter 3

The focus on human rights abuses as linked to crimes such as robbery and kidnapping brought to the forefront a focus on security rather than on human rights. Human rights, as in the case of human trafficking, were used to discuss how to fight crime, not actual needs for protection for, and human rights of, migrants.

On a final note, regarding other professionalized services linked to humanitarian work, Father Paulino noted the value of human resources and capacity building (represented as donations rather than volunteer work) from the United States and Europe.

> We cannot be that naive or abusive. What is donated needs to be compensated. For example, there are international or church organizations that cannot support with food or construction, but they can help with humanitarian action by training professionals. For example, x organization from Germany directs the professionalization of the team. The Episcopal Conference of the USA, they do not give money, for example, to set up bathrooms, but give a subsidy for psychologists, lawyers.

There was value added by international actors that was appreciated by human rights defenders but criticized in the development literature. Despite the cogency of criticisms—there was an obvious need for bathrooms, food, and construction—what was donated was the professionalization of staff. This help shaped specific subjects of care yet was not always geared toward the most basic needs of the shelter or of those accessing shelters. Migrants did not come to shelters to get psychological support, but for food and a place to sleep. On the other hand, many had suffered from abuse that affected their health or solicited legal advice.

To conclude, the services that entered the shelter claiming the humanitarian mantle with reference to assistance had fragmenting and contradictory consequences regarding who was the subject in need of support and what kind of support was actually given. On the one hand, donations and direct and indirect assistance were identified as following a liberal humanitarian logic that prioritized security, offering services designed for victims of crime such as "humanitarian" repatriation services and humanitarian visas. Shelter engagement in antimigration campaigns and other antiviolence activities also presented clashing practices on the ground. These campaigns could have antipolitical effects like supporting the affirmation of strengthening border regimes. The shaping of the suffering body as sick, violated, or disabled could have antipolitical effects if these were the markers emphasized to legitimize suffering. As Ticktin argues, obliging the irregular migrant to barter for protection and rights using their body is the very embodiment of inequality (2011:24).

On the other hand, the shelter's charitable assistance and spiritual support were identified as important sources of solidarity with migrants. The assistance provided by the shelter itself was presented as an important act of subversion against repressive migration controls and border enforcement by some human rights defenders and received as much-needed help and support by migrants. Nevertheless, it faced the restrictions of needing to collaborate with actors that did not necessarily share the same goals. Support was manifested in the liberal humanitarian agenda, which prioritized security and fighting crime, supported rational-legal authority, and paradoxically created the need, in liaison with the state, for a humanitarian space to (re)appear.

Thus, shelters filled an important void created and left in their hands by the state and the international community, at times cooperating with these actors shaping a fragmented humanitarian subject. This cooperation was seen as the path to keeping a community of dialogue open, yet, in the bigger picture, it had limited unitary effect in mobilizing the agenda of free movement as a humanitarian concern rather than one of control.

Conclusion

Charity has often been problematized as sustaining the status quo of the needy and being based on an unequal relationship of power between giver and receiver. Yet, as discussed in this chapter, charity does not function isomorphically, and there are other social connections developed in the chain of giving. When it comes to considering precarious mobility, there is, on the one hand, the issue of freedom of movement and, on the other, what migrating safely implies. This puzzle seems more fragile than we can imagine through simplistic arguments that give accountability to the problem in isolation as coming from the migrant, criminal organizations, and dysfunctional states expelling the migrants.

Rather than framing this problem in isolation from those affected, behind the logic of solidarity and/or alleviating suffering through direct and indirect assistance and infrastructure, the emergency imaginary is actually about the human consequences of social inequalities between the Global North and South and their impact on safe, orderly migration. The humanitarian act and what it implies for freedom of movement becomes less ambiguous if we consider it from where those assisted are assisted, by whom, under which conditions, and why they are assisted under a humanitarian premise.

The shelter, as an emerging humanitarian complex, translates into the provision of fragmented services that attempts to incorporate all assistance offered but results in a highly disjointed constitution of humanitarian assistance in relation to borders, detention centers, repatriation schemes, visas, and migration controls. More broadly, there is a distinction within movement-associated humanitarian work between assistance as humanitarian from an ideology of solidarity and assistance as humanitarian emerging from the need to shape a humanitarian subject governable by the humanitarian policies of nonstate and state actors from the top down. If we take into account the involvement of all these actors, we see the shelter as an oxymoronic site of compassion and repression, threat and human worth. It empowers and disempowers; it opens the doors to victims and heroes but also to criminals, humanitarian action, human rights, and actors linked to the INM. The shelter embraces the poor and their value—it judges and supports the decisions they make.

The disjointed agendas gathered in the shelter simultaneously fill and create a gap in the struggle for dignified transit and against social inequality. They fragment the subject into different levels of assistance and therefore lack a unified agenda clearly delineated for the purpose of free transit as a universal human right. The emerging humanitarian subjects are the victims of crime and prioritized if they are women, children, or sick. Yet the shelter is also open to serve all (highly mobile) migrants in need. Most importantly, in practice and through the distribution of food and water, the shelter's support makes visible perpetrators, survivors and rebels.

Shelters' solidarity in supporting dignified transit, versus liberal humanitarian logics that support security agendas, reflects at different levels of authority where different dependencies emerge. Shelters can be interpreted as bringing actors together in solidarity with migrants, as Father Alberto often explained, or as facing constraints and contradictions to the agenda of free transit through collaboration with liberal humanitarian actors that support security over freedom of movement and validate this choice through human rights; that do not contest the role of the state; that abide under liberal humanitarian principles to remain apolitical yet cannot avoid being used by the more powerful states that fund them. This tension between humanitarian assistance and antimigration (security) activities was difficult to separate on the ground.

The humanitarian act, as much as volunteer work and charitable giving through the transfer of goods and other forms of aid to the disadvantaged and suffering, has been widely criticized as not being a viable, long-term solution. It can lead to emergencies being prolonged from months to years to decades (Calhoun 2008). However, it is also important to consider that economic assumptions of classic gift theory underestimate the power of spontaneity and altruism (Komter 2005:4). As noted earlier, there is a contrast between different ways of helping those in most need: providing help as someone who also has needs, as the Christian thing to do, or as the path to support movement versus addressing its risks through earmarked funding, relief aid intended to alleviate an emergency situation with one-off donations, or services that frame suffering as psychological, as a health issue, or as one of violence or crime. Charity and relief can be seen as sustaining the status quo of migrants preserved in a state of emergency, but, in the case of the shelter, support emerges as a unique form of solidarity with the poor through food, a place to sleep, and a welcoming community that strives for free transit. Humanitarian assistance as solidarity, through making and sharing meals with migrants, shows the need and value to finding *shelter on the journey*. Even if only for a handful, the shelter's gift is to (re)imagine the ebb and flow of migrants and their right to move on.

4

"The Shelter Is a Garden in a Mine of Oil"

The Humanitarian Project under Threat

Next to the shelter, by the train tracks, the body of a local man is found. He has been dismembered. Members of the Group of Urban Rescue (GRU), a vigilante group associated with the municipal authorities, tries to publicly blame migrants for the murder. Promptly, a journalist starts to spread rumors around the community that migrants mutilated the man with a machete. This journalist has been criminalizing the shelter for a while. He uses anything and everything to slander migrants, the shelter, and the human rights defender who founded the shelter. A frequent accusation is that the father is protecting migrants, whom the journalist frames as criminals, and the police normally agree.

The rumors are shared through the *perifoneo*, a system of cars with loudspeakers that relay news in Mexican neighborhoods: *What these Central Americans are doing is too much. We need to put an end to this. We need to try and close the shelter.* "The police and this journalist do and say whatever they want. There is no law against defamation in x Mexican state," Father Alberto explains.

Threats from the community start arriving. Rumors reach the shelter that people from the community are saying that they will start giving the migrants poisoned tacos and *tortas* (sandwiches). Father Alberto investigates to confirm that it was not migrants who had murdered the man and goes to photograph the body. It is thought he was run over by the train. Father Alberto decides to go to the man's wake to clarify with the family that migrants did not murder him and forestall any potential plans to lynch migrants or attack the shelter. As night approaches, he asks me and one of the volunteer nuns if we want to accompany him. He explains to me the value of bearing witness: this is our value as identified by Father Alberto. We drive out with two of his bodyguards. He talks about "lynchings"—attacks by vigilante groups—endured by him and the shelter while we drive to the wake.

When we arrive, we are received by the relatives of the deceased. The men have been drinking. Father Alberto offers to bless the dead body, and the mother accepts. He gives a short sermon, saying that migrants did not kill this young man and calls on the community to stop their xenophobic attacks against migrants and instead express their solidarity. He reminds those present that many migrants are children and women. A handful of men stand up with a disapproving grunt and leave the house. Some minutes later, one of the bodyguards approaches me and tells me there is trouble brewing outside: men are preparing to attack the priest, and we must leave immediately.

At last Father Alberto comes out, accompanied by the family members of the deceased. Later, I learn that the priest had been told that a hitman had been hired to kill him. Over the coming days, he meets with actors from DPMH to decide how to proceed, and urgent action is triggered by a well-known INGO.

The challenging environment in which different actors worked in the shelter brings to light other associations in the making of assistance as humanitarian and the emergency imaginary in Mexico. Father Alberto went to the local man's wake to clarify the truth and perform "damage control" and political advocacy. In this case, his actions meant receiving death threats and being subjected to smear campaigns. What was really at stake was how migrants were used by different actors and why shelters and human rights defenders like Father Alberto posed a threat. There was no debate over the evidence of suffering mobile bodies, yet this suffering was often relativized and represented in diverse ways along the lines of vulnerabilities in other terrains of the humanitarian project and migration. As overviewed in Chapter 3, vulnerability was a type of resource under which each humanitarian actor attempted to legitimize its work to funders—which, for some, included the state—and the community. In shelters, this was a negotiation not only about absolute victims but about human worth and mobility.

This chapter goes to the heart of *shelter on the journey* and the politics to dignify free transit. It is about the tensions between the industries that emerge around the transit migrant situation and the politics of action and exposure implied, which threaten the very heart of the humanitarian project itself. This chapter argues that beyond control and freedom of movement, a business was made out of the transit migrant situation in Mexico. Shelters

108 / Chapter 4

were threatened not only because they helped perceived criminals but also because they were seen as a threat to this business.

This chapter outlines opposing political effects concerning the conceptualization of emergency in shelters, the justifications for intervention, and the diverse levels of exposure between different humanitarian actors. Human rights defenders from shelters appeared on the scene to confront INM authorities, xenophobia, criminals, and the authorities. Human rights defenders were threatened, as were the shelter sites. There was cautious appearance of international humanitarian actors. The obstacles humanitarianism faced when confronting liberal principles of security, freedom, and peace from receiving states in the Global North while attempting to humanize free transit instead of criminalizing it often went unresolved within a business that seemed to be proliferating in every direction. Indirectly, the business of profiting from migrants brought to light not only the issue of migratory status but also of who was deemed unworthy to migrate through legal channels and was exploitable to paying very high fees to *coyotes*, requesting money from family members to be released from kidnappers, and finding ways to survive after being robbed. Beyond other forms of suffering, this group often suffered from poverty and destitution along the way.

The chapter considers the question of industries, the link between criminalizing migrants and illicit business and its associations with humanitarian assistance and precarious migration. It explores the relationship between the criminalization of migration and the criminalization of humanitarian assistance (Cook 2011; Fekete 2009) within the boundaries of the nation-state that come from the adoption of definitions provided at a supranational level by the UN concerning human smuggling. The arguments of the chapter are grounded in examples gathered in the field, showing the effects on transit communities where shelters are based and exploring links with poverty. The chapter concludes with a review on the politics of the actions and exposure taken by different actors (i.e., decisions of whether to interfere and how), showing how these politics influenced differing positions on interfering in a mobility-driven crisis held by different humanitarian actors.

Industries: Humanitarians and Coyotes

The business made out of the criminalization of the migrant was an important condition faced by shelters that confronted and/or denounced two major groups of actors: criminal syndicates and corrupt government officials. One group was framed as having bad intentions and the other as profiting from migrants. These intentions raised questions about how the business being made out of the migrant flourished, as an issue of crime or of rights. In the words of Father Alberto,

Here, there are two sources of criminalization: one is the bad intention that comes from the drug traffickers, from organized crime, and the other from corrupt public officials, from public servants who have profited [*lucrado*] from the migrant. All of them have in one way or another exploited the migrant, and as a minimum they should not do that. They live off of migrants, of stealing [*cachuquear*], of exploiting, of coercion. Why do they do that? Because they want the migrant to be merchandise, a business.

Within this context, an emerging body of literature has focused on addressing an academic gap regarding international migration as an industry and the usefulness of understanding what facilitates or controls this industry. Castles et al. (2013:235) define the "migration industry" as embracing a

> broad spectrum of people and institutions who have an interest in migration or earn their livelihood by organizing migratory movements. Such people include travel agents, labour recruiters, brokers, interpreters, housing agents, immigration lawyers, human smugglers and even counterfeiters who falsify official identification, documents and passports.

Herein, there are no clear delineations of (il)licit actors. Gammeltoft-Hansen and Nyberg Sørensen (2013:6) instead demarcate two groups involved in this industry: controllers and facilitators. They argue that the migration industry constitutes not only the service providers facilitating migration "but equally 'control providers' such as private contractors performing immigration checks, operating detention centers and/or carrying out forced return" and nonstate actors becoming involved with the migration industry. Gammeltoft-Hansen and Nyberg Sørensen include actors who are not (solely) involved for financial gain, such as NGOs, social movements, and faith-based organizations. They suggest the latter two groups be treated as different subcategories of facilitation, rescue, and control within the migration industry (ibid. 7). Missing in this overview are the risks and threats faced by some NGOs, such as shelters, and how threatening these organizations legitimizes the proliferation of the industry. This last point is considered in this chapter.

Andersson's definition of the "illegality industry" in part "highlights how the 'management' of irregular migration is a particularly expensive—and lucrative—field within the larger migration industry" (2014:14). This characterization is similar to Salt and Stein's influential characterization of the business as having two components: legitimate/legal and illegitimate/illegal (1997). The latter is linked to what they referred to as "human trafficking" well before the related UN protocol was drafted and ratified. The

110 / Chapter 4

authors cite an estimated $5–7 billion in global revenue from human trafficking already in 1994 (Salt and Stein 1997:469–472).

Concerning migration, what is presented as bringing in the most money is still human smuggling, which is alleged to be one of the fastest-growing businesses of organized crime—in the case of the U.S.-Mexico border, it was valued at $5 billion in contracts with private companies (Gammeltoft-Hansen and Nyberg Sørensen 2013:2). Instead, Ngai (2004) situates the case of the United States' response to migration and the production of "impossible subjects" (like "illegal" aliens) as one of law, history, the nation (nationalism), war, and citizenship. The argument put forward in this chapter is that in order to understand the illegality industry, we need to situate who is engaged in this production and business: the state? If so, which states? From the Global North, the Global South, or both? Transnational agreements? Criminals? Private companies? It is also necessary to situate the power asymmetries between the Global North and South that demarcate who becomes prey of such industries.

At an international level, revenues from drug and human trafficking have helped mobilize a globalized agenda to legitimize the securitization of migration (Bigo 2002, 2006, 2008) and are materialized in the UN Convention Against Transnational Crime (United Nations 2000). Yet the absence of rights (to migrate) that underlies this business has never been acknowledged by the international community. As discussed in the Introduction, illegality is not only produced by states but also increasingly regionally produced. And, in line with the UN Convention, it is globally produced and legitimized by state signatories. Beyond the financial gains, this industry has substantial impacts.

Within migration studies, there has been a multiplication of definitions of industries linked to migration. Among them, and relevant to the Mexican case, are the "rescue industry" (Agustín 2007) and the "aid industry" (Barnett 2011; Duffield 2012). The rescue industry, a term coined by Agustín (2007), is defined by the strong victimization of its clients, who are subject to human trafficking (Connelly 2015), while the aid industry is normally confined to military interventions and natural disasters. Andersson's (2014) definition of the illegality industry includes critical voices on how illegality is forged and fought and how disparate actors, including aid workers, participate in it: "Critical voices are certainly marginal to the industry—in it rather than of it—yet still awkwardly bound to its core through shared sources of funding commonalities, of concern, or similarities in working methods" (ibid. 15). Yet within these critical voices are nuanced differences, which this book addresses. Some critical voices have no funding commonalities and instead opposing working methods. The humanitarian field linked to the illegality industry in Mexico is not homogeneous, and there are stark differences between actors operating in the field as detailed in Chapters 2 and 3.

I draw on my time in shelters to schematize the divergences and convergences of humanitarian actors in relation to the profits being made out of illegality. Unpacking the humanitarian agenda helps understand that what is happening on the ground is not only about business—even if profit is an important driver of the problem, not the solution. This chapter argues that focusing only on economic aspects as opposed to impacts on migrants leads to confusion, misinterpretations, defamation, smear campaigns, and serious threats to shelters and human rights defenders.

Who Is the Coyote? Humanitarians and Criminals

Illicit migration has changed across time in Mexico. Before, it was more of a familial transaction; usually, a family member helped cross the border. Now, it was done through human smugglers, linked to some kind of criminal syndicate, and this was something even the so-called *coyotes* or *polleros* lamented.

I was in a town I will call El Azul with a group of researchers working on a separate project. We often hung out in the center of the communities where we conducted interviews. One day, as I sat in a plaza with Isabel (a student researcher), a man asked us what we were doing there. I explained that I was conducting interviews with migrants. He said he was a migrant himself and wanted to be interviewed. I opted to proceed. Isabel left us to speak more privately. As the interview evolved, he explained that he was actually a *coyote*, taking people over, and was aspiring to retire from this kind of activity as it had become too dangerous. He was visiting family but was normally based in Tijuana. He told me that at that time (during 2012), to cross "on the line," you might pay up to $10,000. He said he was tired of the business. He now had to pay a toll fee to the *narco* of $500 for every person he took across the border.

At La Esperanza, Central American migrants shared stories of being helped by *coyotes*: during the journey, *coyotes* gave them medicine when they were sick, found them places to sleep, and got them food. This did not mean that migrants were not being cheated, abused, kidnapped, or even tortured by *coyotes*. Nevertheless, many migrants saw migration as a strategy for survival, and the portrayal of the *coyote* was thus heterogeneous. Zhang et al. (2018) have contributed to our understanding of the smuggler as a complex relationship between migrants and those who guide their journeys—at times it has been relatives and close friends or acquaintances. In these lived experiences between migrants and the people behind their journeys, there is the value of reducing the hazards of traversing but also of succeeding to arrive at the destination intended.

As the man I spoke to in the preceding vignette explained, things have changed in Mexico in how this loose illicit network works. The military is corrupt and known to work with criminal organizations, while many criminal syndicates control the territory where they operate, including the border (Andreas 2003; Grillo 2011). His experience of paying tolls exemplifies this. Ultimately, in this context for the migrant, assistance crossing the border alive is a humanitarian act.

Sánchez (2015) has documented extensively the complicated social nature of human smuggling, the important issues that arise from the victim/criminal duality, and how the human smuggler has been conceptualized by looking at flawed understandings and misrepresentations of smuggling and extra-legal crossings that promote policies that ignore racialized, classed, and gendered inequalities. During my time in Mexico, it was apparent from the many migrants I interviewed and hung out with that there were fewer trustworthy networks available for Central Americans than for Mexicans (see also Abrego 2014; Basok et al. 2015; Brigden 2018; Menjívar 2000; Vogt 2018). In a report by the Migration Policy Institute on transnational crime in Mexico and Central America, Dudley (2012) underscores that migrants who could not afford a *coyote* were at higher risk of being kidnapped, abused, and held for ransom. This interpretation of help is of course subjective. Assistance does not mean that a person is being good to you; it should be understood as making things easier and providing support, in this case by facilitating movement as a necessary decision for survival. This is the first aspect that functions as a threat and a mechanism of survival embedded within the proliferation of industries and highlights what is at stake beyond monetary gains: support and survival in movement. For better or worse, the migrant puts their life in the hands of the person(s) who will help them traverse.

Human Smuggling and the Criminalization of Humanitarians

Good and evil as two faces of a coin—of assistance as a humanitarian act versus a criminal act—manifest across human history. In Anne Frank's diary, the humanitarian act materializes in the story of a family illicitly hiding another family in very challenging circumstances in order to save them. There are certain commonalities in terms of the ultimate impact on migrants—of saving their lives—and there may be stark differences in how these lives of migrants and Anne Frank's family are saved and from what.

In the Mexican context, we need to clarify the differences in the roles of actors not (solely) involved for financial gain and classified as the rescue industry and consider other structures, histories, cultural dynamics, and geopolitical relationships that might help escape the conditions that produce the need for rights, which are instead conceptualized as criminal activity. In this chapter, the focus is on the relationship between criminalizing migration and criminalizing those who help unauthorized migrants along their journey. As noted by Father Alberto,

> But they do not want the shelter because we hinder them, as we defend the migrant and stop their business. The shelter and I personally are constantly stopping the exploitation of the migrant. They do not like this; this is why they act to criminalize migrants, so that they do not have defense here in the shelter. They want to close down the shelter, but given that we defend them, they want to put us aside. That is the truth. This is why there is this criminalization against us and against me.

The definition and criminalization of human smuggling has led to the criminalization of those helping migrants. As a result, human rights defenders have had contradictory roles at many levels: they have received human rights prizes from the state, been imprisoned, lauded as the saviors of migrants, and depicted in smear campaigns as *coyotes* themselves. It is useful to consider the definition of human smuggling and its use in criminalizing assistance. Fighting organized crime has been a key mobilizer not only for criminalizing migrants but also for criminalizing those who help them cross borders without documents. This grave issue plagues humanitarian actors in the United States and many in Mexico.

At an international level, the UN took on the task of designing a protocol to fight human smuggling under the UN Convention against Transnational Organized Crime. Smuggling of migrants is defined in the Protocol against the Smuggling of Migrants by Land, Sea, and Air as

> the procurement, in order to obtain, directly or indirectly, a financial or other material benefit, of the *illegal* entry of a person into a State Party of which the person is not a national or a permanent resident. (United Nations 2000)

The protocol contains the term "illegal." In this case, one can understand illegality as being constructed through both the act of the smuggler and the consensual act of the migrant crossing a border as "not a national or permanent resident." The individual and the smuggler can then be seen as becoming the site of state authority. The migrant's agency in the process is used by the state to criminalize him or her, while the smuggler is criminalized due to the financial or other material benefit attained. Problematically, the definition of human smuggling has been used by states to criminalize any person who assists an irregular migrant, even those providing help without financial interest or doing so for humanitarian reasons, as a life-saving practice.

In the United States, assisting undocumented migrants is a federal crime and carries a penalty of up to five years imprisonment (American Patrol Reference 2016). NGOs helping migrants are limited to finding disappeared persons (mostly dead bodies), leaving (but not giving) water in the desert, and confronting civilian groups such as the Minutemen. Even with cases of successful contestation from civil society actors and native populations (see, e.g., Burridge 2009; Gentry et al. 2019), the civil society actors I met during my fieldwork expressed the strong limitations imposed by the law on their humanitarian work.

Father Horacio shared his experience of working in the United States and how the shelter he worked with in Arizona had to be closed. By helping irregular migrants, the shelter staff were creating the risk of the shelter being shut down or for the staff to be deported themselves. He was told, "We are unfortunately an international congregation and where most of us are foreigners, and we are exposing ourselves to being expelled." He explained that this was

> a bit of my experience of frustration and failure and the assistance there. And when the shelter was shut down, I did not want to work there (in the United States) anymore, because the intention of going there was to work for the Hispanics. This was also a depressing experience for me, to have to close down such a good project, and that is when I decided to return to Mexico.

Prior to Mexico's National Supreme Court ruling in March 2008, all those providing humanitarian assistance to irregular migrants in the country were subject to prosecution (Amnesty International 2010:7). After intense lobbying from civil society, in May 2008 a National Supreme Court order ruled that people who assisted migrants without financial gain were not committing the offense of human smuggling. Yet efforts like those of the *Programa Frontera Sur* failed to halt mobility, paradoxically granted criminals more control over the border and transit communities (Buscaglia 2010; DMPH 2012:28–29), and could be used to escalate threats against human rights defenders and shelter sites. Criminalizing humanitarian assistance risked hindering access to what might be some migrants' only lifeline for survival.

In Mexico, solidarity in the form of assistance provided by the poor to the poor was problematized and criminalized. This is not exclusively a Mexican issue: the unprivileged in society have been recurrently and historically pitted against each other for the sake of the privileged. In the larger picture, the production of illegality, especially as it affects the poor and low-skilled workers, is not exclusive to the Americas today (see Chap. 1) but rather nested in the colonial history of labor globally (Santos et al. 2009:71).

Critically, the criminalization of humanitarian assistance is reaffirmed in UN protocols on smuggling, shaking the pillars of the humanitarian project. It presents a crisis that invites debate grounded in empirical evidence and fieldwork to assess its effects versus its politics. Indeed, other transit communities face similar problems, from Morocco to Greece to Turkey (Baldwin-Edwards 2007; Hamood 2006; İçduygu 2000; Papadopoulou 2008).

It is undeniable that actual investments in resources for protection and safety mechanisms for humans in movement across international borders are concentrated in those who can travel by air and have access to legal channels to move. On the other hand, as Chapter 3 shows, it was the poor in Mexico who expressed the greatest solidarity with migrants on their journeys, and it is they who were threatened: the shelter, human rights defenders, and migrants themselves.

Between Criminalizing and Supporting Shelters: Transit Communities

In the Americas, the increased demand for human rights and debates around entitlement to protection manifest in the words of Juan Villoro, who depicts the border as a gaze in Mexico on the United States (Mars 2016)—a magnet whose pull stretches north to south of the border and is used by politicians to legitimize and prioritize a security agenda over humanitarian considerations as an issue of rights. Moreover, as noted in Chapter 1, the liberal humanitarian agenda has been moving from security toward peace as a motivation, and humanitarian assistance and human rights discourse in turn are increasingly managed as concerning the security of migrants, as with *Programa Frontera Sur.*

Yet beyond the borderlands, severe human rights abuses committed against migrants pervade clandestine migration routes across transit in Mexico. The increased vulnerability of migrants and their criminalization has had profound consequences for the people living in communities through which migrants pass on their journey. In response, transit communities have developed complex relationships with the irregular migrants. It should be noted that clandestine routes and shelters are set up in communities already suffering from poverty. In the south of the country, three key transit states, Chiapas, Oaxaca, and Veracruz, are among the poorest in the country, with Chiapas being the poorest. During 2018, 42.1 percent of the Mexican population lived in poverty (World Atlas 2018).

On one hand, criminal networks and corrupt local officials with social ties to the transit communities through which migrants passed played a role in predation. They kidnapped, robbed, raped, and exploited migrants in passage. In fact, one of the states with the most consistent robbery reports by REDODEM was the state of Chiapas (see REDODEM 2014, 2015, 2017, 2019). On the trail of shelters, people with social ties to transit communities expressed solidarity with irregular migrants, as outlined in Chapters 2 and 3.

Thus, one could suggest that the nascent transit communities along clandestine routes were sources of danger but also potential resources for migrants in passage. Concerns regarding security were seldom considered for the poor of the Global South, who became trapped in a vicious cycle that represented them as threats and as a problem to be hunted down. Within transit communities, the sentiments evoked were polarized between xenophobia and solidarity. Migrants and human rights defenders constantly reiterated that shelters were approached by the poorest migrants who did not have resources to pay a *pollero*. In light of this assertion, we can depart from the premise that two unprivileged groups were pitted against each other on the ground.

In the Mexican case, the criminalization of migration was imbricated with religious beliefs predominant in transit communities. The fragmentation here came from attitudes toward potential sinners. As Father Paulino shared in Chapter 2, some Catholics believed that helping someone "illegal" was a sin. Father Alberto noted at a human rights event at a university: "Migrants in the south of Mexico were treated as criminals and being harassed. On the other hand, there was recrimination for the treatment of Mexican migrants in the United States, but for the Central American migrant there was no compassion."

In its 2010 report *Invisible Victims*, AI found that even after the 2008 law decriminalized assisting irregular migrants, many Mexicans still feared prosecution. Many were also driven by xenophobia and wanted shelters to close down. Indeed, the neighbors of one of the shelters I visited had banners hanging from their gates demanding its closure (see Fig. 4.1).

As discussed in Chapter 1, the persecution of migrants did not happen overnight. This form of migrant hunting, as with the witch hunt during colonial times, took time to start with politicians and authorities presenting their anxieties about the spread of migration over the course of many decades in the United States and later on in Mexico. As in a witch hunt, people in communities opposed to migrants shared methods to identify them—

"The Shelter Is a Garden in a Mine of Oil" / 117

Figure 4.1 Banner stating "the neighbors of x demand that the shelter be closed."

their caps, knapsacks, and tennis shoes—and threats were made to punish those who assisted them. One piece of the advice often given in La Esperanza was for migrants to "take off their migrant uniform."

Alonso, a migrant I interviewed in La Esperanza in 2012, had taken the same route several years ago and recounted: "In 2008, I was here in the shelter; a lot of people came with sticks and wanted to burn us. Father Alberto found out. They had said that a Nicaraguan had raped a girl. They wanted to lynch us. All should pay the price." Alonso continued to enumerate the abuse, the violence, the suffering. In 2008, when people from the community had tried to burn and stone the migrants, Father Alberto had stepped in.

I inquired to Father Alberto about this event, and he also recalled it as noteworthy, remembering even the date.

> There are three moments: the first is when they want to burn me and burn the shelter but also close it down because there supposedly had been a rape by a migrant who had come out of the shelter. He had not come from the shelter nor raped anyone. The purpose was to criminalize the shelter. All the people were against us. I was sitting in the dock, being accused. They made people feel like we were the worst, criminalizing us to the maximum. It was true anguish . . . a terrible social lynching. . . . There were the death threats, very vivid,

very strong for me. The second was the internal lynching in the town council with the whole union insulting, criminalizing me, threatening me, telling me they were going to close the shelter, to accept or who knows what was going to happen. It was terrible. . . . The third moment was that same day, I had to go for the migrants across the river, because they still wanted to lynch them. There were stones, sticks, and gasoline. But I would not allow anything to happen to the migrants. I stood in front of them, and apart from some shoves they gave me, they did not dare do more.

Some human rights defenders said policy was to blame; others said it was society, yet others asserted that it was both. As shared by two other human rights defenders who were priests at a university event in April 2012,

It is the fault of a lack of migration policy from the Mexican state; the Mexican people are not at fault to be locking their doors with locks and bars. . . . It is the fault of the war that the Mexican government has, the federal government has, against drug trafficking. They are telling us that what is different in the foreigner is bad. This is a new risk we need to work on.

This is a problem of everyone, not only the government. We as society also occupy a fundamental role in the solution of many problems we have in Mexico—and who better than the youth?

Such perceptions created a tension in transit communities between seeing migrants as enemies and as brothers to be helped. Struggling against the criminalization of migration, human rights defenders constantly attempted to keep migrants out of "trouble," as they put it. Father Alberto shared another example.

I was talking to the Sindico today because—you remember that *borrachito* [diminutive for drunk] that we asked to leave? You know who he is? [I nod.] Well, we asked him to leave yesterday and the day before and three days ago as well. And he keeps drinking. I spoke with the Señor Sindico to prevent a tragedy because if he keeps drinking, he may do something to people, and they might recriminate us, or they might do something to him also. As he is, he might be going to bars right now, and he can do anything.

Human rights defenders constantly worked on damage control that many times derived from rumors, not truth. Yet they struggled with defending an unrealistic representation of the migrant as only good.

Given the imbalance in the representations of the migrant, this damage control was perceived as needed. As noted in Chapter 3, migrants interpreted this reality on the ground with the proverb *justos pagan por pecadores*: one does the harm, and another bears the blame. Many migrants saw their precarious traveling conditions as the fault of migrant criminals who had tainted their reputation, not as an issue of the state or coming from transit communities.

Alonso, the migrant at the lynching who had been stoned and threatened with sticks, shared that the shelter (embedded within a transit community) for him was a place to sleep, eat, and get clean water. He felt that the shelter was helping his sense of freedom and that he was there out of real need.

"It saved lives; there should be a shelter at each station," he said.

The Politics of Interventions

It is thought that when politics fail, humanitarianism appears (Barnett and Weiss 2008). If we consider the Western-dominated system of humanitarianism, the politicization of assistance has been confined to military intervention, open insurgency, and responses to security concerns (Duffield 2012:477). Within this context, the politicization of assistance has been criticized as responding to the decline of security with "self-generated risks." Humanitarians are divided within this debate, and the politicization of assistance has been framed as responsible for increased risk for aid workers. Beyond the politicization of assistance, other problematic aspects include the culture within Western aid, the lifestyle of international aid workers, distrust between agencies, and inequalities between international and local staff, among other factors (ibid. 478). These problematic aspects brings to light contradictions within humanitarianism as a universal institution and how diverse humanitarian actors rationalize their choices of which causes to intervene in (implying which lives to risk and save). Fassin (2012:226–227) refers to this rationalization as the "politics of life." In order to reach the loci of humanitarian logic he proposes to analyze the choices made and practices by humanitarians. He argues that by looking at these choices and practices the production of hierarchies of humanity emerge. By hierarchies of humanity he means distinctions made between sacrificed and sacred lives. Following Fassin (2012), I consider the inequalities that emerge from this implicit hierarchies.

A Missionary Conscience in Action

In the midst of increasing violence against migrants, before setting up the shelter, Father Alberto conducted a kind of exploratory mission through his own fieldwork. He observed and followed police and officials from the INM on raids for one year. This meant facing threats, being beaten up, and even being put in jail. Migrants were not always well received in the church, and this worried him; hostility toward migrants even came from the Catholic Church, he said. "They would go around abandoned like sheep without a shepherd, and I saw how they [criminal and corrupt officials] abused them; they raped them, attacked them in one thousand ways."

Fassin (2010:38) writes that

> Humanitarian government links up with "pastoral power" as characterized by Michel Foucault: it is exercised on a "multiplicity," that is the "flock," it is "fundamentally beneficent" in the sense that "its only raison d'être is doing 'good'"; and it is "an individualising power." The shepherd directs the whole flock, but he can only really direct it insofar as not a single sheep escapes him, and the shepherd owes everything to his flock to the extent of agreeing to sacrifice himself for its salvation.

Within this context, assisting migrants implied losing fear, receiving threats (including death threats; OEA 2014), engaging in hunger strikes (Agencias 2013; Peinado 2013), appearing on top of freight trains (Hernández 2012), and traversing the desert—radicalizing.

In Mexico, priests emerged as the first figures to provide assistance to migrants and began to refer to this assistance as humanitarian and to themselves as human rights defenders. Most missionaries explained their actions as dictated by a missionary conscience: "I am a missionary; I have a missionary conscience, and I saw myself provoked to respond, and I had to fight with the very structure of the church. . . . I left the church, and for me, I decided to not go back to the [church] system." Father Alberto also explained that his actions set a precedent and were followed as an example in Mexico.

But this missionary conscience was often experienced differently in action. Human rights defenders explained that some migrants approached the church, some human rights defenders approached the migrants, and other priests were assigned to the shelter by their parish. Courses of action ranged from fulfilling basic needs to providing a place of safety amid the violence. But the understanding of courses of action varied. Another priest explained to me that migrants approached the church and shelter for food, saying, "Food is what we could give, but we did not have shelter. The church did not have space for forty to fifty persons. We had a hall for meetings. I would put them there, but I would occupy it very often, every day. We had to get them out. So this motivated me to start a shelter where I could house them." Priest

Federico also shared: "The shelter has been working here for fifteen years since migration settled in; the migratory flows around the Franciscan parish started to receive those who came to the city center. As the flows settled, a ministry had to be structured, which came to be the shelter with humanitarian help. . . . I was sent to take charge of this project of the Franciscans."

There were notable nonreligious groups as well, though they were less widespread. The founder of a soup kitchen run by a group of students told me: "In 2007, we started a project to search for migrants. We wanted to integrate a project where we worked with migrants. Since we did not find them, we started looking for them on the tracks. We would take what we had at home—tuna [cans], bottles of water, socks—and we slowly started to receive donations." The Patronas, often in the media, cooked and went to the train tracks to provide food and water to migrants every day, following their (Catholic) values and beliefs to do good, as narrated in a short documentary *El tren de las moscas* (*The Train of Flies*, López Castillo and Prieto 2011).

Again paradoxically, some human rights defenders received protection from the state. One had four bodyguards, for example, though most had none. Despite the desire and efforts to protect shelters from violence, as an interviewee from DPMH noted, the responsibility of shelters was seen to be not to protect but to provide food and water. Thus, there was a conscience in action that associated the crisis with assistance as humanitarian and considered it not only an issue of violence, of extreme need, but also of confronting institutions and opposing the structures that refused to step up. In some cases, human rights defenders were threatened by the authorities, yet some received protection from the state.

Other Humanitarians in Action

Beyond the heads of shelters and shelter staff, there were hundreds of human rights organizations, and some international organizations and humanitarian assistance actors crosscut the humanitarian and human rights debate of migrants. These actors entered shelters with other ethics in action and had diverse responses and exploratory missions.

In the challenging environment of the shelter, international actors had only a limited presence distinguished by "bunkerization" (Duffield 2012)—taking an undercover role, not confronting the authorities, and staying apolitical—which countered and fragmented the definition of the crisis among the humanitarian actors involved. This "bunkerization" was highly problematic, as it reaffirmed the official humanitarian community as involved cautiously or silently in a generous venture yet actually experiencing social, intellectual, and emotional withdrawal from the society in which they were working.

122 / Chapter 4

According to Duffield, bunkerization occurs "where there is a perception among aid agencies that they are facing external risk and physical segregation is not only taking place in regions marked with insecurity" (ibid. 477). In the case of the INGO at La Esperanza,

> A need was identified, but also the security conditions allowed us to work. We saw it was more difficult to work in zones like Tamaulipas and the northern border. Here there is a concentration of migrants. It is an area where Central American migrants pass in a reduced geographical space; in the north, there are three thousand kilometers of border, so reaching migrants is more difficult. Also, the security did not allow us. In other places, there is more risk of suffering aggression toward humanitarian actors. . . . We decided it was good to begin with but in the future, we plan to go up [north]. . . . It is a long story because the first exploratory mission took place in 2009–2010. There is a proposal in 2010, and it is approved in 2011, and in February of 2012, the project is launched.

Location was key in the context of this intervention. A doctor affiliated with the INGO added that the exploratory mission had come about through asking the secretary of health for data on the shelters and organizations dedicated to assisting migrants. The differences between the INGO and the shelter had to do with two issues concerning the emergency organization: logistics and staying apolitical. As noted in Chapter 2, the key actor of the emergency organization affirmed, "We do not have a stance; we are not pro- nor antimigrant." Another European staff member shared her personal view.

> This type of migration project is a bit different; it is a vulnerable population, a forgotten population I would say, sometimes by organizations and the state. Since I am here, I have no doubt of the importance of the project. I think that it is necessary because even if the Mexican state in theory covers the needs of migrants, in practice there are limitations.

On the ground, a key difference between shelter staff and staff from the emergency organization was that the latter arrived together, in an escorted vehicle, with a guard carrying a machine gun who stayed outside their offices during their working hours. This presented immediate visual and material differences between the value of lives of international humanitarian actors, volunteers, and migrants. It raised questions about the hierarchies present among humanitarian actors. The message that came across was that certain causes were not rescuable, given the absence of the INGO across the country. This actor in particular appeared to be governed by the bunkerization effect.

The CNDH was subject to an ethics of action guided by the principle that it could only issue recommendations and was subject to Mexican law. The exploratory mission to La Esperanza came from its own research on where the INM had local subdelegations and where trains converged. Since the shelter was here, the CNDH decided to establish an office to cater to citizens and foreigners in relation to their human rights or any authority that abused them. "We belong to the Fifth Committee; we have the program of threats and abuses against journalists and human rights defenders, matters of human trafficking, and obviously the program focusing on migrants. The work includes working with the shelter and delegation of the INM in the surrounding areas," said an official. This community was chosen as a strategic place, he said. Like the emergency organization staff, CNDH staff entered the shelter according to set schedules and at key locations. They did not arrive with escorts.

IOM worked very closely with the Mexican state. A member of staff explained to me that different offices across the country provided different services to the state characterized by the migratory flow. The IOM exploratory mission to La Esperanza was in line with services by the state.

> For example, the office in x city is for Mexican returns and repatriation of Mexicans. . . . They help them to get back to their place of origin. In xy city, they cater to the flows of Central Americans. In the latter office, there is a regional program on information. The poster campaign is called "Learn about your journey," for example. And the project of direct assistance is to victims of sexual violence, human trafficking. The dynamic is very different at the northern border and at the southern border because of the flows. In the north, we are talking about Mexicans. People are constantly returned. In the south, the flow of Central Americans is totally intense, very intense. Of numbers I am not clear.

He clarified that they worked with humanitarian actors, such as the Red Cross, but not human rights actors, such as AI. "With shelters, it has been the campaign, infrastructure, materials, and medicine but not as much livelihoods such as food. In this case, the organization appears intermittently in accordance with government-funded projects that focus on the criminal dimension or emergency-like scenario."

In short, most actors external to the shelter appeared at their convenience, with earmarked funding or time-limited projects, unable to escape

124 / Chapter 4

collaborating with the state, and also more strongly prioritized security concerns, addressed criminal issues and/or emergency-like situations in relation to movement, and most importantly, sought to remain apolitical. Human rights defenders, on the other hand, geared their missionary conscience to a politics of action based on the violence and basic needs they bore witness to, denouncing authorities and opposing migration and border controls through supporting transit. I associate these ideas with a type of emerging progressive politics.

Local priests and limited volunteer staff were on the ground assisting migrants regardless of the conditions, be it threats from the community, criminals, or the authorities themselves. As they testified, their moral duties were used both for and against them. They were represented as threats by criminals, authorities, and journalists and as the only moral defenders in the migrant situation by other human rights defenders and themselves. The relationships among all these stakeholders were, confusingly, collaborative, as outlined in Chapters 2 and 3. This type of dependency and collaboration by the shelter should not be confused or carelessly linked to the illegality industry defined by Andersson (see earlier in the chapter). It was, as Father Alberto noted, cautiously established as a mechanism of survival and as the path to creating social and moral consciousness and transformation.

Politics of Exposure: Losing Fear

Attempts to delegitimize the mobile poor from Central America and Mexico as "wetbacks," "criminals," or "rapists" appeared in print and in the speeches of politicians, manifest in the bank accounts of corrupt officials and under the mattresses of houses decorated with gold statues of lions. For human rights defenders, intervening in the violence and suffering linked to the criminalization of migration and border enforcement meant not only providing help without an established protection regime but also inviting threats, attacks, and smear campaigns. The need to shed fear and denounce what was happening created political advocacy practices including sharing testimonies, bearing witness, holding hunger strikes, confronting law enforcement, protesting, and portraying the *viacrusis* (stations of the cross, used for advocacy and referred to as *viacrusis del migrante*), to name the most important. There were also caravans for mothers seeking justice and their disappeared children and other migrant caravans that materialize in the struggle against the border regime (Álvarez Velazco and De Genova 2023).

This action turned pastoral workers into human rights defenders (DPMH 2012:108). De Sousa Santos (2002:45–46) has pointed out more broadly that human rights activists have become the target of the state. It is important to note that, historically, there has been a narrative alleging that human rights activists work for criminals and against society in Latin America (Chillier and Varela 2009:73). For example, a report produced for the UN Security Council highlighted special concern around the designation of human rights defenders as "terrorists," "enemies of the homeland," and political adversaries by the Mexican state authorities (Sekkagya and la Rue 2010:12). Yet human rights actors are necessary for democratization processes to thrive. This is not unique to Mexico. Terrorists and human rights defenders alike pose a challenge to the sovereignty of the state because both confront its politics (Ophir 2006).

On the ground, human rights defenders lost much of their fear—they had been radicalized and confronted both the authorities and criminal actors directly. But this radicalization was accompanied by victimization in the face of targeted threats as severe as death. Beyond distinctions between the assisted and assisters, the value of lives fluctuated even among humanitarian workers, as discussed earlier in this chapter. There were numerous targeted death threats, attacks, imprisonments, versus campaigns calling for the protection of human rights defenders. This situation became especially relevant within a debate on democratization processes necessary for the Mexican state outlined by the international human rights community (Sekkagya and la Rue 2010). Responses included urgent actions from AI, the granting of bodyguards by the Mexican state, and finally a law for the protection of human rights defenders and journalists that came into force on June 25, 2012 (Congreso General de los Estados Mexicanos 2016). Yet Mexico remained one of the most dangerous countries for human rights defenders and journalists. Human rights defenders continued to be represented as terrorists and enemies, exposed to forced disappearance, arbitrary detention, and torture (WOLA 2015).

Radicalization was needed, one human rights defender explained: "2008 was the worst year and most intense; in January, they started with savage migration operations with the federal police, the municipal police, the navy, and the army. . . . I was threatened by the Zetas. It is thanks to [a renowned human rights defender] that the operations were suspended as he took pictures of the operations and circulated them."

Priests constantly put their lives at risk as a consequence of the threat they posed to the flourishing business being made out of migrants. More specifically for human rights defenders, losing fear was seen as necessary to be able to help. In the words of Father Alberto,

> There has been a considerable change, very considerable. But that happened in the measure I started to lose fear. . . . I remember that during a meal on a Tuesday, they launched a migration operation. I called the press that day and denounced them. The operation was a

failure because it ended with the mutilation of a fourteen-year-old girl. So I denounced it, and the immediate response was—I had barely left the hospital, it was ten to fifteen minutes, and I was called—*Take care because they are going to detain you. They are going to put you in jail.* It was in that moment I think that I received the first threat. My answer was straight, not to accept blackmail. . . . I am not afraid if you put me in jail. I will be acting from jail . . . and I discovered it was not only that I was not afraid: it was that they did not know what to do. So I moved forward, and they had to back down. Because they only had one alternative—either they eliminated me or they let me pass . . . and every time they threaten me and they do not kill me, I move forward; I become stronger and continue the mission, and that is why I do not have fear. I have God's strength, and I know who I am defending. . . . The threats have multiplied. . . . Only death, a shot here [pointing to his head] will stop me; otherwise I will not stop.

The situation of human rights defenders was precarious, and many were subject to threats (including death threats), harassment, intimidation, forced disappearance, and extrajudicial executions. The severity and nature of these threats varied according to the field they worked in (Velasco Yàñez 2012). Human rights defenders for transit migrants were threatened and faced the same criminalization and harassment migrants faced from local authorities and the community even as they were recognized as defenders of human rights. For example, a human rights defender was awarded a human rights prize, but this same defender had been threatened and harassed by local authorities, imprisoned, and physically attacked by authorities.

Shelters and the priests running them faced smear campaigns from local journalists accusing them of housing and aiding criminal businesses. These sites also confronted actual infiltration by criminals as explored in Chapter 2. Finally, media coverage of criminal incidents linked to shelters spread rumors about the risks of residing in shelters and created a reputation among migrants of shelters being a site of risk. Many migrants were therefore hesitant to access shelters (Amnesty International 2010; Martínez 2014). However, the coverage of criminal incidents also attracted the attention of a plethora of humanitarian actors who stayed temporarily to collaborate and cooperate with the shelter in the distribution of assistance. This attention made shelters into an emerging and unusual space of assistance for irregular migrants, establishing a relationship of mistrust for some and where false defamations continued to be spread.

The relationships between the Mexican state and human rights defenders were contradictory. Although human rights defenders denounced abuses by the authorities, bodyguards were sought from the state. At the same time, lack of trust in the authorities led to stress and rapid turnover of bodyguards, as it was never felt that they were there to protect, rather to pass information on to corrupt authorities. Finally, even though a law was in place protecting human rights defenders, some faced prison time. Such confrontations represent the very motor of progressive politics and are, at times, the most conclusive test of antipolitics, especially when risks to human rights defenders are used to reaffirm the need for further security as a human rights issue.

Conclusion

A flourishing business emerged out of the production of irregularity of migrants in Mexico and elsewhere. Although the issue of migration was framed as business, non-business-like aspects linked to the migration strategy went beyond economic structures and were linked to the survival strategies of the poor confronted by the making of enemies. These framings informed assistance as humanitarian.

In particular, the links between humanitarianism and the human smuggling paradigm emerged as a form of antipolitics when humanitarianism and human rights were used to support a security agenda. Most importantly, the (mis)use of the definition of human smuggling that trickled all the way down to transit communities, implicating migrants and shelters themselves, had serious repercussions, putting the humanitarian project under attack by states and the international community. This (mis)use of human smuggling linked the poor further to a criminal context, putting poor citizens in opposition to criminalized poor noncitizens and their helpers and leading to a general environment of threat, which the Mexican state used for its own purposes—for example, to validate the implementation of *Programa Frontera Sur.*

The Mexican state both created a humanitarian space and the need for its existence. Human rights defenders received human rights prizes for assistance and protection by law (Cámara de Diputados Federal de México 2012) yet were linked to the criminalization of migration and jailed by the state when they opposed INM officials. In short, human rights became Janus-faced: as human rights defenders geared them toward dignified (humanitarian) movement, they were linked to human smuggling and used to make humanitarian assistance in shelters vulnerable to attack by the state and wider society.

The international humanitarian community was seen as being cautiously involved in a generous venture that enabled it to legitimize its absence. Meanwhile, human rights defenders stood in the limelight as radicals, moral leaders, and targets. Intervening in the criminalization of migration and border enforcement crystallized in limited protections for human rights defenders, no protection at all for shelters, and the ambiguous presence of international actors whose knowledge and expertise was valued by human rights defenders despite its clear limits. This crystallization, as argued by Fassin (2012:221–242), shows the inequalities inherent in the humanitarian project, illuminated by the hierarchies of lives that, in this case, made especially manifest the differences between locals and international actors. These hierarches are situated in power asymmetries between the Global North and South and not exclusively in humanitarian interventions.

Ultimately, human rights defenders filled a void in institutional mechanisms to protect human rights and provide humanitarian assistance. As Hagan notes, the Mexican government depended on the shelters for humanitarian assistance (2008:99) yet also threatened them. The paradoxes manifested in the contradictory political effects of humanitarian assistance in shelters need to be further acknowledged in the practice of humanitarianism and human rights discourse in general.

The fact that, despite their humanitarian goals, shelter sites became actual targets of threat not only from criminals but from the authorities shows both the critical situation experienced in shelters and by humanitarian actors and the power of transformation that emerged from them. Beyond the industries plaguing migrants and communities, real exposure was constructed across this humanitarian trail as a loss of fear and a resilient and transformative ethics in action.

5

"That They Do Not Keep Expressing That Mexican Territory Is a Cemetery for Central Americans"

Advocating Free Dignified Transit

We arrive in Mexico City after a long bus ride, Father Alberto, his assistant, and I. He had booked a room in a high-end hotel in the city center. He attempts to sort out a place for me to stay. I told him not to worry, but he was always trying to take care of everyone: migrants, visitors, implementing actors, friends, foes, me. His assistant told me we could both stay at a hostel that also housed refugees.

At the hostel, there is four other women in my room, one of whom had been granted refugee status in Mexico. We chat as I unpack. She tells me about being persecuted, robbed, and threatened by INM officials. She describes the problems she had faced back home in Honduras, the death threats she and her husband had received. They had been at the hostel for a week now. The next day, she was going to a meeting for help finding a job, but, she tells me, what she wants is to continue her journey to the United States. She does not see a future in Mexico for herself and needs to help her family in Honduras. In Mexico, she would earn the same salary or even less than back home.

This woman evokes, in very concrete ways, what makes of movement a human right and what not—what it implies for the subjects targeted, the context they live in, and, more importantly, the context they aspire to live in. She had been offered refugee status as the only viable solution, yet it did not align with her needs: to support her family back in Honduras. As noted by Boehm (2011), holding migrants up for protection by defining categories of victims and criminals does not do justice to their heterogeneous experi-

130 / Chapter 5

ences. Along the so-called *corredor de la muerte*, there was a mobility of "mixed senses" (ibid.). As Jorge, the key actor of the DPMH, shared,

> [The situation of migrants] is different; the realities are different, but they suffer the same. The fact that for example they are deported after twenty to twenty-five years from the United States, and they are deported to a border that they do not know, without money nor documents, with no one to orient them in their own country. In their own country, authorities coerce and beat them up. They put them in jail. Sometimes they are given to organized crime to kidnap. So what persons in transit suffer is different from those at origin, but they suffer the same. We could not determine who suffers more or less. The realities are very similar.

The next day, we headed out to an event in the Senate titled "The Legislative Balance on Human Rights and Migration, Advances and Challenges, 2012." The place was full, and there was a big banner with pictures of migrants on top of a train, smiling and waving. The vice president of the Senate took the podium. He greeted other officials from the Senate and the CNDH president on his panel.

> In their name, I make a greeting that has implicit in it the compromise we have not only to make this balanced panel but also to continue until the last day of this legislation to pass [on to others] the enthusiasm and compromise for the next legislation in the fight for the dignity and justice for the people transiting [Mexico]. This implies the abandonment of what is theirs [the migrants'] to go some other place; that implies accepting foreign conditions, far away from the dignity that migrants have. So that our Mexican and Latin American brothers and in general all human beings who find motivation in one way [or another] try to reach their destiny can change that very destiny—this is the rumor and the expression of compromise of institutional organs, of the organs of government and direction of politics and the law of the Senate of the Republic.

The vice president's speech exemplified the challenges human rights defenders faced in promoting and defending the human rights of migrants. From his words, it appeared a battle won; the speech began and ended by recognizing the issues faced by the woman I met at the hostel. Yet the implementation of the law was far from reflecting these fine sentiments. In Mexico, there was no protection regime for irregular migrants, with the exception—and inherent limitations—of the humanitarian visa. Deaths of Central

Americans in perilous transit across Mexico (and deaths across borders and beyond) were not considered crimes against humanity. Human rights were used to reinforce a national security agenda within migration policy and border enforcement as exemplified through *Programa Frontera Sur* rather than supporting transit or, in the words of the official, having legislation that allows Mexicans and Latin Americans to reach their destiny.

As discussed in the Introduction, the Tamaulipas tragedy was a turning point in Mexico in relation to debates circulating transit migration. Yet the situation has not much improved. Shelter actors denouncing the humanitarian crisis maintain an expansive, complex, and often disjointed assessment. Some link state violence to impunity. Some link criminal violence and need to poverty in the country of origin and structural abandonment. Others share an understanding of Mexico's INM as an institution that abuses power, as corrupt to the core and in need of being dismantled. Activists understand migration management and border enforcement as a central component in the making of the humanitarian crisis. Most see Central Americans from the Northern Triangle as one of the most egregiously targeted populations. Others do not take a political standpoint toward migration and borders, while still others support, at times indirectly, strengthened security measures to address issues arising in movement. Who has the power to decide what humanitarian assistance and human rights activism should stand for and who is a humanitarian actor?

This chapter situates the construction of the intrinsically hierarchical idea of what is "human" in relation to movement and advocacy in the shelter, in this case related to ideas of poverty, race, and human rights. This chapter argues that the notion of humanity as mankind (an idea) and humanness (a sentiment) (Fassin 2012:241), used to claim protections and rights to move as universal, are situated in race (Grosfoguel 2011), socioeconomic hierarchies, and struggles in the Americas. Neither race nor poverty are acknowledged within political debates. Some scholars have outlined the making of illegality as a question of race and ethnicity (see Chapter 1) nested in historical struggles that show that the law is not neutral. Other scholars, like Vogt (2018), have pointed out the economic dimension of visa schemes. And others have focused on the making of a cheap, vulnerable workforce (Anderson 2013; De Genova 2004; Ngai 2004; Ticktin 2011).

Still, the evidence of poverty as criteria for exclusion from visa schemes has been less considered (Menjívar 2010). The need to alleviate the multiple maladies that provoke or are provoked by economic needs is cautiously made (in)visible on the humanitarian stage, and suffering from poverty is not recognized as a legitimate reason to migrate. For most humanitarian actors, another type of suffering must be highlighted in order to legitimate a subject of care. Notwithstanding, at the time I conducted fieldwork in

132 / Chapter 5

Mexico, there was much discussion among human rights defenders about how problematic it was to manage a development issue as one of security. The political winds subsequently shifted, as did the situation in Central America and the United States, but it is unlikely that poverty has ceased to be an excluding marker—or one of the main issues that influences Central American migrants in their decision to move. Herein the purpose is not to put a blind eye to other forms of severe violence in Central America propelling movement, but as in the case of the refugee in the hostel, her motivations to move onwards were also fueled by the economic precarity of her family.

This chapter critically analyzes how the emerging social movement constituted by shelters mobilizes the defense and promotion of the human rights of irregular transit migrants in Mexico in relation to their transit. It unpacks first the only legal tool for human rights defenders available in 2012 to legitimate movement: the humanitarian visa. Then the chapter traces registration and data collection as two of the main responses gathered by the Network for the Documentation of Migrant Defense Organizations, commonly known by its Spanish acronym REDODEM, setting the shelters in the national context. The chapter explores two different methods used for political advocacy geared toward free dignified transit: registration practices and data collection in shelters. It argues that the presentation of the transit migrant situation as embedded in crime, impunity, and poverty struggles against the general portrayal of the humanitarian subject as suffering from torture, abuse, persecution, and so on. I continue to examine how the subject of care is represented through the practice of sharing testimonies at diverse events and how this framing has implications over who counts as the humanitarian subject in the making. The chapter argues that in the midst of an increased production of illegality spreading in the region, the humanitarian crisis must be addressed by considering extended geographies of transit and how these are affected. Nation-states in the region need to revisit the current refugee protection regime, an ill-matched instrument to the vulnerabilities and suffering of the mobile in this context. The role of poverty, violence, and climate refugees as excluding markers to protection and at a policy level needs to instead be geared toward a more universal approach. Finally, safe and dignified transit as a universal concern needs to be prioritized.

Legal Tools

Over the decades, Mexico has experienced ongoing calls by the United States to improve the migration situation. Paradoxically, the United States itself has not ratified any human rights treaties since 2002. Moreover, the United States is the only country, with the exception of Somalia, that has not ratified the Convention on the Rights of the Child, the most widely and rapidly ratified human rights treaty in history. It is one of the only seven countries in the world to have not ratified the Convention on the Elimination of All Forms of Discrimination against Women (CEDAW). Other important treaties that have not been ratified include the Convention for the Protection of All Persons from Enforced Disappearance, Convention on the Rights of Persons with Disabilities, and the Optional Protocol to the Convention against Torture (Human Rights Watch 2009).

Mexico, on the other hand, has ratified most human rights treaties (University of Minnesota 2016) and is one of the few signatories of the UN International Convention on the Protection of the Rights of All Migrant Workers and Members of Their Families. The humanitarian agenda claimed by the country is reflected in the INM guidelines concerning rights of migrants transiting Mexico once they are apprehended. In 2012, these rights covered migrants' stay at MHCs, and two channels were established to legalize their stay in the country: asylum claims and application for a humanitarian visa. There were also special conditions stipulated for children in coordination with the Institute of Integral Development of the Family (DIF) (INM 2014a). Yet we must consider that what we see here is a migration control and border enforcement regime soaked in human rights discourse, which was nevertheless repressive and prioritized national security (DPMH 2012:32).

Given the wide variety of subjects in motion across Mexico, there were norms, programs, and groups involved in the assistance and protection of migrants within the INM. As noted in Chapter 1, in Mexico, nation-building processes have historically excluded the majority of the population from citizenship structures (Quijano 2000) and are therefore not exclusive to migrants. These norms included, to mention only the most important, protection and assistance; protection to Mexican citizens and migrants; the *Bienvenido Paisano* Program (Welcome Back Compatriot, for those returning); the program of humane repatriation, Grupo Beta; offices for child protection (OPIs); the strategy to prevent and address kidnappings of migrants; the humanitarian visa; and assistance to migrant victims of accidents, abuse, and crime. An important tool behind the regularization of migrants apprehended for humanitarian reasons was the Migration Law published in 2011 (Wolf et al. 2013:215). Yet in general, even if there has been considerable legislative activity around migration in general, the number of persons assisted by these programs in Mexico is questionable.

In 2012, applicants needed a sponsor for their humanitarian visa application to be considered. Under Article 9, the sponsor could be a physical person or an institution affiliated with the federal, state, or municipal administration. The sponsor had to assume all travel and accommodation expenses incurred during the application process. The second requirement was that the applicant present an identification document. This was impossible for the many migrants who traveled without documents. Finally, the applicant could not have applied for a visit visa permitting him or her to engage in paid activities (INM 2014b).

During my time in the shelter, a handful of migrants stayed around to apply for the humanitarian visa. I went to the INM offices with them. In our ride to the INM, they confirmed that they would not have applied without the support of, and considerable persuasion from, Father Alberto. Between 2011 and 2013, forty-nine applications were granted of the only ninety-three humanitarian visa applications made all across Mexico. The others were denied or remained pending (Wolf et al. 2013:254–255). These low figures could be justified by a lack of interest in following through with the legal claim, lack of knowledge about the visa, or the complexity of the process (ibid. 254). Insyde notes that at the time, the INM preferred to issue an exit permit, which lasted only fifteen days and did not allow proper follow-up of the case with migrants.

In 2012, the humanitarian visa was the main legal instrument used to temporarily regularize transit migrants. Indeed, other than an asylum claim, it was the only legal channel for regularization. Issued by the INM, the visa was valid for one year. It defined candidates for application: "migrants who have been victims of or witness to a crime have the right to apply for a temporary visa for humanitarian reasons" (INM 2014b). This definition raised two questions. First, why was the Mexican state attempting to reconcile the denial of documents to irregular migrants with the granting of humanitarian visas to victims and/or witnesses of a crime? And second, why could only victims of crimes travel across Mexican borders?

The logic of the visa was presented as humanitarian, but its purpose was mainly to prosecute crime. This logic resonated with the logic behind human trafficking legal tools that also use the language of human rights to fight crime, spelled out in the legal instrument to fight human trafficking at an international level: Palermo Protocol, supplementing the UN Convention against Transnational Organized Crime.

Ten years on, in 2022, the humanitarian visa in Mexico was renamed to "visa for humanitarian reasons" and stated to be aimed at victims of climate change and violence, people whose lives were at risk or in danger, or those who needed to enter the country to rescue someone from an emergency or to support someone with serious health issues (Gobierno de Mexico 2023). Again, it was the INM that issued this visa.

The second actor in this process was the Public Ministry of Social Attention to Victims of Crime (PROVICTIMA), which was created in 2011 to help the families of the disappeared and victims of high-impact crimes such as homicide, kidnapping, extortion, and human trafficking. CNDH, DPMH, and shelters referred victims to PROVICTIMA, yet its representatives did not visit MHCs (Wolf et al. 2013:252). In the previous chapters, the challenges in identifying who is the subject of care in shelters have been outlined, as have the significant discrepancies between liberal humanitarian agendas and the missions of shelters concerning migration. These discrepancies also manifested in the law, public debate, and in data collection (if any occurred). One can therefore argue that for the government, what mattered was showing a response to the suffering of those who were victims of crime, not the actual numbers helped. It was not about the figures but about showing political will and alignment to the human rights agenda, promoted and ratified nationally and internationally. As with human trafficking, the suffering of the transit migrant as a victim of crime was depoliticized and, in the worst-case scenario, used to further legitimate strengthening the border and other control posts along the way. Instead of considering inequality and marginalization responsibility was granted to the specific crime as an individual act.

Data from Shelters

When La Esperanza was first founded in 2006, there was no official register. The priest would simply ask by show of hands where migrants were from. The gathering of data was seen as important in understanding who was being served, yet it could, in turn, be used to define who needed assistance. In the beginning, Father Alberto said, "all [migrants] were lumped together, but you did not know who you were serving. To know the names of persons—they are not numbers—where they are from because their families also ask about them. Sometimes they disappear, and the register helps us to know where they stayed for follow up."

Migrants are received by two male volunteers who ask them to form a queue to enter the shelter. Volunteers are in charge of keeping safety and order. Migrants' belongings are checked mainly for weapons. Migrants are placed in a queue in front of the registration office, where they will answer a survey (the REDODEM survey); this takes no more than a couple of minutes. Women and small children are placed at the front of the line, though not always.

The office is divided into two small, connected rooms. There are four computers for registration. The office space is small, and volunteers and migrants sit right next to each other when registering. Personal and confidential information is requested aloud and in front of other migrants. Everyone in the office, and even in the queue, can hear what is being asked and answered. Some of the migrants are suspicious of the questions. Most simply answer briefly or just nod or shake their heads. After this, they are asked to go into another crammed room to have their picture taken. This is compulsory. If they refuse, they cannot stay in the shelter. During my time, only one migrant refuses to have his picture taken.

There are differences between volunteers and how they approach the migrants. Some are kinder, some skip questions, some are fast, others take their time, and so on. As with any data-gathering exercise, contextual and personal circumstances extending beyond methodological considerations affect the data being collected.

Most women, for obvious reasons given the circumstances under which they register, do not inform volunteers during the registration process if they have been raped. Some wait to find a moment of privacy or until they are prompted by service providers that offer protection against STDs.

Once the registration process is complete, everyone has eaten, and it is time to get some sleep, testimonies become detailed and open. And many times, these are very different from what migrants have briefly shared in the busy registration office. As the sleepless ones gather in groups to talk and smoke, experiences *en el camino* (on the journey) are exchanged.

The humanitarian sector is heavily dependent on statistics—and the nation-state even more so. Foucault (2007 [1978]) argues that national statistics are the science of the state used to group, organize, and control. At times, they are given much weight, and at other times, as noted previously, they are presented as not mattering to politicians. Numbers can be a sensitive vehicle to acquire knowledge depending on context. Yet it is the very absence of statistics on the transit migrant situation that preoccupies REDODEM.

When it comes to transit migration, the battle of numbers is more recent. As discussed in the Introduction, academia did not start collecting data on transit migration until the 1980s (Basok et al. 2015), and it was not until the turn of the twenty-first century that a body of literature began to emerge (see Anguiano and Cruz Piñero 2014; Arriola Vega 2012; Basok et al. 2015; Brigden 2014, 2016; Casillas 2007; Castillo 2003; Nájera Aguirre 2016; Nyberg Sørensen 2013, among others). Beyond the ongoing battle of numbers over legitimate guesstimates of how many people transit Mexico, however, REDODEM is concerned over the absence of data gathered on the transit migrant situation. In general, the debate focuses on the image of migrants constructed with limited empirical referents and facts. Beyond numbers, as noted by Durand and Massey, "immigrants become symbols in a battle of images" (2004:1). This battle of images is often not quantifiable and has to do, on the one hand, with the threat of the migrant and, on the other, with the invisibility of their suffering. There is often a link made by authorities and organizations that, in order to make issues visible, they must first be quantified. Civil society and social movements reporting on human rights issues related to migrants focus on how their undocumented status led to their becoming invisible victims despite the tangible violence they face (Amnesty International 2010; REDODEM 2014). This makes a myth of the suffering within the irregular migration paradigm. Likewise, the making of victims as *invisible* presents complexities over why numbers matter, for whom, and for what.

Within the context of the transit migration situation in Mexico, humanitarian actors and human rights activists needed to instrumentalize suffering as the path to seek recognition and legitimation of the decision to move and seek protection. Within humanitarian legal frameworks like the refugee protection regime, where poverty is not recognized as a legitimate reason to seek protection nor, for that matter, to move, how should suffering be understood? The identification of the transit migrant situation as one of emergency and human rights is inevitably strongly linked to political judgments. What are actual tolerable forms of suffering, and where does legitimate suffering begin for a person to be granted a visa to transit? These kinds of questions revealed different liberal tensions about freedom, movement, and peace over who counts as a subject of rights and who counts as a humanitarian subject, depending on whether the focus was on suffering from poverty or suffering from human rights abuses.

Moreover, emergency organizations and UNHCR made limited attempts to define transit migration of Central Americans. CIDH, OEA, and CNDH also published reports that focused on criminal activities, primarily kidnapping, linked to transit migration flows (CIDH and OEA 2015; CNDH 2009, 2011). As noted in the Introduction and Chapter 4, these attempts simply associated migrants with people smuggling and irregular migration. Moreover, the longevity of the projects collecting information, and the level of actual direct contact they had with migrants, was limited by comparison to shelters, which registered migrants on a daily basis for several years.

In general, irregular migrants were defined by their lack of documents and irregular status. As the humanitarian project became more professionalized, attempts were made to characterize subjects as needing assistance, which, it could be argued, served to legitimize the emergence of humanitarianism as a needed institution. Yet it is also noteworthy that part of the vision of the shelters was, rather than assistance, supporting free transit.

The Servicio Jesuita de Migrantes (SJM, Jesuit Service of Migrants) constituted REDODEM, which comprised fifteen shelters throughout Mexico in 2012. This network was the only one systematically collecting data on migrants on a daily basis and compiling a database as a registration tool used for political advocacy. By 2019, REDODEM's database yielded a cumulative

138 / Chapter 5

sample of around two hundred thousand entries, making it by far the largest extra-official database of Central American migrants in Mexico.

Shelters expressed an interest in contributing data on the transit migrant situation. Although the REDODEM database initially emerged from the need to track disappeared migrants, it grew into a project seeking to publish statistical information about migrants to make their characteristics visible, as was detailed in an interview with a REDODEM official. La Esperanza became part of the REDODEM pilot and stopped working with the CNDH database.

At the shelter, I observe several issues with the registration process. There is no resources to train staff on interviewing techniques, even considering the sensitive context. Interviewers elicited answers in their own unique ways. Time is of the essence so migrants could eat and sleep, but haste made it challenging to create a rapport in which information would be shared. Space was another issue: the office was crammed, so migrants had to answer questions within hearing range of each other and the queue outside. This problem is also noted in other shelters.

Most importantly, there seems to be no consideration of why questions were asked or how they might be used, except for the broad goal of characterizing the migrants' situations. As with any similar tool, what is characterized about the migrant situation is defined by what was asked. The agency of the migrants lay in how they answered but was limited by the framework.

During registration, some migrants lied about their age. Many perceived being underage as an obstacle that might lead to their apprehension and did not want to end up in a government shelter or "repatriated"—deported. The actual needs of migrant children were seldom addressed and flags issues around forcing protection onto them without considering their actual needs. The issue of children and protection has been vastly problematized with child trafficking, where the protection delineated rarely concerns the agency or human rights of the child, often with grave effects (Montgomery 1998, 2007; O'Connell Davidson 2005).

The problematic nature of imposed protection in Mexico could be illustrated by such extreme cases as that of Noemi, a twelve-year-old girl who committed suicide in a Mexican government shelter, not being able to reach her destination and having already completed the journey from Ecuador to Mexico twice (Dwyer 2014). Such cases demonstrate the importance of providing protection for children that actually upholds their rights rather than framing deportation and detention as protection. However, while the tragedy of minors transiting Mexico is of great scale and relevance, it is out of scope for this book. In short, data collection, such as that performed by REDODEM, was an attempt to provide visibility to those being helped in shelters on their terms, but it occurred through a logic that did not necessarily exist or comply with the reality of all transit migrants.

Beyond the limitations described, the value in the database compiled by REDODEM is its role as the only independent source of quantitative information on transit migrants within Mexico. The data gathered and reported between 2013 and 2019 yielded a total sample of 204,702 migrants. Based on all REDODEM reports, Solano and Massey (2022) gather both a profile of the excluded and the cost of human exclusion. In the framing of the transit migrant profile, gender is accounted for. Of the total sample, 90.2 percent reported being male, 9.7 percent reported being female, and 0.1 percent reported a nonbinary identity. Age was also tabulated, although in 2013, only half of the migrants reported age, and in 2019, only the age of young persons was counted. The modal category of eighteen to thirty years of age was the most reported, at 53.9 percent. The vast majority of those who reported their nationality were from the Northern Triangle, 89.3 percent, followed by Mexico with 5.5 percent and Nicaragua with 3.7 percent. Years of education were also compiled, revealing that most migrants (70.2 percent) had not completed more than primary education. The majority of transit migrants in shelters, as reported by REDODEM, were male, between the ages of eighteen and thirty, came from the Northern Triangle, and had no more than primary education (Solano and Massey 2022).

Finally, the reports aimed to gather data on crimes and abuses experienced by the transit migrant en route across Mexico. The most common transgression reported was robbery, accounting for 72.1 percent of the incidents reported, where the large majority of crimes and abuses committed by public authorities were carried out by the police force. In the year 2019, REDODEM took on the task of documenting mistreatment in the process of apprehensions and within MHCs (ibid.). Within the reports themselves, it is not possible to grasp which are crimes and which are human rights abuses, as the reports gather the statistics as crime yet speak of these issues as human rights abuses.

Beyond the shelters and Mexico, these kinds of data is not captured by the humanitarian regime under formalistic requirements for protection and the right to migrate. Suffering is imagined in the refugee protection regime as taking place there, not here—in this case, at origin, not in transit. Currently, the alleviation of suffering in movement in shelters is addressed not in line with this data collection but with short-term goals to feed, give a place for respite, and cure. These same short-term goals are framed as a form of subversion that contests the current global order of borders; human rights activism geared toward free transit visas does not address the needs manifested in the data collected. Ultimately, the data collected to lobby for free transit is restricted by the predominant national security framework led by

140 / Chapter 5

the Mexican government making it very challenging to accommodate data for the purpose of free transit as one based on basic needs and vice versa.

Whose Voice?

Humanitarianism has elevated the importance of sharing testimonies and bearing witness as a process of bringing politics back to the victims (Fassin 2010:250–254; Ticktin 2011:81). This activity has been criticized, as humanitarian actors unavoidably end up speaking for their subjects instead of with them. In this process, there is an attempt to reconceptualize the humanitarian subject and the humanitarian crisis. Turton (2003:2) explains that conceptualization is about constructing something into an object of knowledge or, in Foucault's later work, a "subject" of knowledge (Foucault 1982), which is in turn about a representation, not a definition of the knowledge it attempts to construct. In this case, the irregular as a humanitarian subject is not something discovered but made—and this is where the power of conceptualization lies. The power of knowledge not only assumes the truth but also can make itself true (Foucault 1988). Yet for power to work, there need to be technologies and strategies of application through historical contexts and institutional regimes. As Arendt (1967) pins down, the chances of factual truth to survive power in such contexts are minimal. The Mexican state, in this case, continues to not acknowledge the humanitarian crisis spilling across the country.

Human rights defenders were the protagonists presenting the transit migrant situation. Much of the time, therefore, they ended up speaking for migrants. Irrespective of political or apolitical goals, contradictions and asymmetries in distinguishing first-hand experience from lives told by those who could tell them may emerge (Fassin 2010:253)—even if migrants participated in events organized for potential funders or were part of the *via crusis* of the migrant, mother and migrant caravans, and so on. These activities as speaking for potential funders were limited political milieus, and if such events became visible, visibility was sporadic. The political life of the shelter was present in the human rights defenders who became spokespeople for migrants, even if they did not want to be identified as speaking for the migrant in this kind of collective identity.

In Mexico, human rights defenders shared testimonies at events ranging from government to university events, participating in documentaries, reports, and book launches, among other mediums. It was these human rights defenders who championed not only the vulnerabilities but the need of migrants to have free, safe transit across the country. Their better position allowed them to exercise this type of role. Thus, politics entered the shelter—when human rights defenders spoke in the name of migrants—and with it, the decriminalization of movement and the making of the migrant as vulnerable.

This section focuses on the case of irregular transit as precarious in the language of extreme violence, and the humanitarian crisis. On the one hand, this language is indicative of irregular precarious transit being presented as a matter of human rights; on the other hand, it introduces the language of protection into the logic of migration and border regimes (Anderson 2013).

Extreme Violence: Poverty, Crimes, and Human Rights Abuses

When human rights defenders called out the suffering and violence to which migrants in transit are exposed, a strong victim narrative took centerstage upholding often an anticapitalist agenda through denouncements of extreme violence, crime and human rights abuses, and the vulnerability of women and children. In this case, the figure of the victim as noncitizen and poor became enmeshed within a criminal and violent scenario, an "evil" scenario, a holocaust, a cemetery. As cited in the media (Díaz 2013), a human rights defender denounced: "It is a holocaust because it seems like they are exposed to all kinds of violence, from beginning to end, from when they leave their countries of origin and arrive in Mexico, where we have an estimate of ten thousand migrants disappeared, and that figure is low compared with reality." He added that civil society and shelters have documented "hundreds of thousands of extortions, women raped that are not being treated, persons whose whereabouts we do not know," and commented on the role of the Mexican state, "the torment *calvario*, [stations of the cross] the Mexican government contributes to through the Instituto Nacional de Migración [INM], not only to inhibit the transit of the migrant, but to punish him, there is an authorized crime by omission and the government is guilty." He finally denounced the persecution faced by migrants in the United States: "Even if the country needs cheap labor, it fills its jails with migrants. If all of this is not a holocaust, then what is?"

Weizman argues that humanitarianism has been obsessed with totalitarianism and that the Holocaust has been the crime against which humanitarianism measures all crimes. The Holocaust trope is the greatest validation of humanitarianism and human rights activism: "never again" (Weizman 2011:66). This comparison raises an important issue. It creates a consensus among all actors that violence should be stamped out, having a postpolitical effect. No debate—we need to eliminate this problem.

Human trafficking literature in particular has highlighted how creating consensus by evoking extreme cases of violence and suffering has had undesired antipolitical effects, supporting the strengthening of a border legitimized in the language of human rights (Anderson 2008; Anderson and

142 / Chapter 5

Andrijasevic 2008). In Mexico, the *Programa Frontera Sur*, for example, was designed with the purpose of protecting migrants, but in practice was denounced as a migrant-hunting activity. And indeed, examples of extreme violence were often part of events at which human rights defenders spoke.

At the Mexican state event, a human rights defender shared examples that had been visible in the media or were more extreme:

> That the inhumane condition of these migrant persons from Central America does not become worse, that they do not keep expressing that Mexican territory is a cemetery for Central Americans, that they do not talk of themselves the way testimony speaks of a Salvadorian migrant—the migrant is a dead body without name nor burial.
>
> Who knows if the Mexican state through its officials knows about the skulls of the dead bodies of living people that were kidnapped in the clandestine ditches of Tamaulipas and were destroyed because the kidnappers/hired killers obliged the kidnapped men to fight with each other to the death with hammers until they broke each other's heads? And do you know whether the Mexican government has found the fields where they disposed of the bodies of children dissolved with acid?

In most events, audiences cringed at the grotesque stories shared. In our conversation after he recounted a story at an event about a migrant forced to rape his own mother, Priest Paulino emphasized the need to share these extreme stories. "I know it is too much," he said, "but people needed to know what is happening in Mexico." Another well-known priest working at the U.S.-Mexico border for over two decades shared at one of these occasions that no violent movie can depict the extreme violence witnessed in the region. Yet to use vulnerability is very different from being vulnerable. This type of denouncing shed light on the *pathology* of the society where it was occurring but did not aggregate to "our understanding of the society's normal state" (Bauman 1989:1). The issue was often made a Mexican problem, a "one-item set." Within the context of the language of extreme violence, one must consider that in dialogues at the policy level, when strong victim narratives and horrendous experiences are shared, often no one dares to speak. This brings the dialogue to an end and shuts down the political debate. In a way, then, speaking silences, with the possible effect of dampening rather than igniting social struggles. On the other hand, sharing these testimonies and bearing witness was crucial to contest the blind eye turned by the Mexican state to the humanitarian crisis spilling over its territory.

There were other recurrent themes under which the situation of transit migrants was presented. There was the anticapitalist agenda of the poor that

"Do Not Keep Expressing That Mexican Territory Is a Cemetery" / 143

emerged within the shelter. In events, the anticapitalist agenda was linked to exploitation, abuse, and violence against the poor at origin and during transit. These links have been highlighted along all chapters (see also Hagan 2008). In the context of human rights defenders, testimonies were shared in ways that were at times paradoxical, oscillating between denouncing the violence or even death that came with poverty, discussing how to stop the violence and death, and motivating migrants to follow their dreams. For example, Central American countries were widely referred to as *países expulsores* (countries that expel their citizens) and Mexico as a death threat to the migrant. Poverty was identified as a key culprit of violence. Priest Paulino spoke out the following words:

> We have to be concerned with analyzing why people fall . . . and how to attack these causes . . . not only moral failings but also of the situation we live; the rural areas have fallen. Many of the migrants who come are from rural areas and are indigenous people who have left the countryside because they would stay in the countryside only to share a grave.
>
> To talk about forced Central American migration, of the violations of their rights, we will not only talk about human rights destroyed but also listen carefully [to the talk] of the representatives of Central American consuls. I told the honored ambassador from Honduras when he deigned to visit our shelter: How can you allow this house to receive four hundred teenagers each week, between thirteen and eighteen years old? You are allowing the bleeding out of the best of Honduras to inhumane labor conditions. . . . And I tell the consular representatives of Central America to dare to find out what is happening—why don't you dare?

Priest Federico, another protagonist leader of the movement, elaborated, "They come from a torn social fabric. Poverty has impacted and disarticulated everything, all their values; poverty has destroyed everything. So those people not only have economic and material needs, but they also lack a sense of respect with a minimum of dialogue." He added: "We cannot keep sending slaves to the empire as we did in the sixteenth century. . . . The world is subjected to an unjust economic order that increases inequalities and makes a ruling of death of those who are left over; however, in Mexico it is migrants who are tearing down the empire." Father Alberto spoke out at an event fervently.

> Do not leave this only to us and demand radical explanations for this crime of the state. . . . In your conditions of poverty, you have trusted

Mexico with the masses of your poor, marginalized, forced migrants in search of life. And Mexico has returned them massacred, disappeared. They have even faked the return of bodies, not with the real family member massacred but with dirt and meat that is not human.

As the ultimate victims, children and women were (and continue to be) key vulnerable groups and constantly reappeared in the debate. Women especially were linked to sexual violence and exploitation. Despite the importance of noting the vulnerabilities and nuances of the precarity faced along the journey by females and children, it was mostly males who transited Mexico and accessed shelters, as noted in the REDODEM reports. Carpenter (2003) has delved into this issue in the case of war, noting that gender beliefs shape strategies used to design civilian protection advocacy and constrain access to protection on the ground for the most vulnerable: males.

Within shared testimonies, there was also the objectification of the migrant: seen as merchandise, treated as an animal, and suffering as the body of Jesus Christ, to name some of the most prevalent representations. In the case of merchandise, a human rights defender vocalized in an event, "The crime permitted is that of human migrant flesh that becomes *merchandise.*" Another chimed in and said,

The greatest risks are criminals because the migrant is seen as merchandise. There are people in the communities who dedicate themselves to stealing, and they find out there is a migrant on the way, and they organize to rob the migrants. But it also comes from the authorities that abuse, that hit them, that rob them. Abuse is general when it comes to the migrants; that is where we see the real vulnerability. They rob, assault, discriminate, and even kill them.

There was also the conception of the migrant as Jesus Christ (see also Hagan 2008:98). This often came up during my time in the field and was mentioned at a sermon during a *viacrusis*:

We remember historically how Jesus' clothes were taken from him. He was at the foot of the cross; they had to take everything. They had to leave him naked. They tried to take his own dignity. On occasions, you have experienced them trying to take your things; they have robbed you, assaulted you. They have taken your belongings. Tell.

Such depictions created a challenge to identify a person under these markers, which can be construed as narrow conceptions of victimhood (Enns 2012). Also, these representations often do not accurately align with the realities experienced by most transit migrants. Identification of victims under specific markers has been problematized by migration scholars as pacifying the victim (Anderson 2007; Andrijasevic 2003; Sharma 2003; Yun 2004) and as being geared toward where cash can be invested (Enns 2012).

In this context, the victim presented was one who wore abuse on his body, was objectified as merchandise, and lived in animal-like conditions— a suffering Jesus Christ unidentifiable as an individual. This case made the migrant an absolute victim, voiceless and without agency. In short, the migrant was reshaped from enemy to victim, drawing on depictions that, at times, could not be identified on the ground. Such depictions focused on the violence, crime, and abuses migrants experienced through their objectification rather than on the individuals themselves. As I outline in the following section, this objectification was not unilinear and was often accompanied by other forms of progressive politics that (re)constructed freedom of movement as universal—this was a particularity of the social movement of shelters.

There was a struggle between defining and representing abusers, perpetrators, crimes, and human rights abuses. Both the CNDH and DPMH affirmed that criminal syndicates were responsible for kidnappings and extreme torture to impose power and expand business (CNDH 2009; DPMH 2012). Kidnappings and the disappearance of thousands of migrants was described by human rights defenders as their main preoccupation, the most serious human rights violation in shelters and beyond. These were an important component of the representation of the humanitarian crisis in Mexico at the time. Another human rights defender said at an event, "Right now what is most common and grave are kidnappings and what they suffer during the kidnapping. This is the most serious human rights violation right now for Mexicans and foreigners." There was a great deal of ambiguity over the involvement of state authorities in the abuse, coercion, and kidnapping of migrants. Moreover, the industry of kidnappings had historically been a business for criminal networks in Mexico (Ochoa 2015). The impunity of the authorities was common, and links to criminal networks steered the debate toward a criminal issue. Human rights defenders referred to these atrocities as part of the humanitarian crisis, but there was no clear line about kidnappings as state crimes.

The Case of the Caravan for Serenity

There are different forms of collective migration as a form of advocacy that have been occurring in Mexico for more than fifteen years. There is for example the Caravan of Migrant Mothers and the Migrant *Viacrusis* (Stations of the Cross) that goes across Mexico during Holy Week. These caravans surge out of the urgent need for migrants that leave their country. The caravan that I will refer to as the Caravan for Serenity is an important event that highlights the tensions between security and humanitarianism outlined previously. It is detailed here to clarify these ambiguities. A few months after the 2011 Tamaulipas tragedy, dozens of migrants traveling on the Beast were kidnapped at a shelter exit. This kidnapping led to a he-said-she-said tug-of-war between the INM and CNDH. While the INM maintained that the kidnappings never took place and that there was no evidence the train tracks had been obstructed by a criminal group from the locality, CNDH maintained that the kidnappings had occurred.

The then-coordinator of the DPMH network of shelters and founder of the shelter where the victims had gathered before the kidnapping shared testimonies of the migrants widely with the media, confirming that they had indeed been kidnapped. The chancellery of El Salvador also insisted that the kidnapping had occurred, noting that there were fifteen women and children among the victims. Shelters were pivotal in launching the Caravan for Serenity, which gathered in a city center to raise awareness of the violence in Mexico and draw media attention toward the incident. It drew the attention of other actors to migrants' needs and vulnerabilities. In the midst of these events, all actors gathered to protest against violence—aligning with common liberal humanitarian goals. Peace/security agendas have been especially targeted toward the Global South (Wæver 2004), as elaborated in Chapter 1.

Manuel described to me how the Caravan for Serenity gathered three to four thousand people (a possibly inaccurate figure), including the governors of two states, who even provided buses for participants including undocumented migrants. Migration control posts allowed the migrants to pass. The train stopped running and ever more migrants joined the march. Even the navy watched over the event, he recounted.

In the aftermath of the march, a wide variety of actors (government, INGOs, NGOs, humanitarian action actors, international organizations, and private donors) offered charitable donations, earmarked funding, and/or services to be provided in La Esperanza. The caravan was presented as a historic event by Father Alberto's assistant because of the diverse actors that participated, coming together in the same space, albeit with different agendas, behind a vague notion of peace.

Despite the symbolic value of the caravan, things were less positive on the ground. In the shelter itself, the victims of the kidnapping who decided to denounce the kidnapping received death threats when they left the shelter premises. Father Alberto also received death threats. In the media spotlight, the authorities moved the migrants to Mexico City. An urgent action by an international humanitarian actor was triggered.

Though the event was used to create a consensus for peace, it also created a feeling of concession, showing the two-faced practices of the Mexican state. As in Chapter 3, human rights defenders agreed to come together with state actors, this time in the name of peace and with solidarity with migrants. But the actors gathered with different understandings of what this solidarity implied.

The discursive idea of peace has a stronghold, yet this type of consensus does not mean that borders or migration controls disappear—quite the opposite. Border enforcement is proliferating rather than slowing down. When other migrant caravans began in 2018, President Andrés Manuel López Obrador (popularly known as AMLO) welcomed the migrants and granted the migrants humanitarian visas that allowed them to reach Tijuana. Yet there was a turnover as Donald Trump stigmatized the caravans as an "invasion" of undesirable migrants: the poor (Álvarez Velasco and De Genova 2023:38). In March of 2019, AMLO created a sixty thousand person National Guard (see Introduction) and ordered its deployment throughout the nation with the purpose of combatting undocumented migration and the migrant caravans. In that year, deportations escalated to 150,000 and detentions went up to 183,000 (Meyer 2019). Notwithstanding, migrant caravans continue and are part of the politicization of freedom of movement that intersects *shelter on the journey.*

Dignifying Transit

Mobilization for a free transit visa and the elimination of visa requirements for Central Americans were key items on the agenda for human rights defenders (Sánchez Soler 2014). As religious workers, they had an important role in exploring social action linked to migration due to their social and political resources, their influence in mobilizing followers, and their ability to challenge public policy (Hagan 2008:89). How human consequences of transit were understood had much to do with freedom rather than control and with dismantling migration institutions like the INM rather than strengthening and expanding their outreach.

> We want them to have free transit; we want to put them down from the cross, as we want Jesus to come down from the cross, take away the nails of this situation he is living in. (*Viacrusis of the migrant*, manifesto in participant observation)

Since the 1990s, border enforcement in the United States and Mexico has come under fire (ibid. 88). According to Hagan, religious actors have been working on the legitimation of the right to cross borders when migrants find themselves in situations where they need help. Although the religious groups she looks at did not challenge the right of sovereign nations

148 / Chapter 5

to control borders, she points to the long tradition of Catholic social teachings defending the right to migrate. This social teaching has created tension between the Catholic Church and nation-states. The first group to challenge border enforcement by the United States was, in fact, a peace church along the border in 1987 (ibid. 1460).

Human rights defenders in shelters were known to work with the church but also against the structures of the church at times. They showed up in a diverse array of events held by governments and universities and in local, national, and international debates on the human rights of migrants. Activities such as demonstrations and hunger strikes delineated the contours of a growing activism in favor of free transit. More specifically, at an event in the Mexican Senate, a human rights defender stated,

> We have proposed that they eliminate the visa for Central Americans. . . . The organs of civil society that are working with this campaign for a migration without violence . . . we presented our transmigrant proposal, and we have done everything possible to present this initiative, even if the visa is annulled for Central American countries, that they take away the visa, or that they work with transmigrant visas but in real conditions, not as presented in the guidelines [of the Migration Law].

By "eliminating" the visa, he and other human rights defenders meant there should be no requirement for one. This elimination of the visa was mainly framed along the lines of human rights in regard to dignity but also at times in confusing and contradictory messages that acknowledged national security goals. Another human rights defender presented the following proposition at a government event:

> We demand guidelines that adhere to human security and national security. Today, for example, Don Joaquín told us in the morning how guidelines are coming out that in order to give a humanitarian visa or to give a migrant person a visa, they are asking for economic solvency. How can they ask the Mexican government for economic solvency for thousands of migrants who are on top of a train? From here, we ask civil society, the Catholic Church that has fifty-six shelters in the country, the other churches, to demand from the executive that the guidelines are in line with reality. We cannot demand what these migrants cannot comply with.

Thus, there were demands on the human rights defenders to adhere to demands of national security that were seen as unrealistic, in the case of economic solvency of the migrant. Moreover, shelters within the network and social movement did not define free transit along the same lines. A human rights defender affiliated with La Puerta, for example, pointed out its neutrality on the topic, as it needed to find a way to define the position of no borders politically. This neutrality was seen as beneficial as it allowed shelter staff to go to migration offices to request humanitarian visas. But he also noted that volunteers had limited time and that the effort of defining free transit visas went above the everyday duties. It was difficult to follow up on and hard to design an authentic policy for the shelter. "There is no effort in saying 'down with the border,' but what do we support this with if we have no evidence? . . . The liberty we look for is one without violence where there is a dignified transit, dignified for the migrant, without this need to expose their lives on top of the train."

Within political advocacy, human rights defenders attempted to denounce the Mexican state as responsible for what was happening to migrants, unlike most other humanitarian actors, who chose to remain apolitical and neutral. Civil society also sought the dismantling of the INM as a corrupt institution beyond reform. There were attempts toward radical change.

> Even if considered harshly, we have even asked for the National Institute for Migration [INM] to disappear as an instrument for migration policy because of all the loopholes [*vacíos*—gaps] and abuses it has committed. We have precisely discovered a great number of corrupt officials, either for their use of resources—resources from the United States, Mérida Initiative—not to improve their migration techniques and services but for other matters or also for matters regarding the fence. They have even collaborated instead of giving assistance and safety to the migrants; they have collaborated with organized crime to the extent that we have a very harsh questioning of the three powers [*poderes*] and also of the instruments of migration policy. We are radically seeking not only new legislation but a completely new migration policy that understands.

Another human rights defender added at the event,

> The private guards of the trains, they have allowed them (the guards) to be the first torturers and murderers of migrants. Then they have protected the *Mara Salvatrucha* [a gang], and now they allow the lords of organized crime to do the dirty work so that Mexico stops the transit of migrants. We cannot keep tolerating this. We demand truth from those revising the guidelines and that they modify the

150 / Chapter 5

guidelines—that they make up their minds between lives and visas or that visas are eliminated for our brothers from Central America.

There was also a denouncement of the capitalist nature of borders (see quote in the Introduction), where borders are represented as manipulations with economic interests. Father Alberto's words continued stating:

> International workers, they cannot pass. They are the only illegal ones, but everything else of financial capital that is highly immoral [can pass the border]. Because it is immoral, it is theft; this can pass. And they congratulate those rich people of the plutocracy. They call them successful and publish them in magazines very elegant, with a white collar; they put them as a model of progress, but they do not state that it is at the expense of destroying the planet, of impoverishing millions of human beings. Concentrating richness is a total irresponsibility and little manhood of governments in the face of financial capital. Political submission decides in the face of money, and that is not fair.

Here we see a delineation of the victims of capitalism but also an important denunciation of a system that exploits and does not grant rights to a specific segment of the population—in this case, in reference to poor labor migrants.

Human rights defenders were known to organize humanitarian and social protests and processions like the *viacrusis*. Holding hunger strikes, chaining themselves to the INM offices, riding the Beast, and the like were among the more radical activities undertaken by human rights defenders in Mexico. There were ecumenical events that, as Hagan notes, sought to mourn the dead or create social awareness of the social and political contexts in which poor migrants died searching for a better life (Hagan 2008:106). In such cases, the church, shelter staff, and some civilians were seen as taking the side of irregular migrants by scholars, civil society, the state, and some in society at large. Yet this assumption often left unquestioned the fact that being on the side of the irregular migrant was itself a privileged position that only certain actors could take. At the same time, many of these actors were putting their lives at risk and were confronting and being attacked and punished by state actors.

Finally, human rights defenders called for more unity and support from the very heart of the social movement. In general, human rights defenders following a Christian logic were key in resurrecting the right to migrate, especially for Central Americans, in the context of national security in Mexico.

The racism and classism behind the migrant discriminated into migrating illegally was rendered invisible by a liberal humanitarian agenda that presented racial and poverty struggles as having been overcome through the universal discourse of human rights. While human rights were called on by the radical Left in Latin America to demand rights (de Sousa Santos 2002), a clearer delineation of how human rights could be put into practice within the context of the humanitarianization of freedom of movement for poor, irregular migrants from Central America was needed.

Thus, emerging political advocacy was not well delineated, and a united front was not clearly identifiable. At the level of political advocacy, a more concrete agenda was, and remains, in the making. While human rights defenders in Mexico had as their goal to influence policy and some measures were taken in response (including systematizing the transit migrant situation and political advocacy), there was no clear agenda other than the suggestion of a free transit visa or lifting visa requirements for Central Americans. These suggestions did not present a suitable resolution to the human rights issues of movement or limits as to how movement may be defined as a human right. The truth of lives lost, though denounced by families and human rights defenders, remained to a certain extent obscured, debated, unacknowledged, without a name, without documents, without bodies to grieve within the Mexican nation-state.

Conclusion

The objective of this chapter has not been to deprecate the efforts—or the need—to shape the humanitarian subject but to better understand the constitution of the humanitarian subject and potential (anti/post/progressive) political effects in relation to dignifying movement. The violence and suffering of migrants across Mexican territory is not ceasing, nor is border enforcement. There is an open humanitarian space to be appropriated, upheld, and respected by Mexico and the international community and a discourse to be set into practice that serves the purpose of mobilizing social struggle instead of foreclosing it. Today, many social and ethnic movements have put forward a critique of human rights as perpetrating racism when misused by states and humanitarian actors. This book presents a strong demand to continue to reevaluate the knowledge and practices of human rights concerning issues of poverty intersecting with freedom of movement. In the words of Arendt: "The calamity of the rightless is not that they are deprived of life, liberty and the pursuit of happiness or equality before the law and freedom of opinion—formulas which were designed within communities—but that they no longer belong to any community whatsoever" (Arendt 1976 [1968, 1966]:295). This is what creates a devaluation of life. "Only the loss of polity itself expels him (man) from humanity" (ibid. 297).

Understanding shelters as belonging to a social movement helps locate the contradiction of a political project attempting to legitimize the suffering of noncitizens without being able to escape the victimization of the subject. Notwithstanding, beyond victimization, there was a more prevalent agenda mobilized by shelters: supporting free transit. The ethics of human rights agendas that demarcate which activities are universal (and which are not) are undoubtedly important yet quite removed from the lives of those whose access to such activities—in this case, movement—has not been constrained, as is the case of citizens from the Global North. Yet the human rights abuses linked to these restrictions can more clearly be articulated to their concerns.

Even if shelters' humanitarian advocacy efforts for free transit visas were trapped in a tension between humanitarianism and security and had contradictory effects and limited potential to trigger social change or raise social consciousness, they provide a window for reimagining movement and human rights. Human rights defenders were plowing a path for progressive politics, attempting to use human rights discourse as the instrument to universalize freedom of movement as a matter of human worth and dignity and calling for dismantling migration agencies like the INM. Suggesting that institutions that demarcate protection and legitimate movement are necessary solutions to enhance dignity and security ignores that this very mechanism creates insecurity, vulnerability, and dehumanization.

Conclusion

Dreaming on the Journey

During my time at La Esperanza, I spent downtime with the volunteers living at the ranch. Among them was Carlos, the young boy who claimed to be twenty-one but looked more like he was twelve or thirteen years old, with whom I went to the market. He frequently reminded me of his survival skills, learned living on the streets of Guatemala City. He was often around adults who disregarded his youth and was exposed to the everyday realities and experiences of older men, both in Guatemala and en route through Mexico. He claimed to enjoy sleeping under the stars, so he did not actually have a bed in the ranch. He often climbed up to the roof of the male dormitory, taking a flattened cardboard box on which to sleep.

He kept with him a book called *Gotitas de Felicidad* (*Bits of Happiness*). It contained short passages, stories, poems, reflections, and anecdotes on how happiness in life was about giving, not receiving. When there were not many people around, he would ask me to read for him. He had just begun to learn to read from one of the nuns.

I learned a great deal from Carlos. First, beyond desperation, those in transit carry with them dreams and aspirations for a better life. Second, even if movement begins with a goal in mind, for most, wandering becomes a way of survival. Like Carlos, many are stuck in transit for longer than they expected. Third, most of those who transit Mexico are, like Carlos, young and male and acquired resilience and sharpened survival skills at a young age.

Finally, as they travel across Mexico, the dreams of migrants are criminalized by states: migrants do not pass the test of political judgment, of recognition and legitimation. From the moment of departure, these young boys and men struggle to confront their demonization and dehumanization, the criminalization of their dreams (Ong Hing 1998). This criminalization deprives dreamers of a better life, of escaping violence and gangs, of finding a job, of helping their families and escaping poverty. I, like the others who came to the shelter, eventually left Carlos. He kicked the dirt furiously when I told him I had to go. Despite his maturity and survival skills, he was still a young boy in many ways.

Many of these young boys and men, these dreamers, end up in so-called cages or iceboxes. Hundreds were separated from their families under the zero-tolerance policy pursued by the Trump administration. They continue to be framed as enemies, dehumanized as dangers, as animals, as rapists. Their actual dreams are silenced, and their devastation is justified. Some end in clandestine graves, never to be found, never to be mourned.

The cover of this book is Diego Rivera's *Sleep, The Night of the Poor*, 1932 (*El Sueño, La noche de los pobres*). The dreams of Carlos and others like him are far from the narratives of DREAMers in the United States, whose paths opened thanks to such policies as Deferred Action for Childhood Arrivals (DACA) under President Obama. That dreamer narrative tells of merit-based exceptionalism centered on education and capitalist productivity (Abrego and Negrón-Gonzalez 2020). The dream of Carlos was of traveling with dignity and freedom, finding the transition from damage to hope.

In her 1967 essay "Truth and Politics," Hannah Arendt explores the challenge of speaking the truth in front of nations. This issue emerges, she notes, in the face of politics—and not only when refuting charges. "The chances of factual truth surviving the onslaught of power are very slim indeed; it is always in danger of being maneuvered out of the world not only for a time but potentially, forever. Facts and events are infinitely more fragile things than axioms, discoveries, theories" (Arendt 1967:297). National movements operate in ways where people support causes and ideologies they would reject if national attachments did not exist. The challenge nationalism poses to truth therefore goes deeper than politics, to the "irrational psychic attachments that supersede logical instrumental ones" (Stevens 2010:xiv). By way of example, Stevens highlights the rapid shift executed by President George W. Bush from initially encouraging an open border with Mexico to locking up tens of thousands of Mexicans in detention centers. Shelters emerge out of nationalist goals but with their own volition, understanding the human consequences of transit as a matter of freedom, poverty, and human worth. Shelters do not operate under a specific policy but in answer to a social instinct to police, detain, and deport. Shelters witness the transit migrant conundrum as one of needs, rights, and reaching a destination; it is their daily life.

This book explores social, economic, and (a)political contexts within shelter sites marked by a splintered yet unified Christian and bureaucratic logic that I refer to as "dignifying transit." In *shelter on the journey* we find the emancipatory politics of the freedom of movement and struggles within a dominant environment of control.

When dissecting what is meant by the logic, politics, moral economy, and socialization of humanizing transit migration, this book considers that, in sociology, the mode of knowing is intimately connected to the dissection of social meaning. One of the main endeavors of sociology is to shed light on how relationships, spaces, the law, subjects, and structures are socially and culturally constructed. This book relies on this social constructivist framework. If we consider the world as shaped by knowledge, then discourse and symbols construct the world. They influence the way we act, build relationships, and participate in the world. The lenses through which we see the world shape what we see and what we do not see. In other words, the world is not independent of how we see it. I rely on this way of knowing to cast light on the value of the shelter site beyond its boundaries.

The shelter and transit migration operate within a geography of knowledge that has situated the church as both opposing and supporting colonizing powers. The church elevates the indigenous person from animal to human yet supports civilizing forces that torture, kill, and enslave them. The church and faith have historically led a strong moral agenda around migration and human rights in Mexico. In 2003, the Mexican and U.S. Conference of Catholic Bishops jointly published the first-ever pastoral letter on migration, "Strangers No Longer, Together on the Journey of Hope," seeking the reform of the U.S. immigration system (Hagan 2008:174).

Shelter on the journey involves denouncing the Mexican state and seeking acknowledgment of the calamities, corruption, and violence in border enforcement and its criminalization of movement, not only directed at the migrant but at human rights defenders and shelter sites. As noted in the Introduction of this book, in the Universal Declaration of Human Rights, freedom of movement only applies within the borders of the state, remaining a practice of sovereignty. What happens to some as they attempt to move across and between borders in Mexico is unthinkable. Freedom of movement between borders has also been compromised. Many are captured, detained, or at best simply deported or robbed.

Those who give help along the humanitarian trail can be construed as criminals (even if not by the law): the humanitarian actor seen as a *coyote*. In the United States, helping undocumented migrants is overtly typified as a crime in the law (see Title 8, U.S.C. 1324 [A] Offenses). There is no regard for the lives saved by giving water and food, for help reuniting someone with their family, for finding them a place to sleep: it is a crime.

156 / Conclusion

Shelter on the journey explores the politics of dignifying transit by looking at civil society, humanitarianism, and human rights as inextricably linked with every step of the journey of the migrant and implicated in the reasons why people decide to migrate. Shelters in the Global South propose conceptions of human rights and movement that represent a counterhegemonic human rights discourse to mainstream liberal currents that support controls on movement, exemplifying the politicization of alleviation to suffering related to movement as a situated matter.

Shelter on the journey, likewise, outlines the limitations of this political project, following similar critiques of humanitarian work: shelters also engage in advocacy and distribution of services with antipolitical and postpolitical effects. Ultimately, a central task of their emancipatory politics is to reconceptualize human rights and freedom of movement toward a "globalized localism," the "process by which a given local phenomenon is successfully globalized" (de Sousa Santos 2002:46)—where freedom of movement is supported and universalized, and where the privilege to move stops being about where we come from and how much we earn.

More specifically, the book considers how *shelter on the journey* emerges as both a humanitarian and political project, against the exploitative structures of capitalism and for the legitimation of the transit migrant's right to move on as a matter of social justice. The social dynamics behind the Christian logic of hospitality, solidarity, and advocacy, currently framed as humanitarian assistance, and the defense and promotion of human rights, especially concerning free transit, are constitutive of inclusivist politics. This logic contrasts with the liberal humanitarian logic of international and state actors providing assistance in shelters informed by the principles of liberal peace that, instead, reaffirm the exclusion of freedom of movement as an issue to be addressed and sustain an apolitical stance.

The collaboration of such diverse and contradictory actors within shelters sheds light on the microcosm of assistance as humanitarian and the yet-unresolved paradox of assistance and advocacy, security and rights, threat and human worth, across international borders, especially affecting the poor in the Global South and concerning migration.

Humanizing movement in shelters does not occur in isolated bubbles, as refugee camps are often perceived. Shelters sit astride a wall of violence and of solidarity in Mexico, where migrants suffer from demonization that commodifies them as a danger to be stamped out, seen as merchandise for criminals and corrupt officials to profit from or as brothers and sisters supporting the need to move forward.

The layout of the space and rules of the shelter throw light on the challenges and threats without support—financial or otherwise—from the state and the international community. It also shows how the state and other actors use the space for their own humanitarian agendas. Yet the social layout and space also stands out as a collective of sites of subversion, of spatial dispute that supports and accompanies the migrant.

Humanitarianism and human rights discourse have been critiqued for many reasons: as the detritus of citizenship rights, for ambiguous discourse, having disjointed agendas, leading to antipolitics, being based in racist thinking, and rendering social inequality invisible. However, these discourses have also been an avenue for progressive politics in Latin America. In general, humanitarianism and human rights have had, in Latin America, a story of frustrated hopes and dreams, yet they continue to plow a path toward emancipatory politics (de Sousa Santos 2002).

Human rights defenders not only assist those in need (supporting transit) but attempt, through the constitution of a social movement, to trigger institutional transformations. If we look at the shelter map, a unique humanitarian trail comes to light, one that can arguably be seen as a trail of persecution and escape. The shelter is a site in this trail where the humanitarian subject is shaped under specific conditions. But the humanitarian subject shaped in the shelter is not all-encompassing. On one hand, shelters provide needed social awareness about what is happening to migrants. They make visible the issues many migrants confront, but not necessarily in ways that are representative of the situation of irregular transit migrant in general. Shelters limit and reproduce identity markers as a certain type of population enters to reaffirm them, especially in the interactions between civil society actors and migrants. This map is also one of lived resistances and of solidarity to an exodus that refuses and escapes violence.

Finally *shelter on the journey* is ultimately about the destabilization security has created between freedom and movement, under which territories we see the human consequences spilling over, who is assisting and mostly who is affected by this destabilization.

Motion is prevented not only through walls and barbed wire but through the Universal Declaration of Human Rights, which reproduces, restrictions and protections to exercise the freedom of movement by defining it exclusively as the right to emigrate. Shelters present another possibility of alleviating suffering as political through a unique set of support technologies: open spaces, no classifications on individuals for access and the provision of basic needs and advice to move on. As mechanisms used by shelters to instrumentalize dignity and freedom lies: (i) an ideology, the 'warm' Christian logic that sees migration as a human right, (ii) the apparatuses that are opposed, and (iii) the spaces that are disputed. This book touched upon these layers.

Notwithstanding, the classification of the subject in need of care in shelters is tied to a network of violence that continues to reopen the need for a humanitarian space rather than its foreclosure. This brings me to a final point

158 / Conclusion

raised by Kotef (2015: 140) "Whether here, there or in so many other contexts, freedom and violence within the phenomenon of movement proposes that there are important reasons to have doubts about the possibility of a simple postcolonial or racial justice" or in the words of de Sousa Santos (2002) of human rights being the everyday language of human dignity. The humanitarian trail in Mexico links freedom and movement to the phenomenon of restricting movement as state violence. This does not solve the conundrum posited here, and there but on the move.

Shelters exist because human nature tends toward the pathological (Hume 1896) but also the moral. The moral has both served many political agendas and opposed them. Today, as we witness a global dismantling of social solidarity among those far away, we see a restructuring of social solidarity within communities and across borders. Acts of showing up, giving, helping, defending, and collaborating still provide hope to those in challenging circumstances. The value of this hope and faith, as well as its power, should not be underestimated. It presents a philosophical question I am not able to answer: Is hope as a human emotion and motivation linked to morality, and if so, how can it constitute progressive politics within the realm of human rights and migration without becoming a tool for antipolitics? Ultimately, the assistance and advocacy that emerge in shelters as humanitarian present another possibility for human rights and freedom of movement.

There are many more scholarly journeys to take to better understand the complex field of humanitarianism, human rights, and migration. In particular, there is a growing gap and need to explore the roles of poverty, faith, and spirituality in the situation of those who have chosen migration as a survival strategy—from leaving a village to leaving a city to leaving a country. Prevalent issues persist and bring us back to questions around destination, where migration policy has had a strong restrictionist approach, and at origin, where root causes are meant to be addressed in order to halt mobility. This is the current status quo of the geographies of movement of the poor in the Global South: there, here, and in between. Paths to ensuring safety in movement have been developed for others who travel legally, with passports, across airports, ports, and train stations. I also note an important gap in research on the making of legality of migration, on the rankings of passports and visa schemes. There is a significant dearth of literature in this field with some exceptions.

Despite the burning questions that persist, the story of shelters is indeed one that helps better situate and ground the tendency to frame movement as opposed to security and how this tendency has destabilized the relationship of movement to freedom. Today, this relationship has to do with the suffering this destabilization implies on the way. The issue of movement is highly political rather than neutral. The humanitarian project needs to revisit its missions and visions to work with the current emergency imaginary. Transit migration has grave consequences for poor migrants coming from the Global South this century.

To conclude, *shelter on the journey* is not only a site of alleviation of suffering in movement. It is a site of solidarity that addresses this suffering as a matter of politics, rights, and social justice. It also does not stand in isolation of poverty and race. *Shelter on the journey* attempts to break the silence, support transit through the distribution of food and water, and demand acknowledgment of the *corredor de la muerte* (corridor of death) plowed along its trail. *Shelter on the journey* reveals not only the fatal failures of border and migration controls but the severe limitations of the current humanitarian project to address migration-driven crises and our right to move, be it for a better life or as a survival strategy. Trying to fit liberal notions of freedom of movement, dignity, equality, and human worth within a restrictionist migration regime and such a regime as humanitarian within a liberal humanitarian logic assumes a certain type of *shelter on the journey*. In contrast, the politics of inclusion in shelters, from the bottom up, as non-Western, warm logic—as open (in its ethos), complex (in its distribution), intersectional (in its involvement and activism), and collective (in its target)—manifests in a multifaceted universalism of freedom of movement that should be considered in the humanitarian debate linked to migration.

This book ends with much more to unpack over *shelter on the journey*. I continue to reflect on the dignity seen and felt in migrants on their journey, in their traveling companions, in the shelter staff who assisted them, in the priests who acted as their human rights defenders, and especially the priest and founder of La Esperanza, whom I followed in the field. His words filled many of us with a desire to do good, see that we are good, believe in the goodness of others, and know we are not alone—that wherever there is a dream, there is not only one dreamer.

> Un espejo somos, aquí estamos para vernos y mostrarnos, para que tú nos mires para que tú te mires, para que el otro se mire en la mirada de nosotros. Aquí estamos y un espejo somos. No la realidad sino apenas su reflejo. No la luz sino apenas un destello. No el camino, sino apenas unos pasos. No la guía, sino apenas uno de tantos rumbos que al mañana conduce.[1] (Subcomandante Marcos)

Notes

INTRODUCTION

1. Mainly debated within the borders of the state (Bauböck 2009).

2. Van Schendel and Abraham (2005) point out, there are no clear lines between illicitness and laws of states. Law and criminalization emerge from ongoing historical struggles.

3. All translations from Spanish into English have been done by the author.

4. All interviews, human rights defenders, and shelters are anonymized, and pseudonyms are used in replacement throughout the book.

CHAPTER 1

1. For other examples of the impact of illegality on a person's health, see Castañeda 2009.

2. Such debates on the role of non-Europeans were not unique to the Americas. For example, Thomas F. Buxton, considered a humanitarian and leader of the second generation of the antislavery movement by society at large, organized the 1840 Niger Expedition that attempted to establish a model plantation (commercial and civilized) in West Africa. He was responsible—along with his peers—for the popularization of the notion of African societies as dark and diabolical places that routinely practiced human sacrifice. Such images were part of the call for European intervention. He spread descriptions of a three-hundred-year lack of African "intellectual and moral progress," calling for "proper" colonial governments to provide "care, knowledge, prudence and security" to the ignorant natives who would be saved from slavery—and recruited for colonial or coolie labor (Gott 2002:23).

3. Postcolonial/decolonial scholars trace modernity back to colonization and the exploitation of labor. In the history of geographies of knowledge, a European horizon

has formulated modernity as an exclusively European phenomenon developed in the Middle Ages (Dussel 1999:3). But, as Dussel notes, that typically unacknowledged "first modernity" was constituted during imperial and colonial expansion and marked by the discovery, conquest, colonization, and integration ("subsumption") spreading through the Americas. He notes that in this we see the "management" of the centrality of the first world system (ibid. 112).

4. This account does not relate nor consider "social suffering" (Kleinman et al. 1997), which is at the core of understanding the reproductions of social inequalities but is currently outside the framework of protection of migrants as refugees, whether victims of trafficking or illegal.

5. For example, in March 2011, during an official raid in Boca del Cerro (southwestern Mexico), an indigenous woman from Honduras was chased by a machete-wielding border official from the Instituto Nacional de Migración (National Institute for Migration, INM), and found herself forced into the water. He continued to wave the machete to deter her from attempting to step into Mexican territory. The woman was forced to stay in the water, struggling to stay afloat, fighting for survival (Barboza Sosa 2011).

CHAPTER 2

1. Participant observation at an annual gathering of civil society leaders to discuss migration and development in Chiapas, Mexico, February 2012.

CONCLUSION

1. *We are a mirror: we are here to see ourselves, to show ourselves, so you can see us, so you can see you, so that the other can see himself in our gaze. We are here, and we are a mirror. Not reality, but merely its reflection. Not light, but merely a glimmer; not the road, but merely some steps. Not the guide, but merely one of many directions that will take us to tomorrow.* Translation by the author.

References

Abrego, L. J. (2014). *Sacrificing families: Navigating laws, labor and love across borders.* Stanford University Press.

Abrego, L., Coleman, M., Martínez, D. E., Menjívar, C., & Slack, J. (2017). Making immigrants into criminals: Legal processes of criminalization in the post-IIRIRA era. *Journal on Migration and Human Security, 5*(3), 694–715. https://doi.org/10.1177/233 150241700500308

Abrego, L. J., & Negrón-Gonzalez, G. (2020). *We are not Dreamers: Undocumented scholars theorize undocumented life in the United States.* Duke University Press.

Agamben, G. (1998). *Homo sacer: Sovereign power and bare life.* Stanford University Press.

Agamben, G. (2005). *State of exception* (K. Attell, Trans.). University of Chicago Press.

Agencias. (2013). *Solalinde amenaza con huelga de hambre.* http://sipse.com/mexico/sola linde-amenaza-con-huelga-de-hambre-19655.html

Agier, M. (2013). *Managing the undesirables: Refugee camps and humanitarian government.* Polity Press.

Agustín, L. M. (2007). Sex at the margins: Migration, labour markets and the rescue industry. *International Migration Review, 41*(3), 785–787.

Álavarez Velazco, S. & de Genova, N. (2023). "A mass exodus in rebellion"—The migrant caravans: A view from the eyes of Honduran journalist Inmer Gerardo Chévez. *Studies in Social Justice, 17*(1), 28–47. https://doi.org/10.26522/ssj.v17i1.4157

Albergue Hermanos en el Camino. (2023). https://www.facebook.com/p/Albergue-de -Migrantes-HERMANOS-EN-EL-CAMINO-100064357972787

American Immigration Council. (2021). *The cost of immigration enforcement and border security.* https://www.americanimmigrationcouncil.org/research/the-cost-of-immi gration-enforcement-and-border-security

American Patrol Reference. (2016). *Archive federal immigration and nationality act.* http:// www.americanpatrol.com/REFERENCE/AidAbetUnlawfulSec8USC1324.html

164 / References

Americares. (2020, November 17). *Americares responds to Hurricane Iota*. https://www
.americares.org/news/2020-1117-americares-responds-to-hurricane-iota/

Amnesty International (AI). (2010). *Invisible victims: Migrants on the move in Mexico*.
http://www.amnestyusa.org/sites/default/files/amr410142010eng.pdf

Amnesty International (AI). (2011a). *Mexico urged to take action over collusion between
criminal gangs and police*. https://www.amnesty.org/en/latest/news/2011/04/mexico
-urged-take-action-over-collusion-between-criminal-gangs-and-police/

Amnesty International (AI). (2011b). *Urgent action mass kidnapping of migrants in Mexico*.
http://www.iaia-internacional.pt/files/AUrgentes/AU_201_11_Mexico_1Julho2011.pdf

Amnesty International (AI). (2016). *Who we are*. https://www.amnesty.org/en/who-we-are/

Anderson, B. (2007). *Motherhood, apple pie and slavery: Reflections on trafficking debates*.
COMPAS. https://www.compas.ox.ac.uk/2007/wp-2007-048-anderson_trafficking
_debates/

Anderson, B. (2008). *"Illegal immigrant": Victim or villain?* COMPAS. https://www.com
pas.ox.ac.uk/2008/wp-2008-064-anderson_illegal_immigrant_victim_villain/

Anderson, B. (2013). *Us and them? The dangerous politics of immigration control*. Oxford
University Press.

Anderson, B., & Andrijasevic, R. (2008). Sex, slaves and citizens: The politics of anti-trafficking. *Soundings, 40*(Winter), 135–145. http://dx.doi.org/10.3898/136266208820465065

Anderson, B., & Reineke, R. (2023). Migration, death, and disappearance: Education and
engagement. In B. Murray, M. Brill-Carlat, M. Höhn (Eds.), *Migration, Displacement,
and Higher Education*. Palgrave Macmillan. https://doi.org/10.1007/978-3-031-12350
-4_7

Andersson, R. (2014). *Illegality, inc*. University of California Press.

Andreas, P. (2003). Redrawing the line: Borders and security in the twenty-first century.
International Security, 28(2), 78–111. http://www.jstor.org/stable/4137469

Andrijasevic, R. (2003). The difference borders make: (Il)legality, migration and trafficking in Italy among Eastern European women in prostitution. In A.-M. Fortier, S.
Ahmed, C. Castañeda, & M. Sheller (Eds.), *Uprootings/regroundings: Questions of home
and migration* (pp. 251–272). Berg.

Anguiano, M. E., & Cruz Piñero, R. (2014). *Migraciones internacionales, crisis y vulnera-
bilidades: Perspectivas comparadas*. El Colegio de la Frontera Norte.

Arendt, H. (1958). *The human condition* (1st ed.). University of Chicago Press.

Arendt, H. (1967). Truth and politics. *The New Yorker, 43*(25), 49–88.

Arendt, H. (1976 [1968, 1966]). *The origins of totalitarianism*. World Publishing Company.

Arriola Vega, L. A. (2012). Migrantes centroamericanos en "transitoriedad": Hondureños
en Tabasco, México en: Aragonés, María Luisa (coord.) Migración Internacional.
Algunos Desafíos. Instituto de Investigaciones Económicas, Universidad Nacional
Autónoma de México. México, pág. 193–216.

Augé, M. (1995). *Non-places: An introduction to supermodernity*. Verso Books.

Baldwin-Edwards, M. (2007). Navigating between Scylla and Charybdis: Migration policies for a Romania within the European Union. *Southeast European and Black Sea
Studies, 7*(1), 5–35.

Balibar, E. (2003). *We, the people of Europe? Reflections on transnational citizenship*. Princeton University Press.

Barboza Sosa, R. (2011). *Agente del INM persigue con machete a hondureña*. http://archivo
.eluniversal.com.mx/notas/754202.html

Barnett, M. (2011). *Empire of humanity: A history of humanitarianism*. Cornell University Press.

Barnett, M., & Finnemore, M. (2001). *Rules for the world: International organizations in global politics*. Cornell University Press.

Barnett, M., & Gross Stein, J. (2012). *Sacred aid: Faith and humanitarianism*. Oxford University Press.

Barnett, M., & Weiss, T. G. (2008). *Humanitarianism in question: Politics, power, ethics*. Cornell University Press.

Basok, T., Bélanger, D., Wiesner, M. L. R., & Candiz, G. (2015). *Rethinking transit migration: Precarity, mobility, and self-making in Mexico* (1st ed.). Palgrave Macmillan.

Bauböck, R. (2009). Global justice, freedom of movement and democratic citizenship. *European Journal of Sociology, 50*(1), 1–31.

Bauman, Z. (1989). *Modernity and the Holocaust*. Cornell University Press.

BBC News. (2018, May 17). Trump: Immigrant gangs "animals, not people" [Video]. YouTube. https://www.youtube.com/watch?app=desktop&v=WD0VoR-4sZs&fe

BBVA Research. (2020). Mapa 2020 de casas del migrante, albergues y comedores para migrantes en México. https://www.bbvaresearch.com/publicaciones/mapa-2020-de -casas-del-migrante-albergues-y-comedores-para-migrantes-en-mexico/

Berman, J. (2003). (Un) Popular strangers and crises (un) bounded: Discourses of sex-trafficking, European immigration and national security under global duress. *European Journal of International Relations, 9*(1), 37–86.

Bernal, G. G., & Silver, M. (2010). *Los invisibles*. Amnesty International.

Betts, A. (2010). The refugee regime complex. *Refugee Survey Quarterly, 29*(1), 12–37.

Betts, A. (2011). Introduction: Global migration governance. In A. Betts (Ed.), *Global Migration Governance* (pp. 1–33). Oxford University Press.

Bigo, D. (2002). Security and immigration: Toward a critique of the governmentality of unease. *Alternatives: Global, Local, Political, 27*(1), 63–92.

Bigo, D. (2006). Security, exception, ban and surveillance. In D. Lyon (Ed.), *Theorizing surveillance: The panopticon and beyond* (pp. 46–68). Willan Publishing.

Bigo, D. (2008). Globalized (in)security: The field and the ban-opticon. In D. Bigo & A. Tsoukala (Eds.), *Terror, insecurity and liberty: Illiberal practices of liberal regimes after 9/11* (pp. 10–48). Routledge.

Blackburn, R. (2013). *The American crucible: Slavery, emancipation and human rights*. Verso Books.

Boehm, D. A. (2011). US-Mexico mixed migration in an age of deportation: An inquiry into the transnational circulation of violence. *Refugee Survey Quarterly, 30*(1), 1–21.

Boontinand, J. (2005). Feminist participatory action research in the Mekong region. In K. Kempadoo, J. Sanghera, & B. Pattanaik (Eds.), *Trafficking and prostitution reconsidered: New perspectives on migration, sex work, and human rights* (pp. 175–198). Paradigm Publishers.

Bornstein, E., & Redfield, P. (2011). *Forces of compassion: Humanitarianism between ethics and politics*. School for Advanced Research Press.

Bricker, K. (2008). *"Wall of violence" on Mexico's southern border*. http://narcosphere.nar conews.com/notebook/kristin-bricker/2008/12/wall-violence-mexicos-southern-border

Brigden, N. K. (2014). Transnational journeys and the limits of hometown resources: Salvadoran migration in uncertain times. *Migration Studies, 3*(2), 241–259.

Brigden, N. K. (2016). Improvised transnationalism: Clandestine migration at the border of anthropology and international relations. *International Studies Quarterly, 60*(2), 343–353.

Brigden, N. K. (2018). *The migrant passage: Clandestine journeys from Central America*. Cornell University Press.

166 / References

Brković, Čarna. (2020). Vernacular humanitarianism. In A. De Lauri (Ed.), *Humanitarianism: Keywords* (pp. 224–226). Brill. https://doi.org/10.1163/9789004431140_0104

Brown, W. (2006). American nightmare neoliberalism, neoconservatism, and de-democratization. *Political Theory, 34*(6), 690–714.

Burridge, N. (2009). Perspectives on reconciliation and Indigenous rights. *Cosmopolitan Civil Societies: An Interdisciplinary Journal, 1*(2), 111–128.

Buscaglia, E. (2010). *México pierde la guerra.* http://www.institutodeaccionciudadana.org/docs/documentos/5.pdf

Butcher, J. (Ed.). (2010). *Mexican solidarity: Citizen participation and volunteering* (1st ed.). Springer-Verlag.

Calavita, K. (1995). Mexican immigration to the USA: The contradictions of border control. In R. Cohen (Ed.), *The Cambridge survey of world migration* (pp. 236–245). Cambridge University Press.

Calderón, G., Robles, G., Díaz-Cayeros, A., & Magaloni, B. (2015). The beheading of criminal organizations and the dynamics of violence in Mexico. *Journal of Conflict Resolution, 59*(8), 1455–1485. https://doi.org/10.1177/0022002715587053

Calhoun, C. (2008). The imperative to reduce suffering: Charity, progress, and emergencies in the field of humanitarian action. In M. Barnett & T. G. Weiss (Eds.), *Humanitarianism in question: Politics, power, ethics* (pp. 73–97). Cornell University Press.

Calhoun, C. (2010). The idea of emergency: Humanitarian action and global (dis)order. In D. Fassin & M. Pandolfi (Eds.), *Contemporary states of emergency: The politics of military and humanitarian interventions* (pp. 29–58). Zone Books.

Cámara de Diputados Federal de México. (2012). *Ley para la protección de personas de derechos humanos y periodistas.* http://www.diputados.gob.mx/LeyesBiblio/pdf/LPPDDHP.pdf

Capous Desyllas, M. (2007). A critique of the global trafficking discourse and U.S. policy. *Journal of Sociology and Social Welfare, 34*(4), 57–79.

Carens, J. H. (2008). The rights of irregular migrants. *Ethics & International Affairs, 22*(2), 163–186.

Carpenter, R. C. (2003). "Women and children first": Gender, norms, and humanitarian evacuation in the Balkans 1991–95. *International Organization, 57*(4), 661–694.

Carpenter, R. C. (2005). "Women, Children and Other Vulnerable Groups": Gender, Strategic Frames and the Protection of Civilians as a Transnational Issue. *International Studies Quarterly, 49*(2), 295–334. http://www.jstor.org/stable/3693516

Casa del Migrante. (2016). *Hogar de la misericordia.* http://migrantes.webgarden.es/

Casillas, R. (2007). *Una vida discreta, fugaz y anónima: Los centroamericanos transmigrantes en México.* Comisión Nacional de los Derechos Humanos (México) & Organización Internacional para las Migraciones (OIM).

Castañeda, H., Holmes, S. M., Madrigal, D. S., Young, M. E., Beyeler, N., & Quesada, J. (2015). Immigration as a social determinant of health. *Annu Rev Public Health, 36*(Mar 18), 375–92. https://doi.org/10.1146/annurev-publhealth-032013-182419

Castillo, M. Á. (2001). Tendencias y determinantes estructurales de la migración internacional en Centroamérica. In L. Rosero Bixby (Ed.), *Población del Istmo 2000: Familia, migración, violencia y medio ambiente* (p. 187). Centro Centroamericano de Población de la Universidad de Costa Rica.

Castillo, M. Á. (2003). The Mexico-Guatemala border: New controls on transborder migrations in view of recent integration schemes. *Frontera Norte, 15*(29), 35–65.

Castles, S. (2003). Towards a sociology of forced migration and social transformation. *Sociology, 37*(1), 13–34.

Castles, S. (2004). Why migration policies fail. *Ethnic and Racial Studies, 27*(2), 205–227. https://doi.org/10.1080/0141987042000177306

Castles, S. (2009). Development and migration—migration and development: What comes first? Global perspective and African experiences. *Theoria: A Journal of Social and Political Theory, 56*(121), 1–31.

Castles, S. (2010). Why migration policies fail. *Ethnic and Racial Studies, 27*(2), 205–227.

Castles, S. & Delgado-Wise, R. (Eds.). (2008). *Migration and development: Perspectives from the South.* IOM.

Castles, S., Haas, H. de, & Miller, M. J. (2013). *The age of migration: International population movements in the modern world* (5th ed.). Palgrave Macmillan.

Chávez, L. R. (2001). *Covering immigration: Popular images and the politics of the nation.* University of California Press.

Chávez, L. R. (2013). *The Latino threat: Constructing immigrants, citizens, and the nation.* Stanford University Press.

Chibber, V. (2013). *Postcolonial theory and the specter of capital.* Verso Books.

Chillier, G., & Varela, S. (2009). Violence, (in)security and human rights in Latin America. *IDS Bulletin, 40*(2), 70–78.

Chomsky, A. (2014). *Undocumented: How immigration became illegal.* Beacon Press.

Chomsky, A. (2021). *Central America's forgotten history: Revolution, violence, and the roots of migration.* Beacon Press.

Collyer, M., & de Haas, H. (2012). Developing dynamic categorisations of transit migration. *Population, Space and Place, 18*(4), 468–481.

Collyer, M., Düvell, F., & de Haas, H. (2012). Critical approaches to transit migration. *Population, Space and Place, 18*(4), 407–414.

Comisión Interamericana de Derechos Humanos (CIDH), & Organización de los Estados Americanos (OEA). (2015). *Situación de derechos humanos en México.* http://www.oas.org/es/cidh/informes/pdfs/Mexico2016-es.pdf

Comisión Nacional de los Derechos Humanos (CNDH). (2004). *Gaceta de la Comisión Nacional de los Derechos Humanos.* http://www.cndh.org.mx/sites/all/doc/Gacetas/170.pdf

Comisión Nacional de los Derechos Humanos (CNDH). (2009). *Informe especial sobre los casos de secuestro en contra de migrantes.* http://www.cndh.org.mx/sites/all/doc/Informes/Especiales/2009_migra.pdf

Comisión Nacional de los Derechos Humanos (CNDH). (2011). *Informe especial sobre secuestro de migrantes en México.* http://www.cndh.org.mx/sites/all/doc/Informes/Especiales/2011_secmigrantes.pdf

Comisión Nacional de los Derechos Humanos (CNDH). (2013). *Diagnóstico sobre la situación de la trata de personas en México.* http://200.33.14.34:1033/archivos/pdfs/diagnosticoTrataPersonas.pdf

Comisión Nacional de los Derechos Humanos (CNDH). (2016). *Estructura.* http://www.cndh.org.mx/Estructura

Comisión Nacional de los Derechos Humanos (CNDH). (2021). Informe especial sobre la situación que guarda el tráfico y el secuestro en perjuicio de personas migrantes 2021. https://www.cndh.org.mx/documento/informe-especial-sobre-la-situacion-que-guarda-el-trafico-y-el-secuestro-en-perjuicio-de

168 / References

Congreso General de los Estados Unidos Mexicanos. (2016). *Ley de migración*. http://www.diputados.gob.mx/LeyesBiblio/ref/lmigra.htm

Congressional Research Service. (2021). *The Trump administration's "zero tolerance" immigration enforcement policy*. Congressional Research Service. https://sgp.fas.org/crs/homesec/R45266.pdf

Connelly, L. (2015). The "rescue industry": The blurred line between help and hindrance. *Graduate Journal of Social Science, 11*(2), 154–160.

Cook, M. L. (2011). "Humanitarian aid is never a crime": Humanitarianism and illegality in migrant advocacy. *Law & Society Review, 45*(3), 561–591.

Cornelisse, G. (2010). *Immigration detention and human rights: Rethinking territorial sovereignty*. Brill Nijhoff.

Cornelius, W. A. (1989). The US demand for Mexican labor. In W. Cornelius & J. A. Bustamante (Eds.), *Mexican migration to the United States: Origins, consequences, and policy options* (pp. 25–47). Center for US-Mexican Studies, University of California.

Cornelius, W., Tsuda, T., Martin, P., & Hollifield, J. (Eds.). (2004). *Controlling immigration: A global perspective* (2nd ed.). Stanford University Press.

Coyuntura. (2010). La masacre de Tamaulipas. *Quito: FLACSO sede Ecuador, 9*(diciembre), 14.

Davis, D. E. (2006). Undermining the rule of law: Democratization and the dark side of police reform in Mexico. *Latin American Politics and Society, 48*(1), 55–86.

Dear, M. (2013). *Why walls won't work: Repairing the US-Mexico divide*. Oxford University Press.

De Genova, N. (2004). The legal production of Mexican/migrant "illegality." *Latino Studies, 2*(2), 160–185.

de Haas, H. (2005). International migration, remittances and development: Myths and facts. *Third World Quarterly, 26,* 1269–1284.

de Haas, H. (2009). *Mobility and human development*. International Migration Institute. https://mpra.ub.uni-muenchen.de/19176/

de Haas, H. (2012). The migration and development pendulum: A critical view on research and policy. *International Migration, 50*(3), 8–25.

De León, J. (2015). *The land of open graves. Living and dying on the migrant trail*. University of California Press.

della Porta, D., & Steinhilper, E. (2021). Introduction: Solidarities in motion: hybridity and change in migrant support practices. *Critical Sociology, 47*(2), 175–185. https://doi.org/10.1177/0896920520952143

Dembour, M.-B., & Kelly, T. (2011). Introduction. In M.-B. Dembour & T. Kelly (Eds.), *Are human rights for migrants? Critical reflections on the status of irregular migrants in Europe and the United States* (pp. 1–22). Routledge.

Democracy Now! (2014). *"Obama is trying to vanish us": Immigrants fight record deportations with protests, hunger strikes*. http://www.democracynow.org/2014/3/13/obama_is_trying_to_vanish_us

Department of Homeland Security. (2022). *Court ordered reimplementation of the migrant protection protocols*. https://www.dhs.gov/archive/migrant-protection-protocols

Derrida, J., & Dufourmantelle, A. (2000). *Of hospitality* (R. Bowlby, Trans.). Stanford University Press.

de Sousa Santos, B., (2002). Toward a multicultural conception of human rights. In B. E. Hernández-Truyol (Ed.), *Moral imperialism: A critical anthology* (pp. 29–60). NYU Press.

de Sousa Santos, B., (2003). *Reconhecer para libertar: Os caminhos do cosmopolitismo multicultural.* Civilizaçáo Brasileira.

de Sousa Santos, B., (2004). A critique of lazy reason: Against the waste of experience. In I. Wallerstein (Ed.), *The modern world-system in the longue durée* (pp. 157–198). Routledge.

de Sousa Santos, B., (2007). Os direitos humanos na zona de contacto entre globalizações rivais. *Revista Cronos, 8*(1), 23–40.

de Sousa Santos, B., Gomes, C., & Duarte, M. (2009). Tráfico sexual de mulheres: Representações sobre ilegalidade e vitimação. *Revista Crítica de Ciências Sociais, 87,* 69–94. https://doi.org/10.4000/rccs.1447

Deveraux, R., and Ramos, N. (2019). *Journalists, lawyers & activists targeted in sweeping U.S. intelligence gathering effort on border.* Democracy Now! https://www.democracy now.org/2019/3/11/journalists_lawyers_activists_targeted_in_sweeping

Diario del Sur. (2022). *Vuelven los ataques armados contra los migrantes en "la Arrocera."* https://www.diariodelsur.com.mx/local/vuelven-los-ataques-armados-contra-mi grantes-en-la-la-arrocera-7767390.html

Díaz, G. L. (2013). Migrantes padecen un "holocausto." *Proceso.* https://www.proceso .com.mx/nacional/2013/12/18/migrantes-padecen-un-holocausto-en-mexico-solalinde -127119.html

Díaz de León, A. (2023). *Walking together: Central Americans and transit migration through Mexico.* Arizona University Press.

Diken, B., & Laustsen, C. B. (2005). *The culture of exception: Sociology facing the camp.* Routledge.

Dimensión Pastoral de la Movilidad Humana (DPMH). (2012). *Informe de actividades de la DPMH en el periodo 2006–2012.* Área Pastoral de Migrantes, Comisión Episcopal para la Pastoral Social, Conferencia del Episcopado Mexicano. http://www .sjmmexico.org/uploads/TBL_CDOCUMENTOS_71_2_35.pdf

Doezema, J. (1999). Loose women or lost women? The re-emergence of the myth of white slavery in contemporary discourses of trafficking in women. *Gender Issues, 18*(1), 23–50.

Doezema, J. (2002). Who gets to choose? Coercion, consent, and the UN trafficking protocol. *Gender & Development, 10*(1), 20–27.

Donnelly, J. (1993). Human rights, humanitarian crisis, and humanitarian intervention. *International Journal, 48*(4), 607–640.

Dowling, J. A., & Inda, J. X. (Eds.). (2013). *Governing immigration through crime: A reader.* Stanford University Press.

Dudley, S. (2012). *Transnational crime in Mexico and Central America: Its evolution and role in international migration.* Migration Policy Institute.

Duffield, M. (2001). *Global governance and the new wars: The merging of development and security* (1st ed.). Zed Books.

Duffield, M. (2012). Challenging environments: Danger, resilience and the aid industry. *Security Dialogue, 43*(5), 475–492.

Durand, J., & Massey, D. S. (Eds.). (2004). *Crossing the border: Research from the Mexican migration project.* Russell Sage Foundation.

Dussel, E. (1998). Beyond eurocentrism: The world-system and the limits of modernity. In J. Ferguson & M. Miyoshi (Eds.), *The cultures of globalization* (pp. 3–21). Duke University Press.

Dussel, E. (1999). Six theses toward a critique of political reason: The citizen as political agent. *Radical Philosophy Review, 2*(2), 79–95.

170 / References

Düvell, F. (2011). Irregular migration. In A. Betts (Ed.), *Global migration governance* (pp. 78–109). Oxford University Press.

Düvell, F. (2012). Transit migration: A blurred and politicised concept. *Population, Space and Place, 18*(4), 415–427.

Düvell, F., Triandafyllidou, A., & Vollmer, B. (2010). Ethical issues in irregular migration research in Europe. *Population, Space and Place, 16*(3), 227–239.

Dwyer, J. (2014). A 12-year-old's trek of despair ends in a noose at the border. *The New York Times.* https://www.nytimes.com/2014/04/20/nyregion/a-12-year-olds-trek-of -despair-ends-in-a-noose-at-the-border.html?_r=0

Edwards, J. R., Jr. (2007). *The security and prosperity partnership, its immigration implications.* Center for Immigration Studies. http://thesigintreport.com/backgrounder .pdf

EFE. (2008). *Zelaya y Calderón coinciden en defender la migración como un derecho humano.* http://elbohemionews.com/zelaya-y-calderon-coinciden-en-defender-la-mig racion-como-un-derecho-humano/

EFE. (2015). *México se ha vuelto más "deportador" de migrantes que EU, según expertos.* http://expansion.mx/mundo/2015/06/11/mexico-se-ha-vuelto-mas-deportador-de -migrantes-que-eu-segun-expertos

EG. (2012). *Oportunidad de México para avanzar en los derechos humanos de las personas migrantes.* http://pasolibrefm4.blogspot.com/2012/08/oportunidad-de-mexico-para -avanzar-en.html

Egremy, G. (2002). *Confunden y deportan a mexicanos hacia Guatemala.* http://archivo .eluniversal.com.mx/estados/42487.html

El Informador. (2011). *Migrantes eligen ruta del Pacífico.* http://www.informador.com .mx/primera/2011/294583/6/migrantes-eligen-ruta-del-pacifico.htm

El Universal. (2012). *EPN entrega premio derechos humanos al Padre Solalinde.* http:// archivo.eluniversal.com.mx/notas/889061.html

Englund, H. (2011). The anthropologist and his poor. In E. Bornstein & P. Refield (Eds.), *Forces of compassion: Humanitarianism between ethics and politics* (pp. 71–93). School for Advanced Research Press.

Enns, D. (2012). *The violence of victimhood.* Pennsylvania State University Press.

Escobar, A. (1995). *Encountering development: The making and unmaking of the third world* (1st ed.). Princeton University Press.

Escobar, A. (2011). *Encountering development: The making and unmaking of the third world* (2nd ed.). Princeton University Press.

Falcón, S. (2001). Rape as a weapon of war: Advancing human rights for women at the U.S.-Mexico border. *Social Justice, 28*(2 [84]), 31–50.

Fals-Borda, O. (1981). *Ciencia propia y colonialismo intelectual.* Carlos Valencia Editores.

Fanon, F. (1967). *Black skin, white masks.* Grove Press.

Fanon, F. (2004 [1963]). *The wretched of the earth.* Grove Weidenfeld.

Fassin, D. (2007). Humanitarianism as a Politics of Life. *Public Culture, 19*(3), 499–520. https://doi.org/10.1215/08992363-2007-007

Fassin, D. (2010). Inequality of lives, hierarchies of humanity: Moral commitments and ethical dilemmas of humanitarianism. In I. Feldman & M. Ticktin (Eds.), *In the name of humanity: The government of threat and care* (pp. 238–255). Duke University Press.

Fassin, D. (2011). Noli me tangere: The moral untouchability of humanitarianism. In E. Bornstein & P. Redfield (Eds.), *Forces of compassion: Humanitarianism between ethics and politics* (pp. 31–52). School for Advanced Research Press.

Fassin, D. (2012). *Humanitarian reason.* University of California Press.

Fearon, J. D. (2008). The rise of emergency relief aid. In M. Barnett & T. G. Weiss (Eds.), *Humanitarianism in question: Politics, power, ethics* (pp. 49–72). Cornell University Press.

Federici, S. (2004). *Caliban and the witch*. Autonomedia.

Fekete, L. (2005). The deportation machine: Europe, asylum and human rights. *Race & Class, 47*(1), 64–78.

Fekete, L. (2009). Europe: Crimes of solidarity. *Race & Class, 50*(4), 83–97.

Feldman, I., & Ticktin, M. (2010). *In the name of humanity: The government of threat and care*. Duke University Press.

Fitzgerald, D. (2008). *A nation of emigrants: How Mexico manages its migration*. University of California Press.

Flynn, D. (2007). *Human trafficking and forced labour: What perspectives to challenge exploitation?* Platform for International Cooperation on Undocumented Migrants (PICUM). http://childhub.org/sites/default/files/library/attachments/513_546_EN _original.pdf

FM4 Paso Libre. (2013). *Migración en tránsito por la Zona Metropolitana de Guadalajara: Actores, retos y perspectivas desde la experiencia de FM4 Paso Libre*. FM4 Paso Libre. Dignidad y Justicia en el Camino AC.

Fogal, C., Carlsen, L., & Lendman, S. (2010). *Security and prosperity partnership: Militarized NAFTA*. http://www.voltairenet.org/article164650.html

Foucault, M. (1982). The Subject and Power. *Critical Inquiry, 8*(4), 777–795. http://www .jstor.org/stable/1343197

Foucault, M. (1988). *Power/knowledge. Selected interviews and other writings 1972–1977*. Harvester Press.

Foucault, M. (2007 [1978]). 1 February 1978. In M. Senellart (Ed.), *Security, territory, population: Lectures at the Collège de France*. Palgrave Macmillan.

Foucault, M., Bertani, M., Fontana, A., Ewald, F., & Macey, D. (2003 [1976]). *"Society must be defended": Lectures at the Collège de France, 1975–1976*. Palgrave Macmillan.

Frank-Vitale, A. (2015). "Fui migrante y me hospedaron": The Catholic Church's responses to violence against Central American Migrants in Mexico. In A. Wilde (Ed.), *Religious Responses to Violence: Human Rights in Latin America Past and Present*. University of Notre Dame Press.

Friese, H. (2010). The limits of hospitality: Political philosophy, undocumented migration and the local arena. *European Journal of Social Theory, 13*(3), 323–341. https:// doi.org/10.1177/1368431010371755

Fukunaga, C. J. (Director). (2009). *Sin nombre* [Film]. Scion Films, Canana, Creando Films, and Primary Productions.

Gallagher, A. T., & Pearson, E. (2008). Detention of trafficked persons in shelters: A legal and policy analysis. https://ssrn.com/abstract=1239745

Galtung, J. (1969). Violence, peace, and peace research. *Journal of Peace Research, 6*(3), 167–191.

Gammeltoft-Hansen, T. (2006). *Outsourcing migration management: EU, power, and the external dimension of asylum and immigration policy*. DIIS Working Paper, No. 2006:1. Danish Institute for International Studies.

Gammeltoft-Hansen, T., & Nyberg Sørensen, N. (2013). *The migration industry and the commercialization of international migration*. Routledge.

García Aguilar, M. del C., & Villafuerte Solís, D. (2014). *Migración, derechos humanos y desarrollo: Aproximaciones desde el sur de México y Centroamérica*. UNICACH/Juan Pablos Editor.

172 / References

García de León, A. (1985). *Resistencia y utopía: Memorial de agravios y crónica de revueltas y profecías acaecidas en la provincia de Chiapas durante los últimos quinientos años de su historia* (1st ed.). Ediciones Era.

Gatti, G., Irazuzta, I., & Sáez, R. (2020). Los no contados: Desbordamientos del concepto jurídico de desaparición. *Athenea Digital, 20*(3), e2718. https://doi.org/10.5565/rev/athenea.2718

Geertz, C. (1973). *The interpretation of cultures: Selected essays*. Basic Books.

Gentry, B., Boyce, G. A., Garcia, J. M., & Chambers, S. N. (2019). Indigenous survival and settler colonial dispossession on the Mexican frontier: The case of Cedagĩ Wahia and Wo'oson O'odham indigenous communities. *Journal of Latin American Geography 18*(1), 65–93. https://doi.org/10.1353/lag.2019.0003

Gibler, J. (2009). *Mexico unconquered: Chronicles of power and revolt*. City Lights Publishers.

Gledhill, J. (2015). *The new war on the poor. The new production of insecurity in Latin America*. Zed Books.

Global Detention Project Report. (2021). *Country Report. Immigration Detention in Mexico: Between the United States and Central America*. https://www.globaldetentionproject.org/wp-content/uploads/2021/02/Immigration-Detention-in-Mexico-2021-GDP.pdf

Gobierno de México. (2023). *Visas por razones humanitarias*. https://www.gob.mx/tramites/ficha/visa-por-razones-humanitarias/INM74

Goldring, L., Berinstein, C., & Bernhard, J. K. (2009). Institutionalizing precarious migratory status in Canada. *Citizenship Studies, 13*(3), 239–265.

Gordon, L. R. (2006). African-American philosophy, race, and the geography of reason. In L. R. Gordon & J. A. Gordon (Eds.), *Not only the master's tools: African American studies in theory and practice* (pp. 3–55). Routledge.

Gott, G. (2002). Imperial humanitarianism: History of an arrested dialectic. In B. E. Hernández-Truyol (Ed.), *Moral imperialism: A critical anthology* (pp. 19–38). New York University Press.

Grillo, I. (2011). *El Narco: Inside Mexico's criminal insurgency*. Bloomsbury Publishing.

Grillo, I. (2012). *El Narco: En el corazón de la insurgencia criminal mexicana*. Ediciones Urano (Tendencias).

Grosfoguel, R. (2011). Decolonizing post-colonial studies and paradigms of political-economy: Transmodernity, decolonial thinking, and global coloniality. *Transmodernity: Journal of Peripheral Cultural Production of the Luso-Hispanic World, 1*(1), 1–37.

Grosfoguel, R., & Georas, C. S. (2001). Latino Caribbean diasporas in New York. In A. Laó-Montes & A. M. Dávila (Eds.), *Mambo montage: The Latinization of New York* (pp. 97–118). Columbia University Press.

Grupo de Trabajo sobre Política Migratoria (GTPM). (2023). *Mapeo regional de actores sobre movilidad humana*. https://gtpm.mx/organizaciones/

Hacking, I. (1999). Making up people. In M. Biagioli (Ed.), *The science studies reader* (pp. 161–171). Routledge.

Hagan, J. M. (2008). *Migration miracle*. Harvard University Press.

Hall, N. (2016). *Displacement, development, and climate change: International organizations moving beyond their mandates*. Routledge.

Hamood, S. (2006). *African transit migration through Libya to Europe: The human cost*. American University in Cairo, Forced Migration and Refugee Studies.

Haraway, D. (1988). The science question in feminism as a site of discourse on the privilege of partial perspective. *Feminist Studies, 14*(3), 575–579.

Harrell-Bond, B. E. (1985). *Imposing aid: Emergency assistance to refugees*. Oxford University Press.

Harvey, D. (2014). *Seventeen contradictions and the end of capitalism*. Oxford University Press.

Haskell, T. L. (1985). Capitalism and the origins of the humanitarian sensibility, part 1. *The American Historical Review, 90*(2), 339–361.

Hastrup, K. (2004). Getting it right: Knowledge and evidence in anthropology. *Anthropological Theory, 4*(4), 455–472.

Hernández, G. (2012). Denuncian activistas boicot a manifestación en apoyo a migrantes. *Proceso.* http://www.proceso.com.mx/307832/denuncian-activistas-boicot-a-mani festacion-en-apoyo-a-migrantes

Herzog, L. A. (2000). *Shared space: Rethinking the US-Mexico border environment*. Center for US-Mexican Studies, University of California.

Hill, S. (2015). *Raw deal: How the "Uber economy" and runaway capitalism are screwing American workers*. Palgrave Macmillan.

Horstmann, A. (2017). Plurality and plasticity of everyday humanitarianism in the Karen conflict. In D. Smyer Yü & J. Michaud (Eds.), *Trans-Himalayan borderlands: livelihoods, territorialities, modernities* (pp. 167–188). Amsterdam University Press. https://doi.org/10.1515/9789048531714-009

Human Rights Watch. (2009). *United States ratification of international human rights treaties.* https://www.hrw.org/news/2009/07/24/united-states-ratification-internatio nal-human-rights-treaties

Hume, D. (1896). *A treatise of human nature* (L. A. Selby-Bigge, Ed.). Clarendon Press.

Huspek, M., Martinez, R., & Jimenez, L. (1998). Violations of human and civil rights on the U.S.-Mexico border, 1995 to 1997: A report. *Social Justice, 25*(2 [72]), 110–130.

Huxley, M. (2007). Geographies of governmentality. In S. Elden & J. Crampton (Eds.), *Space, knowledge, and power: Foucault and geography* (pp. 185–204). Routledge.

İçduygu, A. (2000). The politics of international migratory regimes: Transit migration flows in Turkey. *International Social Science Journal, 52*(165), 357–367.

Instituto Nacional de Migración (INM). (2011). *Quinto informe de labores*. Secretaría de Gobernación (SEGOB). http://www.inm.gob.mx/static/transparencia/pdf/Informe _de_labores_2011.pdf

Instituto Nacional de Migración (INM). (2014a). *Derechos humanos de las personas migrantes que transitan por México.* http://www.inm.gob.mx/static/pdf/DH_PERSONAS _MIGRANTES_TRANSITAN_MEXICO.pdf

Instituto Nacional de Migración (INM). (2014b). *Visa por razones humanitarias.* http:// www.inm.gob.mx/static/Tramites_2013/visas_solicitadas/VISA_POR_RAZONES _HUMANITARIAS.pdf

Instituto Nacional de Migración (INM). (2016). *Grupos Beta de protección a migrantes.* http:// www.gob.mx/inm/acciones-y-programas/grupos-beta-de-proteccion-a-migrantes

International Commission on Intervention and State Sovereignty (Canada), & International Development Research Centre (Canada). (2001). *The responsibility to protect: Report of the International Commission on Intervention and State Sovereignty.* https:// www.globalr2p.org/resources/the-responsibility-to-protect-report-of-the-interna tional-commission-on-intervention-and-state-sovereignty-2001/

International Federation of Red Cross and Red Crescent Societies. (2006). *Complex/manmade hazards: Complex emergencies.* http://media.ifrc.org/ifrc-pages/ifrc-responsive -footer/

174 / References

International Organization for Migration (IOM). (2016a). *United States of America.* https://www.iom.int/countries/united-states-america

International Organization for Migration (IOM). (2016b). *Fatal journeys: Identification and tracking of dead and missing migrants* (T. Brian & F. Laczko, Eds.). International Organization for Migration.

Islas, A. (2012). *El albergue.* https://elalberguedoc.wordpress.com/

Jacobsen C., Karlsen M., & Khoshravi, S. (Eds.). (2021). *Waiting and the temporalities of irregular migration.* Routledge.

Kempadoo, K. (2005). From moral panic to global justice: Changing perspectives on trafficking. In K. Kempadoo, J. Sanghera, & B. Pattanaik (Eds.), *Trafficking and prostitution reconsidered: New perspectives on migration, sex work, and human rights* (pp. 3–24). Paradigm Publishers.

Kempadoo, K., & Doezema, J. (Eds.). (1999). *Global sex workers: Rights, resistance, and redefinition.* Routledge.

Kempadoo, K., Sanghera, J., & Pattanaik, B. (Eds.). (2005). *Trafficking and prostitution reconsidered: New perspectives on migration, sex work, and human rights.* Paradigm Publishers.

Kleinman, A., Das, V., & Lock, M. M. (1997). *Social suffering.* University of California Press.

Komter, A. E. (2005). *Social solidarity and the gift.* Cambridge University Press.

Kotef, H. (2011). Movement. *Political Concepts: A Critical Lexicon* (2). https://www.political concepts.org/movement-hagar-kotef/

Kotef, H. (2015). *Movement and the reordering of freedom: On liberal governances of mobility.* Duke University Press.

Kovács, G., & Tatham, P. (2009). Responding to disruptions in the supply network—from dormant to action. *Journal of Business Logistics, 30*(2), 215–229.

Kuhner, G. (2011). *Problemas que enfrentan los migrantes en las fronteras sur y norte de Mexico, y en su viaje entre las dos.* BBC. http://www.bbc.co.uk/spanish/especiales /humanrights/entrefront.shtml

La Jornada. (2014). *Deportó México a unos 78 mil centroamericanos vía terrestre en 2013.* http://www.jornada.unam.mx/2014/01/08/politica/013n2pol

La72 Hogar-Refugio para personas migrantes. (2023). *Defendemos los derechos humanos de las personas migrantes y refugiadas.* https://www.la72tenosique.org/

Lee, R. M. (1993). *Doing research on sensitive topics.* SAGE Publications.

Legrás, H. (2017). *Culture and revolution: Violence, memory, and the making of modern Mexico.* University of Texas Press.

León, N. (2022). *Cortan la luz a refugios de emigrantes de Mexicali.* El imparcial. https:// www.elimparcial.com/mexicali/mexicali/Cortan-la-luz-a-refugios-de-migrantes-de -Mexicali-20220120-0014.html

Levy, C. (2010). Refugees, Europe, camps/state of exception: "Into the zone," the European Union and extraterritorial processing of migrants, refugees, and asylum-seekers (theories and practice). *Refugee Survey Quarterly, 29*(1), 92–119.

Liamputtong, P. (2006). *Researching the vulnerable: A guide to sensitive research methods.* SAGE Publications.

Linde, T. (2009). Humanitarian assistance to migrants irrespective of their status—Towards a non-categorical approach. *International Review of the Red Cross, 91*(875), 567–578.

López Castillo, F., & Prieto, N. (2011). *Vídeo: Inmigrantes como moscas.* http://cultura .elpais.com/cultura/2011/01/21/videos/1295564401_870215.html

Magaloni, B., & Zepeda, G. (2004). Democratization, judicial and law enforcement institutions and the rule of law in Mexico. In K. J. Middlebrook (Ed.), *Dilemmas of political change in Mexico* (pp. 168–198). Institute of Latin American Studies.

Malkki, L. H. (2015). *The need to help: The domestic arts of international humanitarianism.* Duke University Press.

Marchena, D. (2016). *Un héroe americano: "Estados Unidos seguirá recibiendo inmigrantes, pero a trozos."* http://www.lavanguardia.com/internacional/20161116/411887180019/alejandro-solalinde-iglesia-hispanoamerica-inmigracion-derechos-humanos-droga-donald-trump.html

Margalit, A. (1996). *The decent society.* Harvard University Press.

Marrujo Ruíz, O. (2001). Los riesgos de cruzar: La migración centroamericana en la frontera México-Guatemala. *Frontera Norte, 13*(25), 7–33.

Mars, A. (2016). *Villoro: "Trump es el gran aliado del gobierno de México."* http://internacional.elpais.com/internacional/2016/04/28/estados_unidos/1461854489_575128.html

Martínez, O. J. (2006 [1988]). *Troublesome border* (rev. ed.). University of Arizona Press.

Martínez, O. J. (2014). *The Beast: Riding the rails and dodging Narcos on the migrant trail* (reprint ed.). Verso Books.

Martínez, O., & Martínez, C. (2012). *Soy parte de un grupo de sacerdotes que no se dejará amedrentar por la excomunión o la inquisición.* http://elfaro.net/es/201209/noticias/9693/Soy-parte-de-un-grupo-de-sacerdotes-que-no-se-dejará-amedrentar-por-la-excomunión-o-la-inquisición.htm

Massey, D. (2013). America's immigration policy fiasco: Learning from past mistakes. *Daedalus, 142*(3), 5–15.

Massey, D. (2020). Immigration policy mismatches and counterproductive outcomes: unauthorized migration to the U.S. in two eras. *CMS, 8*(21). https://doi.org/10.1186/s40878-020-00181-6

Massey, D., Durand, J., & Pren, K. (2014). Explaining undocumented migration to the U.S. *International Migration Review, 48*(4), 1028–1061.

Massey, D., & Pren, K. A. (2012). Unintended consequences of US immigration policy: Explaining the post-1965 surge from Latin America. *Population and Development Review, 38*(1), 1–29.

Massey, D., Pren, K. A., & Durand, J. (2016). Why border enforcement backfired. *American Journal of Sociology, 121*(5), 1557–1600.

Mauss, M. (2000 [1924]). *The gift: The form and reason for exchange in archaic societies.* WW Norton & Company.

McGee, D., & Pelham, J. (2018). Politics at play: Locating human rights, refugees and grassroots humanitarianism in the Calais Jungle. *Leisure Studies, 37*(1), 22–35. https://doi.org/10.1080/02614367.2017.1406979

Meissner, D., Kerwin, D. M., Chishti, M., & Bergeron, C. (2013). *Immigration enforcement in the United States: The rise of a formidable machinery.* Migration Policy Institute. http://www.migrationpolicy.org/research/immigration-enforcement-united-states-rise-formidable-machinery

Meléndez, J. (2015). *México supera a EU en cifra de deportaciones de migrantes.* http://www.eluniversal.com.mx/articulo/nacion/seguridad/2015/10/14/mexico-supera-eu-en-cifra-de-deportaciones-de-migrantes

Meneses, G. A. (2003). Human rights and undocumented migration along the Mexican-U.S. border. *UCLA Law Review, 51*, 267.

Menjívar, C. (2000). *Fragmented ties: Salvadoran immigrant networks in America.* University of California Press.

Menjívar, C. (2006). Liminal legality: Salvadoran and Guatemalan immigrants' lives in the United States. *American Journal of Sociology, 111*(4), 999–1037. https://doi.org/10.1086/499509

176 / References

Menjívar, C. (2010). Immigrants, immigration, and sociology: Reflecting on the state of the discipline. *Sociological Inquiry, 80*(1), 3–27. https://doi.org/10.1111/j.1475-682X.2009.00313.x

Menjívar, C. (2021). The racialization of "illegality." *Daedalus, 150*(2), 91–105. https://doi.org/10.1162/daed_a_01848

Menjívar, C., Simmons, W. P., Alvord, D., & Valdez, E. S. (2018). Immigration enforcement, the racialization of legal status, and perceptions of the police. *Du Bois Review, 15*(1), 107–128. https://doi.org/10.1017/S1742058X18000115

Menjívar, C., & Walsh, S. (2019). Gender-based violence in Central American and women asylum seekers in the United States. *Transnational Criminology, 16*(Winter), 12–14.

Menz, G. (2011). Neo-liberalism, privatization and the outsourcing of migration management: A five-country comparison. *Competition & Change, 15*(2), 116–135.

Mesoamerican Migrant Movement. (2016). *Central American migration.* WordPress Foundation. https://movimientomigrantemesoamericano.org/2016/07/13/central-american-migration/

Meyer, M. (2019). *Mexico's proposed national guard would solidify the militarization of public security.* WOLA. https://www.wola.org/analysis/mexico-national-guard-military-abuses/

Mignolo, W. D. (2000). *Coloniality, subaltern knowledges, and border thinking: Local histories/global designs.* Princeton University Press.

Mignolo, W. D. (2002). The geopolitics of knowledge and the colonial difference. *The South Atlantic Quarterly, 101*(1), 57–96.

Mignolo, W. D. (2006). Citizenship, knowledge, and the limits of humanity. *American Literary History, 18*(2), 312–331.

Milenio Digital. (2014). *México criminaliza a niños migrantes: CIDH.* http://www.milenio.com/politica/Ninos_mujeres_migrantes-vulnerables_en_Mexico-CIDH-derechos_humanos_migrantes_0_356364468.html

Molina, L. (2013). *En la Bestia: "Si no pagan 100 dólares, los tiran del tren."* http://www.eldiario.es/desalambre/inmigracion/La_bestia-accidente-Mexico-migrantes_0_169033650.html

Monsiváis, C. (2003). "Where are you going to be worthier?" (The border and the post-border). In M. Dear & G. Leclerc (Eds.), *Postborder city: Cultural spaces of Bajalta California* (pp. 33–46). Routledge. https://doi.org/10.4324/9781315810935

Montgomery, H. (1998). Children, prostitution, and identity: Case study from tourist resort. In K. Kempadoo & J. Doezema (Eds.), *Global sex workers: Rights, resistance, and redefinition* (pp. 139–150). Routledge.

Montgomery, H. (2007). Working with child prostitutes in Thailand: Problems of practice and interpretation. *Childhood, 14*(4), 415–430.

Mountz, A. (2020). *The death of asylum: Hidden geographies of the enforcement archipelago.* University of Minnesota Press.

MSF. (2020). *Report: No way out—The humanitarian crisis for Central American migrants and refugees.* https://www.msf.org/report-no-way-out-central-american-migration

Muller, B. (2004). Globalization, security, paradox: Towards a refugee biopolitics. *Refuge: Canada's Journal on Refugees, 22*(1), 49–57.

Nájera Aguirre, J. N. (2016). El complejo estudio de la actual migración en tránsito por México: Actores, temáticas y circunstancias. *Migraciones Internacionales, 8*(3), 255–266.

Ngai, M. M. (2004). *Impossible subjects: Illegal aliens and the making of modern America* (1st ed.). Princeton University Press.

No More Deaths and Coalición de Derechos Humanos. (2021). *Left to die: Border patrol, search and rescue and the crisis of disappearance.* https://nomoredeaths.org/new-re port-left-to-die-border-patrol-search-rescue-and-the-crisis-of-disappearance/

Noticias Terra. (2012). *Amnistía inicia campaña para recolectar medias para migrantes.* https://noticias.terra.com.ar/mundo/amnistia-inicia-campana-para-reolectar-medi as-para-migrantes,cd2ca9c2bf915310VgnVCM20000099f154d0RCRD.html

Nyberg Sørensen, N. (2013). Migration between social and criminal networks: Jumping the remains of the Honduran migration train. In T. Gammeltoft-Hansen & S. N. Nyberg Sørensen (Eds.), *The migration industry and the commercialization of international migration* (pp. 238–261). Routledge.

Nyers, P. (2003). Abject cosmopolitanism: The politics of protection in the anti-deportation movement. *Third World Quarterly, 24*(6), 1069–1093.

Nyers, P. (2006a). Taking rights, mediating wrongs: Disagreements over the political agency of non-status refugees. In J. Huysmans, A. Dobson, & R. Prokhovnik (Eds.), *The politics of protection: Sites of insecurity and political agency* (pp. 48–67). Routledge.

Nyers, P. (2006b). The accidental citizen: Acts of sovereignty and (un)making citizenship. *Economy and Society, 35*(1), 22–41.

Nyers, P. (2010). No one is illegal between city and nation. *Studies in Social Justice, 4*(2), 127–143.

Ochoa, R. (2012). Not just the rich: New tendencies in kidnapping in Mexico City. *Global Crime, 13*(1), 1–21.

Ochoa, R. (2015). The politics of crime in Mexico: Democratic governance in a security trap. *Global Crime, 16*(1), 51–54.

O'Connell Davidson, J. (2005). *Children in the global sex trade.* Polity Press.

O'Connell Davidson, J. (2010). New slavery, old binaries: Human trafficking and the borders of "freedom." *Global Networks, 10*(2), 244–261.

O'Connell Davidson, J. (2014). Making politics: Migration, suffering and rights. In B. Anderson & M. Keith (Eds.), *Migration: The COMPAS anthology* (pp. 142–143). Centre on Migration, Policy and Society, COMPAS.

Office of Population Research, Princeton University, & Departamento de Estudios Sobre Movimientos Sociales (DESMOS), Universidad de Guadalajara. (2016). *Mexico migration project.* http://mmp.opr.princeton.edu/

Office of the Press Secretary. (2005). *Security and prosperity partnership of North America prosperity agenda.* https://2001-2009.state.gov/p/wha/rls/prsrl/2005/69848 .htm

Ong Hing, B. (1998). *The immigrant as criminal: Punishing dreamers. 9 Hastings Women's L.J., 79.* https://repository.uclawsf.edu/hwlj/vol9/iss1/3

Ophir, A. (2006). Disaster as a place of morality: The sovereign, the humanitarian, and the terrorist. *Qui Parle, 16*(1), 95–116.

Ophir, A. (2010). The politics of catastrophization: Emergency and exception. In D. Fassin & M. Pandolfi (Eds.), *Contemporary states of emergency: The politics of military and humanitarian interventions* (pp. 59–88). MIT Press.

Organización de los Estados Americanos (OEA). (2014). *CIDH condena asesinato de defensores de derechos humanos de migrantes en México.* http://www.oas.org/es/cidh /prensa/comunicados/2014/149.asp

Organización de los Estados Americanos (OEA). (2015). *CIDH expresa preocupación ante el Plan Frontera Sur de México.* http://www.oas.org/es/cidh/prensa/comunicados /2015/065.asp

178 / References

Organización Internacional Para Las Migraciones (OIM). (2016). *OIM*. https://mexico .iom.int/es

Oxford University Press. (2016). *Oxford English dictionary*. http://www.oed.com/

Papadopoulou, A. (2008). *Transit migration through Greece*. IMISCOE Conference Papers.

Partlow, J. and Miroff, N. (2018). *U.S. gathers data on migrants deep in Mexico, a sensitive program Trump's rhetoric could put at risk*. Washington Post. https://www .washingtonpost.com/world/national-security/us-gathers-data-on-migrants-deep -in-mexico-a-sensitive-program-trumps-rhetoric-could-put-at-risk/2018/04/06/31a 8605a-38f3-11e8-b57c-9445cc4dfa5e_story.html

Peinado, M. L. (2013). Fray Tomás, defensor de los migrantes, denuncia amenazas de muerte. *El País*. http://internacional.elpais.com/internacional/2013/03/20/actualidad /1363744497_788598.html

Pereira da Costa, I. D. (2016). The influence of American exceptionalism on Latin American foreign affairs: A case study of Guantánamo Bay, Cuba. *Encuentro Latinoamericano ELA*, *3*(1), 34–49.

Petryna, A. (2003). *Life exposed: Biological citizens after Chernobyl* (1st ed.). Princeton University Press.

Peutz, N., & De Genova, N. (2010). Introduction. In N. Peutz & N. De Genova (Eds.), *The deportation regime: Sovereignty, space, and the freedom of movement* (pp. 1–32). Duke University Press.

Piketty, T. (2014). *Capital in the twenty-first century*. Harvard University Press.

Portes, A., & Hoffman, K. (2003). Latin American class structures: Their composition and change during the neoliberal era. *Latin American Research Review*, *38*(1), 41–82.

Presidencia de la República. (2014a). *Pone en marcha el Presidente Enrique Peña Nieto el Programa Frontera Sur*. http://www.gob.mx/presidencia/prensa/pone-en-marcha -el-presidente-enrique-pena-nieto-el-programa-frontera-sur

Presidencia de la República. (2014b). *¿Qué es el Programa Frontera Sur?* http://www.gob .mx/presidencia/articulos/que-es-el-programa-frontera-sur

Quemada-Díez, D. (Director). (2014). *La jaula de oro (The golden dream)* [Film]. Animal de Luz Films, Kinemascope Films, Machete Producciones, México.

Quijano, A. (1999). ¡Qué tal raza! *América Latina en Movimiento*. https://repositorio .flacsoandes.edu.ec/handle/10469/5724

Quijano, A. (2000). Coloniality of power, Eurocentrism, and Latin America. *Nepantla: Views from the South*, *1*(3), 533–580.

Rajaram, P. K., & Grundy-Warr, C. (2004). The irregular migrant as homo sacer: Migration and detention in Australia, Malaysia, and Thailand. *International Migration*, *42*(1), 33–64.

Rancière, J. (2004). Who is the subject of the rights of man? *The South Atlantic Quarterly*, *103*(2), 297–310.

Red de Documentación de las Organizaciones Defensoras de Migrantes (REDODEM). (2013). *Narrativas de la transmigración centroamericana en su paso por México*.

REDODEM. (2014). *Migrantes invisibles, violencia tangible*. http://www.centerforhuman rights.org/PDFs/REDODEM_InformeMigrantes2014.pdf

REDODEM. (2015). *Migración en tránsito por México: Rostro de una crisis humanitaria internacional*. http://www.fm4pasolibre.org/pdfs/Informe_redodem_2015.pdf

REDODEM. (2016). *Migrantes en México: Recorriendo un camino de violencia*. Servicio Jesuita a Migrantes. http://redodem.org/wp-content/uploads/2019/07/Informe-Redo dem-2016.pdf

REDODEM. (2017). *El estado indolente: Recuento de la violencia en las rutas migratorias y perfiles de movilidad en México*. Servicio Jesuita a Migrantes. http://redodem.org/wp-content/uploads/2019/07/Informe-Redodem-2017.pdf

REDODEM. (2018). *Procesos migratorios en México: Nuevos rostros, mismas dinámicas*. Servicio Jesuita a Migrantes. http://redodem.org/wp-content/uploads/2019/09/REDODEM-Informe-2018.pdf

REDODEM. (2019). *Migraciones en México: Fronteras, omisiones y transgresiones*. Servicio Jesuita a Migrantes. https://redodem.org/wp-content/uploads/2020/09/REDODEM_Informe_2019.pdf

REDODEM. (2021). *Website of the Red de Documentación de las Organizaciones Defensoras de Migrantes*. Servicio Jesuita a Migrantes. https://redodem.org/

Registro Nacional de Personas Desaparecidas o no Localizadas. (2021). *Versión pública RNPDNO*. Secretaría de Gobernación. https://versionpublicarnpdno.segob.gob.mx/Dashboard/Index

Rieff, D. (2003). *A bed for the night: Humanitarianism in crisis*. Simon and Schuster.

Rodgers, D. (2009). Slum wars of the 21st century: Gangs, *mano dura* and the new urban geography of conflict in Central America. *Development and Change, 40*(5). 949–976. https://doi.org/10.1111/j.1467-7660.2009.01590.x

Salt, J., & Stein, J. (1997). Migration as a business: The case of trafficking. *International Migration, 35*(4), 467–494.

Sánchez, G. (2015). *Human smuggling and border crossings*. Routledge.

Sánchez Soler, M. (2014). *Movimiento migrante Mesoamericano—Caravana de madres Centroamericanas—"Sigo tus pasos con la esperanza de encontrate."* https://www.fundar.org.mx/mexico/pdf/documentocaravana.pdf

Sandri, E. (2018). "Volunteer humanitarianism": Volunteers and humanitarian aid in the jungle refugee camp of Calais. *Journal of Ethnic and Migration Studies, 44*(1), 65–80. https://doi.org/10.1080/1369183X.2017.1352467

Sassen, S. (1999). *Globalization and its discontents: Essays on the new mobility of people and money*. New Press.

Schlee, G. (2010). *How enemies are made: Towards a theory of ethnic and religious conflict*. Berghahn Books.

Scott, J. C. (1998). *Seeing like a state: How certain schemes to improve the human condition have failed*. Yale University Press.

Sekkagya, M., & la Rue, F. (2010). *Protección para periodistas y defensores de los derechos humanos*. Naciones Unidas Oficina del Alto Comisionado de Derechos Humanos. http://www.hchr.org.mx/images/doc_pub/L241110.pdf

Sharma, N. (2003). Travel agency: A critique of anti-trafficking campaigns. *Refuge: Canada's Journal on Refugees, 21*(3), 53–65. https://doi.org/10.25071/1920-7336.21302

Siegel, P. (2005). Using an asset-based approach to identify drivers of sustainable rural growth and poverty reduction in Central America: A conceptual framework. Policy Research Working Paper. World Bank Group. https://doi.org/10.1596/1813-9450-3475

Silver, H. (1994). Social exclusion and social solidarity: Three paradigms. *International Labour Review, 133*(5), 531–578.

Simmel, G. (1911/1971). The adventurer. In D. N. Levine (Ed.), *Georg Simmel: On Individuality and Social Forms*, pp. 187–198. University of Chicago Press.

Sinembargo. (2016). INM ha intentado deportar a mexicanos de comunidades indígenas para cubrir "cuotas." *Vanguardia*. http://www.vanguardia.com.mx/articulo/inm-ha-intentado-deportar-mexicanos-de-comunidades-indigenas-para-cubrir-cuotas

180 / References

Skeldon, R. (1997). Rural-to-urban migration and its implications for poverty alleviation. *Asia-Pacific Population Journal, 12*(1), 3–16.

Slack, J. (2019). *Deported to death. How drug violence is changing migration in the US-Mexico border.* University of California Press.

Solano, P., & Massey, D. S. (2022). Migrating through the corridor of death: The making of a complex humanitarian crisis. *Journal on Migration and Human Security, 10*(3), 147–172. https://doi.org/10.1177/23315024221119784

Solimene, M. (2013). The (strange) life of ethnographers: Fiction and incorporation in anthropological knowledge. https://skemman.is/bitstream/1946/16783/3/MarcoSolimene_Felman.pdf

Stanford Encyclopedia of Philosophy. (2023). Dignity. https://plato.stanford.edu/entries/dignity/

Stephenson Jr., M. (2005). Making humanitarian relief networks more effective: Operational coordination, trust and sense making. *Disasters, 29*(4), 337–350.

Stephenson Jr., M., & Schnitzer, M. H. (2006). Interorganizational trust, boundary spanning, and humanitarian relief coordination. *Nonprofit Management and Leadership, 17*(2), 211–233.

Stevens, J. (2010). *States without nations: Citizenship for mortals.* Columbia University Press.

Stumpf, J. P. (2013). The crimmigration crisis: Immigrants, crime, and sovereign power. In J. A. Dowling & J. X. Inda (Eds.), *Governing immigration through crime: A reader* (pp. 59–76). Stanford University Press.

Suárez-Krabbe, J. (2013). Democratising democracy, humanising human rights: European decolonial social movements and the "alternative thinking of alternatives." *Migration Letters, 10*(3), 333–341.

Suore Missionarian Carlo Borromeo, Scalabriniane. (2016). *Who we are.* https://www.scalabriniani.org/en/

Ticktin, M. I. (2011). *Casualties of care: Immigration and the politics of humanitarianism in France.* University of California Press.

Ticktin, M. I. (2014). Transnational humanitarianism. *Annual Review of Anthropology, 43*(1), 273–289.

Torpey, J. (2000). *The invention of the passport: Surveillance, citizenship and the state.* Cambridge University Press.

Turton, D. (2003). Conceptualising Forced Migration. RSC Working Papers Series, 1–19.

United Nations. (2000). *United Nations convention against transnational organized crime.* http://www.unodc.org/unodc/treaties/CTOC/

United Nations General Assembly. (1948). *Universal declaration of human rights.* http://www.un.org/en/universal-declaration-human-rights/

United Nations High Commissioner for Refugees (UNHCR). (2014). *Children on the run.* Regional Office for the United States and the Caribbean. http://www.unhcr.org/about-us/background/56fc266f4/children-on-the-run-full-report.html

United Nations Human Rights Office of the High Commissioner (UNHROHC). (2016). *Who is a defender.* http://www.ohchr.org/EN/Issues/SRHRDefenders/Pages/Defender.aspx

United Nations Office on Drugs and Crime (UNODOC). (2021). *Homicide data.* https://dataunodc.un.org/

University of Minnesota. (2016). *University of Minnesota human rights library.* http://hrlibrary.umn.edu/research/ratification-mexico1.html

Urrea, L. A. (2005). *The devil's highway: A true story.* Back Bay Books.

U.S. Customs and Border Protection. (2014). *Trusted traveler programs*. https://www.cbp.gov/travel/trusted-traveler-programs

U.S. Department of State. (2007). *Merida Initiative*. https://2009-2017.state.gov/j/inl/merida/#:~:text=Enhancing%20Citizen%20Security,build%20strong%20and%20resilient%20communities

U.S. Department of State. (2008). *NAFTA profession list*. http://www.nafsa.org/_/file/_/amresource/8cfr2146.htm

U.S. Department of State. (2010). *Anti-trafficking projects awarded during fiscal years 2009 and 2010*. http://www.state.gov/j/tip/rls/other/2010/149560.htm

U.S. Department of State. (2011a). *The Merida Initiative: Expanding the U.S./Mexico partnership*. https://2009-2017.state.gov/p/wha/rls/fs/2012/187119.htm

U.S. Department of State. (2011b). *Trafficking in persons report*. https://www.state.gov/j/tip/rls/tiprpt/

U.S. Department of State. (2016). *Visas for Canadian and Mexican NAFTA professional workers*. https://travel.state.gov/content/visas/en/employment/nafta.html

Van Schendel, W., & Abraham, I. (2005). Introduction: The making of illicitness. In W. Van Schendel & I. Abraham (Eds.), *Illicit flows and criminal things: States, borders, and the other side of globalization* (pp. 1–37). Indiana University Press.

Velasco Yáñez, D. (2012). Defensores de derechos humanos en México (2da parte). *Derechos Humanos, 22*(87), pp. 275–298. https://dialnet.unirioja.es/servlet/articulo?codigo=4421282

Villareal, M. A., & Lake, J. E. (2009). *Security and prosperity partnership of North America: An overview and selected issues*. Congressional Research Service. http://oai.dtic.mil/oai/oai?verb=getRecord&metadataPrefix=html&identifier=ADA513873

Vogt, W. (2018). *Lives in transit: Violence and intimacy on the migrant trail*. University of California Press.

Voutira, E., & Harrell-Bond, B. (1995). In search of the locus of trust: The social world of the refugee camp. In E. V. Daniel & J. C. Knudsen (Eds.), *Mistrusting refugees* (pp. 207–224). University of California Press.

Wæver, O. (2004). Peace and security: Two concepts and their relationship. In S. Guzzini & J. Dietrich (Eds.), *Contemporary security analysis and Copenhagen peace research* (pp. 53–65). Routledge.

Weizman, E. (2011). *The least of all possible evils: Humanitarian violence from Arendt to Gaza*. Verso Books.

WOLA. (2015). *El mecanismo de protección para personas defensoras de derechos humanos y periodistas en México*. https://www.wola.org/es/2015/02/el-mecanismo-de-proteccion-para-personas-defensoras-de-derechos-humanos-y-periodistas-en-mexico-desafios-y-oportunidades/

Wolf, S. (2022). Is Mexico's Security Policy Backfiring? Americas Quarterly. https://americasquarterly.org/article/is-mexicos-security-policy-backfiring/

Wolf, S., Aguilar, G., Bravo, A., & Román, A. (2013). *Diganóstico del Instituto Nacional de Migración: Hacia un sistema de rendición de cuentas en pro de los derechos de las personas migrantes en México*. Instituto para la Seguridad y la Democracia (Insyde). http://insyde.org.mx/wp-content/uploads/2014/03/Diagnostico_INM_Insyde_2013_Completo

Wong, D. (2005). The rumour of trafficking: Border controls, illegal migration and the sovereignty of the nation-state. In W. Van Schendel & I. Abraham (Eds.), *Illicit flows and criminal things: States, borders, and the other side of globalization* (pp. 69–100). Indiana University Press.

World Atlas. (2018). *The poorest states in Mexico.* https://www.worldatlas.com/articles/the-poorest-states-in-mexico.html

Wright-Carozza, P. (2003). From conquest to constitutions: Retrieving a Latin American tradition of the idea of human rights. *Human Rights Quarterly, 25*(2), 281–313.

Yun, G. (2004). *Chinese migrants and forced labour in Europe.* https://www.ilo.org/global/topics/forced-labour/publications/WCMS_081990/lang--en/index.htm

Zhang, S. X., Sanchez, G. E., & Achilli, L. (2018). Crimes of solidarity in mobility: Alternative views on migrant smuggling. *The ANNALS of the American Academy of Political and Social Science, 676*(1), 6–15. https://doi.org/10.1177/0002716217746908

Zolberg, A. R., & Benda, P. M. (2001). *Global migrants, global refugees: Problems and solutions.* Berghahn Books.

Index

Abrego, Leisy, 8, 10, 32, 46, 112, 154
Accompaniment, 5
Agamben, Giorgio, 43, 84
Aid agencies, 48, 122
Aid industry, 110; and natural disasters, 110
Anderson, Bridget, 29, 37, 41, 131, 141, 145
Andrés Manuel López Obrador (AMLO), 13, 147
Anticapitalist agenda, 16, 83, 141; counterhegemonic human rights discourse, 16; denouncements of, 141
Anticapitalist spiritual support, 97–99; value on well-being, 97; contesting capitalist goals, 97; form of solidarity, 99; giving worth by supporting transit, 99. *See also* anticapitalist agenda; spiritual support
Antikidnapping projects, 66
Antiterrorism and Effective Death Penalty Act (AEDPA) 1996, 8
Apolitical agenda, 19, 50; minimalist approach, 48; politics fails, 48; activities as technical, 57; humanitarianism's value, 64; speaking for, 140; exclusion of freedom of movement, 156
Arendt, Hanna, 41, 43, 45, 140, 151
Article 2 of the Migration Law, 10
Article 71 of the Migration law, 67

Authority, 57, 59, 60, 64; not devoid of power, 64; use institutional and discursive resources, 64; Western-dominated system, 64; to designate the donation, 94. *See also* webs of power

Baja California, 67
Bare life, 38, 43; between the cracks of the state, 38; stripped of all rights, 43; Giorgio Agamben, 43. *See also* humanitarian subject; subject of care
Barnett, Michael, 17, 18, 19, 45, 48, 57, 60, 81, 88, 96, 119
Bauman, Zygmunt, 142
Beast, The, 1, 31, 71, 146, 150
Bestia, 1; freight train, 1, *2*, 120; cargo trains, 13, 31. *See also* Beast, The
Bienvenido Paisano Program, 133
Biometric data, 12
Border enforcement, 12, 13, 19, 29, 31, 32, 42, 62, 74, 76, 103, 124, 128, 131, 147, 148, 151; linked to poverty, 19; risks linked to violation of human rights, 32; Global South have been tardier, 42; humanitarian agenda that gears, 49. *See also* liberal humanitarian agenda; securitization of borders
Border outsourcing, 12

184 / Index

Border partnership agreement, 9
Brigden Noelle, 18, 24, 30, 31, 43, 53, 112, 136
Bunkerization, 121–123; withdrawal from the society, 121; physical segregation, 123
Bureaucratic logic, 79, 155; governed by specific policy, 79
Bush, George W., 82, 154; Bush administration, 82

Calderón, Felipe, 10
Campaign(s), 89, 90, 94, 102, 107, 113, 123, 125, 126
Caravans for mothers, 124
Casas del migrante, 13, 23, 24
Catholic Church, 14, 61, 98, 148
Central Americans, 21, 31, 43, 44, 46, 106, 112, 123, 129, 131, 138, 142, 147, 150; informal proletariat, 46; feminicide, 46; civil wars, 46; drawn on these networks, 46. See also transit migration
Chain of distribution, 80, 81, 93; involved webs of power, 80; reciprocity of, 93
Chain of giving, 80, 81, 93, 103; givers of assistance, 80; presented a subject, 81; created hierarchies of morality, 93
cheap, vulnerable workforce, 44, 45, 131
Christian logic, 17, 24, 62, 75, 79, 90, 99, 151, 156, 157; migration as a fundamental human right, 17; political advocacy based on, 17; serving those, 75. See also warm logic
Chomsky, Aviva, 8, 41, 44, 46
Citizenship structures, 39–40, 133
Civilizing, 36, 40, 51, 155
Clandestine, 31, 43, 45, 115, 116, 142, 154. See criminalization of migration
Climate change, 43, 46, 134
Cold War, 43
Coloniality, 14, 24; historical world phenomenon, 14; colonial situations, 14; late modernity, 14. See also civilizing; colonial powers
Colonial Power, 34, 41
Commissioner of migration, 93
Complex humanitarian emergency, 30
Congreso General de los Estados Unidos Mexicanos, 10, 125
Convention for the Protection All Persons from Enforced Disappearance, 133
Convention on the Elimination of All Forms of Discrimination against Women, 133

Convention on the Rights of Persons with Disabilities, 133
Convention on the Rights of the Child, 133
Corredor de la Muerte, 5, 130. See also humanitarian crisis
Cortés, Hernán, 36
Counterterrorism, 48
COVID-19, 13
Criminalization of migration, 7–11, 53, 74, 108, 116, 118, 124, 127; racialized and gendered, 9. See also crimmigration
Crimmigration, 9; immigration law overlap with criminal law, 9. See also criminalization of migration

Declaration on Human Rights Defenders, 58
Deferred Action for Childhood Arrivals (DACA), 154
De Genova, Nicholas, 7, 43, 44, 47, 124, 131, 147
Department of Homeland Security, 12
Deportations, 2, 31, 43, 147
Derrida, 53
Detention centers, 10, 13, 31, 38, 54, 100, 104, 109, 154
Deterrence of movement, 46
Díaz, Porfirio, 37
Dignity in transit, 3, 5, 9, 11. See also dignifying transit; the politics of dignity
Direct assistance to victims of trafficking, 89
Documentary regime, 11
Dry Corridor, 46; Central American region, 46. See also climate change
Dry logic, 79; bureaucratic logic of the state, 79; other international humanitarian actors, governed by, 79; security and peace, 79
Duffield, Mark, 30, 99, 110, 119, 121, 122

Earmarked funding, 64, 79, 84, 105, 123, 146
El Salvador, 7, 32, 146. See also Northern Triangle
Emancipation, 50
Emergency imaginary, 14, 29–33, 76, 94, 103, 107, 159; movement associated humanitarian work, 14; human consequences of, 30, 103; temporality, 30; precarious migration linked to, 30
Emergency organization, 63, 64, 65, 100, 122, 123, 138

Emergency Relief Unit, IOM, 6
Emerging humanitarian complex, 24, 25, 75, 76, 104. *See also* shelter on the journey
Extraterritorial spaces, 29
Extreme violence, 61, 141–151

Faith-based civil associations, 4
Faith-based humanitarianism, 4
Fassin, Didier, 16, 17, 22, 23, 28, 38, 43, 55, 56, 68, 69, 72, 88, 93, 99, 100, 106, 119, 120, 122, 128, 131, 140
Father Alberto, 1, 21, 52, 53, 55, 56, 63, 68, 70, 73, 74, 77, 80, 81, 83, 84, 86, 91, 92, 94, 95, 97, 104, 106, 107, 109, 116, 117, 118, 119, 121, 124, 125, 129, 134, 135, 143, 146, 150; protagonist of, 55; moral leader, 55
Father Paulino, 27, 53, 102, 116
Federici, Silvia, 35, 36
Feudal crisis, 36
FM4 paso libre, 6
Forced migration, 38, 50
Foucault, Michel, 120, 136, 140: power of knowledge, 140; assumes the truth, 140; can make itself true, 140
Frank, Anne, 112, 113
Freedom of movement, 4, 5, 11, 24, 25, 26, 27, 28, 40, 41, 42, 49, 50, 51, 54, 55, 81, 103, 104, 108, 147, 151, 152, 155, 156, 157, 159; liberal concept of liberty, 41; mobility of bodies, 41; Northern privilege, 5
Free transit visas, 4, 139, 149, 152
French Red Cross, 99
Frontera portatil (portable border), 11; city life, 11; demarcates worth, 11
Fugitives, 27, 43, 52

Galtung, Johan, 6
Gang violence, 46
Ginés de Sepulveda, Juan, 34
Global humanitarianism, 48
Globalized localism, 156; local phenomenon, 156; globalized, 156. *See also* progressive politics
Good Samaritan, 87
Grosfoguel, Ramón, 14, 33, 131
Group of Urban Rescue, 106
Grupo Beta, 2, 15, 53, 56, 64, 67, 68, 95, 100, 101, 133
Grupo Beta Nogales, 67

Grupo Beta Tijuana, 67
Guatemala, 1, 12, 28, 32, 43, 44, 72, 153

Hagan, Jacqueline, 15, 16, 24, 58, 90, 98, 100, 128, 143, 144, 147, 150, 155
Hierarchies of lives, 93, 123
Highway of the devil, 13
Holocaust, 141
Honduras, 7, 32, 43, 46, 47, 130, 143, 162
Hospitality, 17, 24, 53, 61, 63, 68, 72, 74, 75, 76, 79, 83, 90, 156; unconditional openness to, 53; protectionism of, 53; serve those in need, 74. *See also* Christian logic
Hostility, 72, 76, 120; enemies composite of, 72; conflict theory, 72
human dignity, 33, 74, 158; recognition that, 33; special value linked to, 33. *See also* human worth
Humanitarian advocacy, 52, 78
humanitarian alibi, 49
Humanitarian crisis, 3, 5, 6–8, 10, 14, 29, 33, 43, 48, 51, 68, 82, 131, 132, 140–144. *See also* structural violence; precarious migration
humanitarian governance, 18, 56
Humanitarian logic, 16, 24, 58, 68, 79, 119, 156, 159; of a shared humanity, 58. *See also* Christian logic; bureaucratic logic
humanitarian medical action, 65
Humanitarian reason, 16, 69, 79, 106, 114, 133, 134, 135; sets of responses to suffering, 16. *See also* warm logic; dry logic
humanitarian subject, 10, 22, 24, 25, 29, 43–47, 50, 54, 81, 84, 95, 104, 132, 140, 151, 157. *See* bare life
Humanitarian trail, 3, 5, 29, 59, 77, 82, 129, 155
Humanitarian visa, 71, 85, 102, 130, 132, 134, 148, 149
Human rights events, 3, 56
Human Rights Law, 38
human rights mandate, 66, 67
human smuggling, 1, 8, 110–114, 127; pollero, 1, 3; coyote, 1, 108, 110, 111–113; complicated social nature, 112; racialized, classed, and gendered inequalities, 112
Human trafficking, 20, 38, 67, 82, 89, 102, 110, 123, 134, 135, 141
human worth, 4, 25, 33, 34, 35, 36, 38, 40, 54, 75, 76, 93, 104, 107, 152, 154, 156, 159

186 / Index

Identification, 11, 21, 25, 39, 47, 69, 70, 82, 109, 134, 137, 145
IFE (Institute Federal Electoral), 67
Illegal Immigration Reform and Immigration Responsibility Act (IIRIRA) of 1996, 8
Illegality industry, 109; illicit business, 108; is still human smuggling, 110; as human trafficking, 110; includes critical voices, 110
Impossible subjects, 110; illegal aliens, 110
Indigenous minority, 12, 21
Indigenous people, 10, 33–35, 143
Industries, 108–115; business made out of, groups of actors, 108
Informal proletariat, 46; lacks social security, 46; poverty in rural areas, 46
Iniciativa más allá de Mérida, 9
Iniciativa Mérida (Merida Initiative), 9
Insecurity, 3, 6, 11, 13, 54, 122, 152
Institute of Integral Development of the Family (DIF), 133
Insyde, 134
International development, 48
International Refugee Law, 38
Invisible victims (Amnesty International report), 116
Irregular migrant, 9, 13, 28, 31, 32, 42, 43, 56, 77, 114, 116, 126, 129, 135, 137, 150, 151
Irregular migration, 8, 10, 19, 22, 23, 37, 44, 109, 137

John (apostle), 97
Jungle of Calais, 13

Kidnappings, 32, 89, 90, 102, 133, 145, 146
Kotef, Hagar, 31, 41, 158

La Arrocera, 95, 101
La Jaula de Oro, 1
Las Casas, Bartolomé de, 34; movement to end slavery, 34; human rights language, 34
Latin America, 2, 6, 9, 39, 44, 46, 50, 124, 130, 131, 150, 157
Law for the protection of human rights defenders and journalists, 125
Legislative balance on human rights and migration, advances and challenges 2012, 130

Liberal humanitarianism, 5, 7, 14–15, 24
Liberal peace, 17, 25, 42, 50, 156
Liberal subject, 40–43, 47

Malkki Lisa, 18, 22, 38, 80, 95
Malleus Maleficarum (the Hammer of the Witches), 36
Mara Salvatrucha, 6, 149
Massey, Douglas, 6, 8, 9, 13, 31, 32, 43, 46, 136, 139
Mauss, Marcel, 80
Maximalist state, 47
Medicalization of transit migration, 99–100
Menjívar, Cecilia, 7, 9, 28, 43, 46, 97, 112, 131
Mérida Initiative (Iniciativa Mérida), 12
Mesoamerican Migrant Movement, 3
Mexican senate, 148
Mexican social solidarity, 37; social solidarity, 37, 79, 158; volunteer activity, 37; civil and ecclesiastical structures, 37
Mexico's National Supreme Court, 114
Mignolo, Walter, 14, 34
Migration controls, 2, 11, 18, 19, 49, 76, 103, 104, 147, 159
Migration Data Portal, 3
Migration industry, 109; organizing migratory movements, 109; controllers and facilitators, 109
Migration Law, 8, 10, 30, 62, 133, 148
Migration Protection Protocols (MPP), 12
Migration regime, 159
Missionaries, 15, 36, 58, 60, 62, 99, 120
Missions, 28, 54, 56, 63–68, 76, 121, 135, 159
Modern state-building, 53
Mother caravans, 140; caravans for mothers, 124

Narco, The, 7, 92, 111
National security, 9, 11, 20, 29, 59, 76, 101, 131, 133, 139, 148, 149
Nicaragua, 46, 72, 117, 139
No borders, 42, 149
Nogales, 8
(Non)humanitarian subject, 95–103
North American Free Trade Agreement (NAFTA), 12
Northern border, 123
Northern Triangle, 32, 43, 46, 139; expelled from violence, 43; changed in volume, 46. *See also* Central America; dry corridor
No Way Out (report MSF), 57

Index / 187

Obama, Barack, 154
Obras Pontificias del Papa Benedicto XVI, 84
Office to Monitor and combat Human Trafficking (G/TIP), 82
Offices for Child Protection (OPIs), 132
Open Society Justice Initiative, 32
Operativo Guardián, 9
Optional Protocol to the Convention against Torture, 133

Países expulsores, 143
Palermo Protocol, 134
Partido Revolucionario Institucional (PRI), 7
Pastoral power, 120; exercised on a multiplicity, 120
Pastoral work, 17
pastoral workers, 62, 124
Patrol force, 15, 67
Peña Nieto, Enrique, 13
Perruchoud, Richard, 66
Political advocacy, 15, 17, 20, 25, 27, 49, 62, 107, 124, 132, 138, 149, 151
Politics of care, 63
Politics of dignifying free transit, 4, 6, 15, 49; politics of dignity, 4–5. *See also* social solidarity; free transit; freedom of movement; shelter on the journey
Politics of exposure, 124–127
Politics of interventions, 119–127; increased risk for, 119; culture within Western aid, 119; courses of action, 120
Politics of life, 119; which causes to intervene in, 119; inequalities that emerge, 119; implicit hierarchies 119. *See also* hierarchies of lives
Politics of suffering, 39, 50; entitlement and, 50
Postpolitics, 48; repressing politics, 49
Precarious migration, 5, 6, 25, 29–33, 42, 50, 63, 75, 76, 108; police mentality of persecution, 14; global divides, 4, 11; global market economy, 6; how irregular migrants deal, 31. *See also* humanitarian crisis; structural violence; emergency imaginary; Corredor de la Muerte
Precariousness, 30–31
Production of illegality, 44, 115, 132; as racialized in, 44; security threat, 45–46;

that is exploitable, 45. *See also* cheap vulnerable workforce
Programa Frontera Sur, 13, 131, 141
Programs of assisted voluntary return, 89
Progressive politics, 25, 49, 50, 75, 124, 127, 145, 152, 157, 158; pure act of subversion, 48. *See also* hospitality; social solidarity; globalized localism
Protocol against the Smuggling of Migrants by Land, Sea and Air, 113
Public Ministry of Social Attention to Victims of Crime (PROVICTIMA), 134

Quijano, Anibal, 28, 35, 39, 133

Racial hierarchies, 35; new social identities, 35
Reagan administration, 46
Receiving states, 5, 12, 19, 28, 32, 40, 42, 108
Refugee camps, 69, 70, 84, 156
Refugee protection regime, 7, 38
Registration, 69, 70, 132, 135, 136, 138
Relief centers, 15
Religious actors, 2, 4, 88, 97, 147
Repatriation schemes, 100–101
Repatriation services, 64, 80, 100, 102; *See also* migration controls; repatriation schemes
Rescue Industry, 82, 110; victimization of its clients, 110; subject to human trafficking, 110
Rights of Man, 33, 39

Sanctuary, 40
Sangatte, 99
Securitization of borders, 11–14; insecurity issue, 11; include other transit institutions, 13. *See also* arterial border; migration industry
Security and Prosperity Partnership (SPP), 12
Senate of the Republic, 130
Señor de los trenes, 6
Sense of deportability, 11; carried by the migrant, 11
Service-oriented organization, 65
Sharing testimonies, 17, 124, 140
Shelter governance, authority, 59–63
Shelter on the journey, 3–4, 29, 42, 76, 105, 107, 147, 155, 156, 157, 159; faith-based humanitarianism, 4; spatial disputes, 4;

188 / Index

Shelter on the journey (*continued*)
 unite as a social movement, 16. *See also*
 political advocacy; hospitality; Mexican
 social solidarity; progressive politics; free
 transit
Slavery, 22, 24, 29, 41, 45, 89, 161. *See*
 production of illegality
Social movement, 4, 15, 16, 19, 21, 27, 37,
 42, 48, 55, 58, 62, 132, 137, 145, 148, 150,
 151, 157
Social solidarity, 37, 79, 158
Social transformation, 5, 48, 85
Sock It to 'Em, 94
Socks and Soup, 94
Socks for Refugees, 94
Sonora, 8
Soup kitchens, 15, 21, 24, 121
Southern border, 29, 47, 123
Spiritual support, 16, 19, 85, 97, 98, 99
State crimes, 145
Strangers No Longer, Together on the
 Journey of Hope (pastoral letter), 155
Structural violence, 6, 14, 31. *See*
 also criminalization of migration;
 securitization of borders; precarious
 migration
Stumpf, Julia, 8
Subject of care, 18, 29, 36, 42, 43, 47, 49,
 51, 100, 131, 132, 135. *See* humanitarian
 subject; (non)humanitarian subject,
 fugitive
Subject of rights, 45, 47, 137
Supporting movement, 55, 99

Tamaulipas (tragedy), 6, 131, 136
Ticktin, Miriam, 17, 18, 22, 38, 43, 44, 56,
 59, 65, 88, 100, 102, 131, 140
Transit communities, 4, 16, 53, 75, 87, 108,
 114–119, 127
Transit migrants, 4, 6, 14, 15, 23, 25, 28, 31,
 32, 35, 57, 58, 73, 80, 82, 126, 132, 134,
 142, 145. *See also* Central Americans;
 Northern Triangle
Transit migration, 27–30, 49, 51, 52, 55–57,
 59, 68, 71, 94, 99, 131, 136, 137, 155, 159
Trump, Donald, 9, 10, 11, 46, 147, 154

UN agency, 65
UN Convention Against Transnational
 Crime, 110, 134

UN International Convention for the
 Protection of the Rights of All Migrant
 Workers and Members of Their Families,
 133
Universal Declaration of Human Rights, 3,
 33, 155, 157
Universal freedom of movement, 5
UN Security Council, 125
Urgent actions, 64, 107, 125, 146
U.S. immigration system, 155
U.S.-Mexico border, 13, 14, 20, 32, 61, 67,
 110, 142
U.S. Soviet containment strategy, 46
U.S. Visitor and Immigration Status
 Indicator Technology, 12

Vatican, 17, 61, 84
Viacrusis, 124, 140, 144, 146, 147, 150; of the
 migrant, 140, 147
Victims of crime, 10, 62, 67, 102, 104, 134,
 135
Violation of dignity, 7–11. *See also*
 structural violence; humanitarian crisis;
 precarious migration
Visa for humanitarian reasons, 134
Vogt, Wendy, 11, 12, 18, 24, 31, 43, 53, 112,
 131
Voluntary migration, 37
Volunteerism, 59, 79, 96. *See also* volunteers
Volunteers, 2, 4, 23, 53, 55, 57, 60, 67, 70–72,
 74, 84, 85, 87, 93, 96, 97, 122, 135, 136, 153

Wall of violence, 5–14
Warm logic, 79, 96, 159; nurtured by
 Christianity, 79; focuses on solidarity, 79.
 See also Christian spiritual support
Webs of power, 88–93; keeping while
 giving, 80, 93; personal relationships
 based on, 93; cooperation with, 92. *See*
 also chain of giving
Western dominated system of
 humanitarianism, 19, 30, 57
Witch, 35, 36, 45, 116
Wool Socks for Refugees, 94

Xenophobia, 2, 4, 32, 65, 108, 116

Zelaya, Manuel, 10
Zero tolerance policy, 46
Zetas, 6, 73, 125

Priscilla Solano is a Senior Lecturer in the Department of Global Political Studies at Malmö University in Sweden.